Big Trips

Terrace Books, a trade imprint of the University of Wisconsin Press, takes its name from the Memorial Union Terrace, located at the University of Wisconsin–Madison. Since its inception in 1907, the Wisconsin Union has provided a venue for students, faculty, staff, and alumni to debate art, music, politics, and the issues of the day. It is a place where theater, music, drama, literature, dance, outdoor activities, and major speakers are made available to the campus and the community. To learn more about the Union, visit www.union.wisc.edu.

Big Trips

More
Good Gay Travel Writing

Edited by
Raphael Kadushin

Terrace Books
A trade imprint of the University of Wisconsin Press

Terrace Books
A trade imprint of the University of Wisconsin Press
1930 Monroe Street, 3rd Floor
Madison, Wisconsin 53711-2059

www.wisc.edu/wisconsinpress/

3 Henrietta Street
London WC2E 8LU, England

5   4   3   2   1

Printed in the United States of America

"Return to San Francisco" by Bruce Benderson was published in part in
French under the title "San Francisco païenne" in *Actuel,* July 1998, and the
complete essay appeared in *Attitudes (Chroniques),* © 2006 by Bruce Ben-
derson, translated into French by Thierry Marignac, published by Payot &
Rivages, reprinted by permission of the author; "Taormina" by Duncan Fal-
lowell originally appeared in *To Noto, or London to Sicily in a Ford,* © 1989 by
Duncan Fallowell, first published by J. M. Dent, reprinted by permission of
the author; "Fugitive Emissions" by Mack Friedman originally appeared in
Setting the Lawn on Fire: A Novel, © 2005 by the Regents of the University of
Wisconsin System, reprinted by permission of the University of Wisconsin
Press; "A Wedding in the Sky" by Michael Klein originally appeared in *The
End of Being Known: A Memoir,* © 2003 by the Regents of the University of
Wisconsin System, reprinted by permission of the University of Wisconsin
Press; "The Heart of Paris" by Douglas A. Martin originally appeared in *They
Change the Subject,* © 2005 by Douglas A. Martin, published by the Univer-
sity of Wisconsin Press, reprinted by permission of the author; "A Table for a
King" by Martin Sherman originally appeared as part 1 of *A Madhouse in
Goa: A Play,* © 1989 by Martin Sherman, first published by Amber Lane Press
Ltd., reprinted by permission of the publisher; "Skinned Alive" by Edmund
White originally appeared in *Skinned Alive: Stories,* © 1995 by Edmund
White, reprinted by permission of Alfred A. Knopf, a division of Random
House, Inc.

Library of Congress Cataloging-in-Publication Data
Big trips : more good gay travel writing / edited by Raphael Kadushin.
p.   cm.
Sequel to: Wonderlands : good gay travel writing, c2004.
ISBN 978-0-299-22860-6 (cloth: alk. paper)
1. Gay men—Travel.   2. Travelers' writings.   I. Kadushin, Raphael.
HQ75.25.B54   2008
910.86'64—dc22
2008011964

To
SYLVIA

Every time a door opens,
I wait for you to walk through.

Kol Hakovod l'Eshet Chayil

Contents

Contents

Editor's Note

I had one vague rule in mind when I started collecting the pieces for *Big Trips,* and I broke that rule almost immediately. Initially I considered limiting the anthology to nonfiction travel pieces. But since so much true travel writing is more truly classified as fiction, and since so many strong fiction pieces came in, I quickly decided to include all genres. In the end, in fact, there is more fiction included here than anything else. The stories by Ty Geltmaker, Aaron Hamburger, Trebor Healey, Andrew Holleran, Mack Friedman, Douglas A. Martin, Dale Peck, Martin Sherman, Edmund White, and myself are all works of fiction.

Acknowledgments

First I'd like to thank all the *Big Trips* contributors, who have generously offered their work. No one accepts any royalties on this book; any profit goes directly into funding the University of Wisconsin Press's Living Out series, and the Press's small literary titles.

Second, I'd like to thank the University of Wisconsin Press staff. I have never worked with a group of people who are more dedicated, or so capable of focusing communally on the same worthy goal. Special thanks to Sheila Moermond, for her typically impeccable editing, and eye; to Scott Lenz, for his seamless design and layout; and to Margaret Walsh, for her intrepid work, and for just being Margaret.

Finally, I want to thank Alfred and Sylvia Kadushin, though nothing I say can equal the kind of parents they have been, or the kind of people they are. They are my models of how to love, fully, and how to lead an ethical life. And they exemplify what a really humane human being should be—curious, generous, funny, singular, and always, in the end, absolutely true.

And of course thanks to Tommy, who is my third stroke of great good luck.

Big Trips

Introduction

Raphael Kadushin

An old journalism professor of mine who maybe read too many Hemingway impersonators once informed me, solemnly, that short travel pieces—very short ones—were the truest test of fine writing. Real writers, he suggested, were the ones who could squeeze the essence of a place down into a tight little nub of a paragraph, just a shot-glass worth of writing, a sentence, maybe only a wisp of a clause. A word or two. This advice sounded at the time like the kind of considered wisdom that makes sense but later of course I realized it didn't. Later I realized it was just wrong. Because if you can squeeze the essence of a place down into a couple of lines either the place is Las Vegas or your sense of where you've been, and what you've seen, is so vapid, so translucent, it's worthless.

Unfortunately the really bad advice, with a lot of help from the hyper Internet, has turned it into a national mantra. My professor would be pleased. More and more writers these days are writing in puny sound bites that aren't even bite sized, encouraged by the notion, and maybe the reality, that this is the way most readers read. It's what we're becoming used to and what we're increasingly accepting as the norm. The going standard for travel journalists writing a destination piece now, in fact, has nothing to do with locating the essence of anything at all. It has more to do with sizing up the shiny look of a place and selling it, in a primal PR grunt that approximates carnival barker prose (Paris? Glossy. London? Swinging. Amsterdam? Grrr. Vegas? Ca Ching. DuBai? DaBest.). The goal, in the end, is to avoid scaring the reader with too much actual text, and if the quick word picture of the place needs some plumping up what gets added are lots and lots of lists, lists within lists, and lists of lists. The occasional dead zones that don't contain lists get plugged with savvy hipsterisms (What's in? Mancations.), sidebars, photos that don't just frame the words but swamp them, and, on the Internet, a lot of cherry-picked (i.e., plagiarized) quotes and nuggets from other travel pieces that are reformatted into a dizzy, disconnected heap of misinformation. Is this an exaggeration? Of course. But not as much as real writers and readers would hope. Certainly the wealthier magazine outlets, like Condé Nast, still allow for bona fide, considered travel features. And a few literate publishers still publish thoughtful travel books. But look at new wave travel books (which are increasingly getting reduced to lists themselves, as in the ten-countries-in-five-days-on-a-Vespa-with-one-wheel kind of thing), truncated newspaper travel pages, and mostly the Internet (where a majority of readers now go, and where an amazingly high percentage of that writing consists of camouflaged PR campaigns planted by hotels, restaurants, airlines, and the travel industry) for any semblance of travel writing, and what you'll find is a trip leading nowhere.

That's one disease—the decline and fall of a narrative text—infecting and gutting travel writing, and most other genres. The other literary virus making the busy rounds these days is a form of avid self-absorption and self-promotion that, like the love of brevity, undermines classic travel writing in the most elemental way. If the traditional travel journalist used to focus, fittingly, on the foreign landscape itself, the gaze has increasingly turned back on the observer. The introspective traveler, of course, is a worthy tradition in itself and if the writer's response to the passing scenery tells us something about the scenery, or the nature of wanderlust, or what it means to be human, it resonates. And in fact probably the majority of the pieces in *Big Trips* have an introspective cast. But finding the shared experience in the personal is a subtle, complex form of alchemy and very few writers can do what Edmund White does: burrow so deeply into his own private story that he comes out on the other side and locates something universal. That is a quickly dying art. At a time when everyone is busy telling his own story for its own opaque, thoughtless sake, in too many autobiographies and blogs and MySpace profiles that comprise an exhibitionistic din, the contemporary confessional isn't really designed as a shared confession. It is either just a tic, because what people do now is tell their stories to strangers, so it becomes part of a democratic stew of voices, or it is designed, instead, to promote the person as click-worthy, stylish, and desirable, as someone whose iPod playlist and favorite clothing brands will brand them too, as a Friendster for life; it's designed as a form of speed dating. And that new kind of tinny autobiographical voice—simultaneously self-regarding and pandering, because it just wants to be liked, and invite more hits, or join the exhibitionistic party because that has become the norm—increasingly colors travel writing. Ultimately the story of the trip focuses less on the story of the place than the glib adventures of the writer himself, who usually packs too many shoes (he's fun!), finds the underground network of louche clubs (he's hip!), and fights off the avid attentions of all the excited locals (he is—and this of course is the essential message—a very sexy thing).

Both of these diseases—the shrinking text and the self-regarding one—are only going to get worse, since they're both partly (okay, largely) inventions of the ever-expanding, equally self-regarding, and largely small-minded Internet. And while it's crucial to salvage all kinds of literature it's especially important to save travel writing since the genre is, in its original state, the natural antidote to the puny and self-important. That's because the observant travel writer is forced to interact with something bigger than the self; he's forced to at least consider a larger world. And because the journey also forces the writer back into his traditional role as a literal outsider, as someone at least momentarily unmoored observing something un-known, it makes the writer consider layers of meaning, metaphors, and a new vocabulary. The best trips resist clichés and easy punch lines; they aren't glib and they aren't list-worthy.

But who is going to do the difficult job of taking back the expan-sive, thoughtful, narrative travel writing? I'm going to say the gays, despite the fact that of course there is nothing punier or more preen-ing than a lot of current gay travel journalism. But it wasn't always that way. Just the contrary. In fact, if there is a genre that is in some way quintessentially queer, it's travel writing, partly because every travel writer becomes, for a moment, queer by throwing himself into a strange world where he becomes a misplaced oddity, where he isn't just observing the exotic but turning into something exotic too. And no group is better at navigating their oddness than queers, who are old hands at being outsiders and who develop, from birth, all the natural skills of a travel writer. Maybe this will change. But for now growing up gay still means that even your own hometown is a slightly foreign, unforgiving country. And that in turn means every queer kid becomes a patient ethnographer who has to read his cul-ture closely and decode the most subtle social signs, like a seasoned traveler, if he is going to stay safe.

It's no surprise then that many of our best travel writers are gay or bisexual, from Paul Bowles and André Gide to J. R. Ackerley, Bruce Chatwin, and Robert Tewdwr Moss. But the list grows much longer if we include all the gay writers writing a form of travelogue, even if it comes ostensibly shaped as a novel, short story, or play. Certainly some classics of modern literature like Christopher Isherwood's *Berlin Stories,* a withering portrait of a demented place, are as much dark travelogue as fiction. Is this mixing genres? Yes, but not really. All travel writing is a form of fiction, in the sense that we're always imposing our own sensibility on a place, projecting our own fictions, and reinventing the landscape. And because we call a work fiction, instead of a travel story, doesn't necessarily make it any less of a travelogue, if its story is framed and informed by a trip, and if one of its major characters is the destination itself. Colm Tóibín's portrait of Argentina in *The Story of the Night,* Alan Hollinghurst's Lowlands backdrop in *The Folding Star,* and John Weir's homage to New York, in the gorgeous and oddly overlooked *What I Did Wrong,* all qualify as profoundly telling travel stories that consider their settings as fiercely as their characters.

The sheer wealth of all this gay talent made it relatively easy, or easier than expected, to pull together this anthology. In fact, every gay writer I admired, and approached for a contribution, had a travel narrative on hand. And the sheer range of those narratives proved impressive, starting with the obvious: geographic range. The following pieces, simulating the most adventurous trip, skip all over the world, from Prague to Florida, from Corfu and Rome to Vienna, Taormina, London, Paris, and San Francisco.

But what these stories and personal essays—and yes, we're mixing genres—really demonstrate is a different kind of range; travel writing, if it does rediscover its brain, can intersect with every kind of journey and explore the deepest themes. One of those themes, of course, is on some level, love. But that's to be expected. Wanderlust itself is a form of lust and what drives our need to travel—the pull of the unknown, the drama of discovery, the urge to feel deeply, and exuberantly—is what impels us to risk falling in love. That impulse is thrown into clear relief in Aaron Hamburger's "Lukas's Story." Assuming a double risk—the dare of the unknown place and the unknowable lover—Hamburger's superficially tough, but tender-to-the-touch, narrator flirts with both Prague and a teenager named Lukáš, and never really divines either. Dale Peck's "The Law of Diminishing Returns" captures a similar voyage out, a young man's cautious but brave embrace of the world itself (in this case London) and the world of men, while in Michael Klein's "A Wedding in the Sky" the place, Provincetown this time, becomes a running metaphor for the state of desire; in the quintessential summer town, where "sex was too much in the air," everyone is fully alive, and everything is permitted. Duncan Fallowell evokes the more subtle shape of eroticism in his portrait of Riccardo, whose ancient Sicilian beauty recalls the ambisexual lure of those ripe Taormina boys photographed, wearing togas and laurel leaves, by Edwardian queens who swanned south, drawn by their dreams of some liberating neoclassical nirvana. Ty Geltmaker's narrator shares his memory of Rome when the city really did approximate la dolce vita. And in Edmund White's "Skinned Alive" (one of the previously published pieces in this collection, but worth repeating because no one blends genres—autobiographical fiction, romance, travelogue—better than White), twin romances, with a Frenchman and an American, are framed by two trips: a sojourn in Paris and a journey to Morocco, through a "lunar valley."

These are some of the stories gathered in the first part of the anthology, a section titled "Going Out" because it features one kind of travel story. This is the voyage out, the trip that is fueled by exuberance and hope, since the traveler is happily leaving (often fleeing) home, and seeing things fresh; his story is an adventure. But there is a second kind of travel story that is more of an elegy, and this kind focuses on the traveler moving, more slowly, less hopefully, in the opposite direction, back to the place he left. Driven more by hunger for stasis than for movement, these travelers are haunted by a sense of how travel failed them, and how all the bad trips, or the sad ones, underscore their need for a real home, or their lack of one.

That translates, in many of the pieces collected in the anthology's second section, "Coming Back," as an almost desperate desire to find some resting place for the narrator, his memories, or—in both Trebor Healey's "Saint Andy" and Mack Friedman's "Fugitive

Emissions"—a loved one. Healy's protagonist, Seamus, biking cross-country with his lover's ashes, sees grief everywhere, so even the scroungiest back-roads dogs seem to sniff the scent of the boy he lost and all the small-town main streets come draped in black crepe. For Friedman's narrator, Ivan, Mexico may be the place he can finally bury his own bag of ashes, the remains of his mother, after they take one last trip together.

Usually, though, in "Coming Back," the narrator is just trying to find a place to plant himself. Demonstrating the way even a mundane road trip can embrace a much bigger story, Andrew Holleran's odyssey through the wastelands of Northern Florida operates partly as social satire but more tellingly as an emblem of the narrator's abiding sense of dislocation. And in Bruce Benderson's return to San Francisco, once hippified and now guppified, the journey travels back through decades, to a place that once evoked the promise of life, and a real home, and now seems uninhabitable.

It's the collection's final piece that evokes both kinds of travel stories, the need to leave home and the need to find it, because it includes kinds of travelers. Martin Sherman, probably best known for his pioneering play *Bent,* wrote *A Madhouse in Goa* in the late eighties and the play was first presented at the Lyric Theatre, London, in 1989, starring Rupert Graves as David, the traveler just setting out, and Vanessa Redgrave as Mrs. Honey, the spent traveler trying to land somewhere. The self-contained first act, set in Corfu in 1966, proves that good travel writing really can take any form, although Mrs. Honey seems skeptical of travel herself. "When we travel," she laments, "we pick up impressions, that's all. Never the truth. We're never invited inside." Well, not usually. But when we travel well we do see inside something. Sometimes that is the place itself, the foreign country. And sometimes that's just our own intrepid, or lonely, or disconnected selves, thrown into a world that can be both welcoming and wholly unforgiving. But in either case the record of what we see, if it's a complete record, can come close to capturing some kind of truth, even if it is only a passing one.

1
Going Out

Lukas's Story

Aaron Hamburger

I followed my so-called boyfriend up to San Francisco after we graduated from UCLA. My parents thought he was a room-mate and that we'd decided to move to San Francisco for the architecture.

Two days after we hauled our queen-size mattress up three flights to our bachelor pad in the Western Addition, the so-called boyfriend informed me "our thing" was over. Translation: he was dumping me (insofar as you could dump someone you weren't having a relation-ship with) because he wanted to pick up strange men in gay bars and fuck them.

We weren't really boyfriends since I wasn't really "gay." In fact, I'd never even been inside a "gay bar." The so-called boyfriend and I met while I was trashed at a frat party. I made out with him because that's what I did sometimes when I was trashed.

From the beginning of our thing, I set down limits. For example, it didn't matter how many times my so-called boyfriend explained that giving head was no big deal and I should pretend it was just a hot dog. I didn't do hot dogs. He claimed he was fine with just mak-ing out and jerking each other off. But if by some chance I might change my mind and want to try something new, not that he wasn't already completely satisfied with everything we did . . . which of course was a total fucking lie since if he had been completely satis-fied he wouldn't have dumped me (insofar as you could dump some-one you weren't having a relationship with).

Instead of looking for a real job, I temped at Charles Schwab. Their offices were downtown, where the glass buildings were flat, tall, and new. The people clutching briefcases looked like they were about to cry all the time.

On my way home from work, the bus passed through the Castro, San Francisco's gay "ghetto." (I'm still not sure about the use of the term "ghetto." Can a ghetto be said to have more over-priced bou-tiques, hair salons, and bars than you could dangle a limp wrist at?) Sometimes I'd get off the bus there and walk around to stretch my legs, and that was how I noticed Lucas.

Lucas was a teenager with smooth, airbrushed skin whose home was a box in the window of a gay video store. A caption cut off his bare chest at the waist: "A touching *cuming* of age tale in a charming

European setting." Lucas didn't look like a typical queen. He seemed too young, too pretty, too free of HIV.

I decided to walk in. I don't think anyone saw me.

The back of the store was devoted to gay porn, which fell into categories like "bears" and "water sports." I found *Lucas' Story* under "classics." Lucas smirked up from his box, daring me to take him home. But to do that you needed to take out a membership, which meant you needed to give the store your name and address so they could record on their computer what you'd done.

I stood closer to the video racks to make room for a guy hovering behind me like he wanted to get past, but he didn't move. "You like Czech boys?" he asked. The man was bald and had a crooked nose and wide hips. "Czech boys are hot," he lisped. "I've heard they hang around the main train station in Prague and for a few dollars or German marks, the toughest straight boys will do anything." He lowered his voice, as if we were surrounded by KGB spies, and touched my arm.

I jerked my arm away and ran out of there, past a gay bank, gay cafés, and the gay post office, painted sunburn pink. Then I had to stop running because the sidewalk was clogged up with gays, standing shirtless in circles, holding hands or kissing each other's dogs, spilling beer over the sticky floors of the Lure, the Inferno, the Midnight Sun, their doors all flung wide open for ventilation. If I so much as glanced in their direction, the old trolls parted their dried lips, ready and desperate to suck.

"What the fuck are you staring at?" I yelled at no one in particular and ran into the street, where I almost forgot to dodge the oncoming traffic.

Two months later I joined the flock of fifty thousand confused young American twits who'd migrated across an ocean to teach English. For the price of a plane ticket I became a foreigner. I could have gone to Africa or Japan, but in Eastern Europe, the guys would look like Lucas.

Before leaving, I sat for five intensive Czech lessons with a private tutor, a Slovak poet with a dirty maroon beret and a ponytail of grey hair. I learned to change Latin-based words like "information" or "integration" into Czech by substituting "ce" for "tion," with the results of *informace* and *integrace.* However, my tutor warned me about *poluce,* which wasn't "pollution," but "wet dream."

Why the Czech Republic? he wondered. Did I know anyone there?

"Yeah," I said. "A guy called Lucas. Is that a common name?"

"Lou-KASH?" he repeated, pronouncing the name in its Czech form. "It's not uncommon."

Somehow, without my saying a word about liking men, the tutor thought I might like to know there wasn't such a big gay scene in Prague except the prostitutes at the train station. I told him that was just what I wanted, but it wasn't until the night before I left, while lying awake in my parents' house in L.A., that I realized he could have interpreted my answer to mean that the prostitutes at the train station were "just what I wanted" instead of "not such a big gay scene." I tried to call him to clarify my statement, but a woman with a British accent answered his number and said he didn't live there anymore.

During my first week in Prague, I stayed in a hostel. Then I transferred to a private room, then another private room, and finally I moved in with an American girl I met in an expatriate café. The night after I moved into her place, I felt like stretching my legs, so I put on a pair of tight jeans and decided to head to one of the gay bars in my guidebook. There was L-Club, which sounded suspiciously to me like the L stood for lesbians, and something else called "Hollywood." Leaving the hall lights off, I tiptoed out of my room and had just reached for the front doorknob when my roommate shuffled up behind me in her fuzzy green slippers.

"I've never heard of Hollywood before," she said. "But there's a good bar just up the street. It's called U-something-or-other. Hold on, I'll put on my shoes."

So I had to explain just what kind of bar Hollywood was.

"Really," she said, looking disappointed. "Really?"

Really. The entrance to the bar was around the corner from its street address. I walked past the door three times and then sat on a park bench across the road and breathed slowly to collect myself. When I finally stood up, I felt nauseous.

The bar had low tables and palm trees with nylon leaves. When I ordered a beer, the bartender said something I didn't catch, then asked in English if I was from America. "Canada," I said and handed over a twenty-crown note. He stood there grimacing like a lobotomy victim. "You want to take my picture?" I asked. No one besides the bartender paid me any attention, but I didn't take it personally. The men were all fat, horrible, puffy-faced Russians in jogging suits. The women wore silver-spangled leather belts buckled around out-dated, oversize sweaters. They snapped their fingers out of time to the music, mostly soundtracks from '80s teen movies.

After that night's disaster, I stayed away from gay bars and taught English in a school that operated out of a trailer next to a highway. The door to my room had a poster of a trained monkey beating a drum. Teaching was easy. I peppered my lessons with Bill Clinton jokes. I played American pop songs. I let out class ten minutes early.

During their free time, my fellow Americans hunted for cheap beer and fifteen-year-old pussy, the age of consent in Prague. To avoid being asked to join in, I pretended to be in a perpetual Bad Mood. I leafed through Proust and *Teach Yourself Czech* in my room. (I preferred *Teach Yourself Czech* because I liked hard, mean books with no frills.) I tried to take up smoking. I wandered around the train station late one night and pretended I was going to Paris or Berlin. I didn't notice any of those fabled male prostitutes in the train station, though I wasn't really looking very hard.

One evening my students forced me to join them in the pub. They all wanted to know: "Why have you come to our country?"

"Chci vidět vše že změnil tady," I said, which meant I wanted to see all the changes in Prague. I wanted to visit their liberation while the prices were still cheap.

They toasted me with pints of golden beer that cost thirty-five cents each. They slapped my back and told me I was a lucky man; they had sisters. *"Zlaté české holky,"* golden Czech girls. "Good kiss!" they said and poked my ribs so hard my sides hurt.

What was it about those girls? The magnificence of their beauty verged on a national obsession. Homosexuality, on the other hand, came up only once in my classes, after a discussion of contraception (for), partial-birth abortion (against), and sexual harassment (didn't

17

understand what it was). A jovial computer engineer who enjoyed the finer shadings of American slang wanted to know, "What is street term for *homosexuální?* I hear this word 'poofy.'"

"'Poofter,'" I corrected him. "That's a British idiom."

So that was my life, for a while. I taught. I ate a shitload of potatoes and dumplings. I masturbated. Then spring brought out mobs of couples kissing in parks by the river, or under the pretty architecture. I watched those pert-nosed, pink-cheeked young men, flowers of their country's pride, as they tongue-wrestled with girls in the metro, on the street, in cafés.

And finally I became so frustrated with my right hand I decided to visit the other gay bar in my guidebook: L-Club. Even if "L" did stand for "Lesbians," dykes sometimes had faggot friends.

I left my apartment so late the metro was closed and I had to take a night tram. The driver dropped me off at a stop haunted by teenage boys in thick coats with hoods hanging down their backs. L-Club, number 49, was a steep, crumbled stairway next to a store that sold tacky lingerie. Halfway down the steps, I froze and thought, God, you see how I have to degrade myself? How pathetic, to stand for hours hoping some queeny gay guy will talk to me because he happens to like my face.

My other thought was that I should have looked up how to say "only jerk off" in Czech.

The door was locked so I rang the bell. Entrance cost fifty crowns, a bit under two dollars at that time. The burly cheeked bouncer didn't seem too happy to take my money, but that was the Czech Republic for you. Tram drivers snarled if you asked questions. Women clutching recycled plastic shopping bags marched down the sidewalks with their heads bowed.

Inside, the walls were painted white and lit with blue fluorescent tubes. Videos, calendars, and copies of *Soho Gay,* the national homo magazine, were spread out on a card table behind the bouncer. The miracle of free enterprise. The men wore white T-shirts, jeans, black boots with metal strips clamped to the heels, and vinyl jackets sewn with chains, snaps, and zippers. The more metal the better was the rule of thumb. A gaggle of British queens disappeared into the bar in back, which was wood-paneled like a traditional Czech pub.

As I paid for my cheap beer, I caught the eye of a short man wearing a black suit and a sheer T-shirt underneath. His nose and cheeks were dotted with freckles and beads of sweat, and his curly brown hair was slicked back with gel, like he'd been slapped in the face by a tidal wave. I took him for a tourist.

I got bored with my beer, so I danced, just to stretch my legs a bit. The man in the suit danced too, near me. He kept pulling at the air with his small hands and shaking his hips in time to the hands, repeating the same motion for dear life like it was the only move he'd ever learned. (I had students who spoke English the same way.) The man stared me right in the eye once. I couldn't help it. I looked back and then glanced at his alligator shoes.

He left the dance floor and stood by the table of videos for sale. I sat on a stool across the bar and waited for him to come over. He didn't. Finally, the prospect of sex knotted up my stomach so tightly it propelled me out of my seat like a jack-in-the-box.

I swallowed a few times and asked how he was, in Czech.

In Czech, he answered that he was fine. He smelled expensive.

I admitted I was American.

But you speak Czech, he said and smiled. He had small teeth, bright and even.

"Chceš radost?" he asked, which translated literally as, "You want joy?"

I thought he was a bit forward, but after months of roughing it, I wasn't going to pretend to be modest. Why not, I said recklessly. Okay. Okay to joy.

He led me out of L-Club without looking over his shoulder to make sure I was following. Outside, his polished pointy shoes clicked an exotic, almost Latin rhythm against the pavement. It turned out we were heading not literally for "joy" but a popular New York-style ex-pat bar whose name meant "joy" in Czech: Radost FX. American artists repainted it monthly in gold or leopard print, and once with faces of movie stars. I'd never imagined real Czechs going in there. The beer cost three dollars.

We shared a purple plush couch. Now came the part where I had to make interesting conversation until he decided whether to take me home.

"Why you no smile on me when I smile on you in L-Club?" he asked me.

I couldn't think of a reason. Our thighs brushed and I let them.

He looked up a word in my pocket dictionary. "You are shy boy."

I wasn't going to split hairs. If "shy" could get me to his house, then I was shy.

His apartment was in a neighborhood of winding pot-holed streets behind K-mart called *Nové Město,* or "New Town" (meaning new in the 1300s). The Baroque building facades were caked with black soot except for one block they'd cleaned for a movie. Students in black sweaters sat in cafés there and shot dirty looks at American imperialists who dared to pull out English newspapers or books. Even *Teach Yourself Czech.*

My new friend shared a bedroom with some woman, so he dragged his mattress into the kitchen and locked the door. We sat in the dark and talked for almost an hour. I wondered if I'd made a mistake until he whispered, "You are pretty boy," and touched my hand. Then I buried my head in his neck, which was a relief, like going to the bathroom after holding it in for a very long time. I pressed my stomach to his and licked behind his ears the way the so-called boyfriend had trained me. The guy tried to pull down my underwear, but I held back his hand and whispered, *"Příští."* Next time. I wasn't ready to go that far with someone I didn't know, probably because I hadn't had enough cheap beer. We kissed until I made him stop and then we lay next to each other with our eyes closed. When he let me out, the sun was coming up. It was orange.

Even though the metro was functioning again, I took a tram so I could admire the architecture like a tourist. The smog had thinned enough to see clearly the jagged spire of St. Vitus Cathedral across the river. At the back of my car, a factory worker in a blue uniform that reeked of whiskey let out a loud fart, then slumped in his seat and snored.

My roommate was still asleep and I wasn't about to wake her up to spread the good news. Safe in bed, I tried to doze, but the telltale taste of cologne kept burning my tongue, even after I brushed my teeth three times.

I met him that afternoon in an over-priced café on Wenceslas Square, not a square but a long avenue of department stores and hotels where the Czechs had their revolutions. He stood next to the dessert carousel in a long brown coat of glistening wool that looked both ridiculous and glamorous. When we sat down, he called a friend on his cell phone just to say hello. *"Ahoj, kurvo, co nového?"* (Hey, you whore, what's new?) He paid the waitress for both of us and left an extravagant tip.

"I must know name for pretty boyfriend," he said. Apparently you could become this guy's boyfriend without telling him your name first. "I am like you. No sex on first date. I too want love, no only sex." Talk about cultural confusion.

His name turned out to be Lukáš, which you pronounced "Lou-KASH," and not "LOU-kiss" like in the video title. He had trouble saying my name because it had too many vowels. His language favored consonants and had even eliminated vowels completely in words like *"trh," "prst," "vrch"* (market, finger, hill). Lukáš had recently been promoted to manager of the newly opened DKNY, though he intended to quit because of "politics."

He took me home. The female roommate was out, at a "rest-house," as Lukáš put it. "I must save money for own flat," he apologized between giggles.

Then he whispered, "Don't be afraid," and touched my zipper. I lay there so quiet I could hear his hand flicking through the coarse fabric of my boxers. Finally I was so impatient for him to touch me, I pulled it out myself. "I want true love like in films," he said with his small hand pumping my penis, which made me feel very tender toward him until I came. Thankfully he took care of himself. I curled up under his Mickey Mouse blanket and pretended to sleep.

"I never have American boyfriend before," he whispered into my hair.

I pictured Lukáš as a sweet, nervous, effeminate young boy in some godforsaken village. "Is it hard for you to be gay in your country?" I asked, turning over to face him.

"I'm no gay. If I want girl in bed I have girl. If I want boy, then boy."

As long as he didn't expect me to give him a blowjob.

He asked me to visit him at DKNY the next day. The store was clean and white with neatly folded clothes in small, incidental piles on the shelves and prices for overnight Russian millionaires. Televisions showing static hung in the corners. Feeling out of place in my flannel shirt with ripped sleeves, I asked a sales assistant wearing a sweater that cost twice my monthly salary to find his boss.

Lukáš came out of the back and argued with one of his assistants. He looked very handsome in a form-fitting brown suit, and I realized he looked more natural dressed up than naked. I followed him into his office. He shut the door behind me, pulled down the blinds, and then stuck his tongue into my mouth like a thermometer.

Manila files were scattered across the floor and the walls were bare. A half-eaten cruller from Dunkin' Donuts sat on his desk.

"I love, love, love Dunkin' Donuts," he said and took a bite. "I eat every day."

He sat by his computer, which was switched off, and opened a shoebox. "How you like new shoes?" They were DKNY flip-flops. "Where you are from in America?"

"Originally? Los Angeles. You know, like Hollywood?"

Lukáš tossed his box of shoes under the desk. "I must save money. I want go to L.A. I want look at good fashions, nice models, good shopping. When you go?"

Actually, I had no plans, though the school year was coming to an end in a couple of months and I had to do something. Even Proust had an ending. "Soon, I guess."

"What mean?"

"*Brzo.*"

"You no go." He wheeled himself at me and pinned my wrists to my chair.

"*Musím odjet někdy,*" I said sadly. I must go away someday.

"Kiss," he commanded, clamping his fingers to my neck. He was a good kisser.

Lukáš wanted to see my apartment. I briefed my roommate beforehand and invited him over. Dressed in her usual sweatpants and T-shirt getup, she shook Lukáš's hand and dealt out cards for Uno. After one round, he got bored and went through my armoire. He picked out a yellow tie and preened in front of my mirror until he noticed my roommate staring at him. Then he quickly rolled up the tie and threw it on a chair.

Later I asked him in bed, "So, how do you like my roommate?"

He sniffed. "She like only books. She is no pretty. She no know fashion."

"I don't know fashion," I said and kissed his temples.

"Yes, you know fashion. You know who is Versace, who is Armani, who is Banana Republic. I like party. I like pretty people and nice music and nice fashion."

He pushed me back on the bed, then kneeled over my waist and pulled my dick out of my boxers, as if to begin a blowjob, but I yanked him back by the hair.

"Why no?" he asked, but I shook my head.

"Why not?" the so-called boyfriend used to ask. "Aren't you tired of doing the same old thing?" Maybe I was, a little. But why should a person change what was safe?

After the fireworks were over, Lukáš wanted to spend the night, but after a quick argument, he agreed to leave in exchange for my seeing him to the tram stop. It was freezing out but I waited there next to him just like a real boyfriend. Thank God he didn't want me to hold his hand or anything. When the tram came, Lukáš started to climb the first step, then suddenly jumped down again and kissed me. The pressure of his lips sucking on mine made me tremble, and for a second I forgot where I was. Then I opened my eyes and noticed the driver arch his eyebrow. Lukáš climbed aboard like any other passenger and calmly chose a seat by the window.

As soon as the tram doors clacked shut, I sprinted back down the hill to my building, where a neighbor was coming down the path to walk her dog.

"Watch out, you moron," I said in English, right in her fat face.

Now there were witnesses.

In class the next day, I had my students read exercises aloud from the text while I looked on. To waste an extra bit of time, I asked them to describe a scene in one of the illustrations: a man with wavy hair in a pink polo shirt.

"Vypadá teply," one man cracked, and they all laughed. He said

the remark in a loud voice, probably assuming that even if I'd understood its literal meaning, "He looks warm," I would not have recognized "warm" as slang for "like a fairy." And even then, what if I had? As far as they knew, I was like them.

When I came home from class, I called Lukáš. "We go in your room," he laughed and pushed me on the bed, though I was much stronger than he was. I could have easily raped him.

I got hard immediately. Lukáš licked my penis and raised his eyebrow at me. "I don't know if I feel comfortable doing this," I said, so he grabbed the pillow, put it under my neck, and went back to licking my penis.

I was afraid. Afraid that licking a penis was disgusting. Afraid he might bite it off or I'd get a disease or I'd forget myself and pee in his mouth or that I really was becoming a fag. But I was also afraid to stop him because his tongue felt cool and scary on the head of my penis, which was streaming out pre-come like it was crying. I braced myself for him to swallow the damned thing, but then he suddenly sat up and looked me in the eye. "I want go with you to L.A. I can save money."

"I don't know," I said.

Lukáš let go of my penis and faced the wall. I had to jerk myself off. He didn't say anything when the mattress creaked, just bounced next to me in silence.

He was gone when I woke up. "Thank you for sleep. Lovely, Lukáš," he wrote on a flyleaf torn from one of my English textbooks. I stared at the "Lovely," then ripped the note into a hundred pieces and threw half of them into the garbage bag in my room and the other half in the garbage bag in the kitchen, just like I did with my credit card receipts so no one could piece them together later. Where the hell did "Lovely" come from? How could he have misunderstood my plain English so horribly? I needed to act.

Flushed with a new sense of resolution, I faced my students that day with a knowing smile, even the sulky teenagers whose parents forced them to come after school.

"Jitka, how about you? What is your favorite room in the house?"

Jitka, who'd buried her head in her arms, picked herself up long enough to say, "No, I am tired," then slumped back down.

"Poor Jitka is tired. I think her favorite room in the house must be the bedroom." Laugh, laugh, laugh. The class's favorite English teacher was back.

I met Lukáš at his apartment. He wore white imitation alligator shoes. When we hugged on the edge of his bed I breathed in the flowery stink of his perfume. Actually, I was starting to get used to it.

"I happy see you. I want see my pretty boy night day night day."

"But you don't know who I am." I let him go. *"Nemužu mít laska,"* I said. I can't have love. So there. "I'm busy."

"I too." He smiled as if this was his idea. "We meet only one, two times week."

He wasn't picking up the hint. For once I'd have to speak plainly. "Maybe we shouldn't see each other at all. I'm leaving soon . . ."

When I began teaching, my boss warned me away from complicated constructions like "shouldn't," "at all," and "actually" when communicating with novice speakers. But Lukáš understood me immediately. He relaxed his shoulders and frowned.

"As you want." He slipped off his white shoes and his wool pants, which he hung in his closet, then went into the kitchen to fix himself a melted cheese sandwich. I sat in a rickety metal chair as the bread and cheese sizzled on his grill. He looked different in just a T-shirt and underwear, a defenseless, poverty-stricken villager. Suddenly he pulled his penis out of the pee flap of his underwear and pulled back the foreskin. The pee hole peeped through his fingers like a smile. When I stepped closer as if to touch it, Lukáš said, "No for you," and put it away.

He carried his plate of food into his room and I followed him because I didn't know what else to do. We sat in different chairs as I inhaled fumes of melted cheese and tried to work out what he'd meant. I knew he was trying to offend me in some way, but I wasn't sure how. When he finished his sandwich, Lukáš turned on the TV and watched a quiz show. The contestants spoke too fast for me to understand, but then maybe I wasn't meant to. I kept staring at the tiny bulge in his grey underwear and thought about kneeling in front of him and burying my head in his lap and then, as he combed through my hair, pulling out his dick with my teeth. I could have forced him—he was too puny to resist—but it wasn't the penis itself I wanted. I wanted him to offer it again.

He didn't, and after waiting almost half an hour, I stood up. Lukáš put on slippers and walked me to the door. His cheeks were wet. I hugged him and pressed my pelvis against his to get something going, but he pushed me back. Just whip it out again, I thought. You were so anxious for me to grab it all those other times. Why not now?

"I have no more boyfriend," Lukáš said, and as the door shut in my face, I almost told him he could come home with me to Los Angeles.

I saw him once more before I left Prague, in the nightclub in the basement of Radost. Thursdays were "Gay Night," and I'd started going there. Once while I was standing in line outside, a couple of drunken Americans passing by paused to check out all the faggots waiting to get in. I remembered them because they were very good-looking. "*Gay* Night?" the blond one said and leered at me, his bugged-out eyes red like he'd been crying. "Are you gay?" he asked, practically spitting in my eye.

I should have lied, but I didn't quite feel like it that night. "Questioning," I said and expected him to hit me or something. Instead the guy's friend dragged him off to hail a taxi that was about to get away.

Downstairs in the club, I spotted Lukáš standing in a circle of friends wearing feather boas, men and women. He wore a transparent silk shirt, and frames for glasses with no glass. I smiled shyly, and he said something in Czech that I didn't catch. "I miss you," I whispered.

"What?" he said in Czech, but I shook my head. Then he laughed and ran to join his fabulous friends on the dance floor. I sat by myself on a stool and watched. And I waited.

Taormina

Duncan Fallowell

One's first impression of Sicily was the lack of road signs, so I aimed to the left as the boys had advised and arrived in Taormina quite quickly. Now I am sitting on a large double bed in one of the most beautiful rooms in the world, chuckling away.

The drive from Messina was via a new motorway with mountains up on the right so there wasn't much to see except prickly pears along the roadside and down on the left water that wasn't blue but the color of fog. Taormina is built high above the Ionian Sea on mountain ledges, Inca-style, and the motorway delivered the car right into the center of it via twirling viaducts on concrete posts sullied with large spray-can graffiti, at which point the feed road contracted abruptly into narrow toy-town streets and I went completely wrong.

The plan was to head for the Timeo, then contact Von, whom I'm dying to see—probably said that before. Back in London Keith Raffan had said, "You must stay at the Timeo because it's the old hotel in Taormina and hasn't been done up and is wonderfully pretty and cheap and there's a super garden with views, well, everything in Taormina has views, but you can get a room with a balcony and the food's quite, not sensational but hotel food never is usually, but there are lots of restaurants and the thing I like about it is the peeling paint is pink and very '20s, you'll see what I mean, but now I've got to go to the House and vote!" Then he repeated everything he'd said but in a different order. Like all good modern MPs, Keith can run on empty when he gets going.

The Timeo, it transpired, was almost inaccessible to motor vehicles but the car just managed it, knocking a plate that I had to pay for off the outside wall of a souvenir shop, only to discover that the hotel was closed—for renovations and general tarting up. Good-bye, Timeo. So the car reversed, tremulously avoiding those plates, and took the via Circonvallazione to allow for an interval of brow mopping. Yes, the ring road, which sounded quite large but was tiny like everything else here. But it could be driven along without plates being struck off walls and sometimes one even got up into third gear—which was the gear I was moving into when a nineteenth-century gothic fantasy swooned into view. It was too batty to pass, so pulling over I investigated and discovered it was a hotel of sorts, more a boarding house. I struck the desk bell and eventually there was the muffled sound of several doors being opened in sequence, each nearer than the last, until a door at the back of the hall opened and there was—Aurora.

She clacked in on high mules, coughing, spluttering, smoking, gasping, small and slight, with pale brown skin, brownish eyes, hair and teeth the color of tobacco juice. No, she didn't have a single room—and gave the sweetest smile. Cough splutter. Yes, there was a double room. Wheeze. She smelt of cologne and grappa. Forty thousand lire per night. As usual in France and Italy, the price of the room stays the same no matter how many use it. She must've been about sixty. Colazione three thousand lire extra. But if I wanted breakfast I had to say so the day before.

Could I see the room?

She unhooked a key and clacked coughingly off round a corner. Room number 6. Double doors into the small hallway of a suite. Turn right into a cream bedroom with fittings and furniture in chocolate wood. It had a high ceiling making it very nearly a cube and was on a corner with lancet windows in two directions. Cream muslin curtains, falling almost the height of the room from wooden pelmets, blew softly in the afternoon breeze like the essence of virginity, as if made from pressed hymens. The windows and shutters were open. There was a side view onto the luxuriant garden next door but the main view was over Taormina with its playful gothic turrets, molar-shaped battlements, and glass houses on rooftops. The windows in this direction were full-length and opened onto a small balcony of wrought-iron lancets from which Aetna was visible to the right. There was a bad oil painting of this volcano in the room. The other pictures were photographs of marble statues, including one of the Virgin. The coldness of marble extinguished the usual insipidity of this image and almost lent it nobility. In the middle of the room was a very large double bed. Bells came tinkling up from the cathedral on cue.

Back to the hallway, and double doors led into the bathroom where all was white and old-fashioned, especially the bath, which was also very big, permitting a full extension of the legs with water left over.

"I'll take it."

The place is called the Villa Isadora and looks as though it were once a grand private house. There are only a dozen or so letting rooms and I'm the only guest. I've stretched out on the bed, with hands behind my head, and find the situation so congenial that I keep breaking into chuckles and whoops of delight. I do a bit of unpacking and the coat rail collapses in the wardrobe. I ease off my shoes—hot blisters from driving in tennis pumps. Run a bath and flush the loo; don't know why but a good job I did because all the water has drained out of the apparatus and none has refilled it. I go and find Aurora in the dining room who buries a fag in the filth of the ashtray beside the TV set, coughs, and comes to the bathroom and says I must treat the mechanism *come una vecchia signora* because it's very old and she demonstrates and it works now. So after my crap I'm about to step into the bath when I realize there's no soap. I pull on some clothes and pad off to find Aurora but discover that the latch on the double doors out of the suite is stuck and I'm locked inside. So I set up a refined howling, whistling, hallooing, and I hear her clack toward the room and say to her through the door in my pidgin Italian that presumably the door is a *vecchia signora* too and she says yes, unlatches it somehow, and I ask for soap, which she goes in search of and eventually returns with, and by the time all this hoo-ha has happened I'm feeling very at home and happy. There's nothing like domestic calamities for getting one on Christian name terms. So I go back into the bathroom where the bath is filling up nicely with scalding water—yes, that's enough scalding water—really, that's enough—Christ, the hot water tap has jammed *on,* so I run in cold water hoping to cool it down sufficiently to enable me to put my hand in and extract the plug but now I have to turn off the cold because really it's getting too full—what can I do now? It will overflow any second. Calm, calm. Adopt the *vecchia signora* principle, grasp the burning hot tap with a cold flannel and delicately vary the pressures around it until, moments before disaster . . . I detect a . . . giving, and off, it's turned. Too full to get in, too hot to remove plug, so I wander to the window overlooking the garden where a young gardener unzips his fly, pees, looks up perchance, and grins in mild embarrassment. Go into the bedroom to sort out money, a necessary and pleasurable task at every major stop. There's Caravaggio with his tremendous, thick-lipped sneer. And Bellini's much less obvious face, a luminous face, childlike, intelligent, feminine, boyish all at once.

The last time I spoke to Von was from France and she said she'd be arriving at the Hotel Villa Kristina about now. I said I'd be arriving about now too but would play the accommodation by ear since the Kristina came as part of a package tour and I didn't. I ring now and discover she's been there for two days. What's more, the hotel is only a few hundred yards up the road and round the bend. At the Kristina reception I ask for Miss Whiternan. The manager opens his eyes wide and says, "Oh, yes . . ." He contacts the room, handing over the receiver through which a voice says, "Io io Pan! Come up, *do* come up! I want to show you something! Io io Pan!"

She's in one of her excited states. We kiss and embrace with mighty hug, and red of face and arms, dressed in a terracotta shift, she drags me across the room to the balcony, saying, "Look, look, look!" It is Aetna, slopes of, the crest lost in cloud. The crags about us are covered with small, square, concrete villas and flats from the horizontal railed rooftops of which Alsatian dogs leap up and down, barking frantically at each other, an aerial community of hate.

"Have you got a view of Aetna?" she enquires.

"If I crane."

"And look!" She pushes me into the bathroom, indicating a bottle of Veuve Clicquot wallowing in water in the washbasin. "We've got a pool. That's where I was when you rang first. Have *you* got a pool?"

"No. It's a sort of private house."

"You can use ours. We get meals. Do you get meals?"

"No, but I get breakfast if I tell them before."

"You can eat here if you like. I should eat here because it's all in. I've brought your post from London."

"Wonderful! I'll take you out for dinner."

"Oh, jolly japes!" This comes in inverted commas. Oxonians put inverted commas round a great many of their expressions.

Taormina was founded in 396 BC by refugees from the Greek colony of Naxos nearby. The resort prospered on tuberculosis. *The winter, especially on the coast, is very mild so that the island in general and Palermo in particular are coming more and more resorted to by delicate persons and phthisis patients. At Taormina the influx of strangers begins as early as the second half of January. The mean temp. of the island in Jan. is 51.4° Fahr.* (from *Baedeker*).

The majority of tourists now are German and Von's tour operator said, "If you wanna job here you gotta speak German." In the main square, which has one side overlooking a steep drop to the sea, tourists sit around at evening in the cafés, stunned by the day's sun, staring out at the young men of the town who parade up and down singly, in couples or groups, laughing, playing with each other, staring in. This playful strutting curiosity of the male is found here to a greater extent than anywhere else in Italy and is at first rather oppressive and has a counterproductive effect. There seems to be no interaction between foreign tourists and Sicilians. I've never been in a place with so much ostentatious soliciting and so little actually happening. It makes Saint Tropez by comparison a very causal, easy affair.

The best shop in the world is on the Corso Umberto. It's called Ginger and is located in an ancient and abandoned gothic stone church. Purple, green, and red neon pours out into the night through the filigree of windows and door. It sells trendy clothes but what it sells isn't the point. This shop is sculpture, not a place to buy things. Von picks up a top and puts it down. She asks the assistant if there's somewhere she can pee—women always need somewhere to pee—and then we find somewhere to eat, a pretty restaurant in a garden off the main *dragette*. Seated under a tree with fairy lights, I start to open my post.

"That one looks interesting," she says.

It's from a Welsh transsexual asking me if I can help her to get her novel published.

"The local prawns are supposed to be extra sweet because of the special algae in Taormina bay," Von continues, shaking her mass of long, wavy, henna-red hair.

"I expect pollution's finished that off."

"Anyway I don't want prawns tonight. I want something big! Did you stop at Paris on the way down? I want to go up Aetna. *Right* up.

And we must see the Greek Theatre. And there's a valley of temples at Agri . . . at Agri-gin—whatever the place is called. Tell me about Noto."

"Later."

"And about that horrible Black Lake."

"Noto sounds Japanese."

"I know. And Taormina sounds Chinese."

We are pulling in slightly different directions. She's just arrived in the Mediterranean and wants to gorge on food and ruins. I've already done a lot of that and want to gorge on people.

"I think those von Gloeden postcards of naked boys in all the shops are wonderful! Though none with erections," she adds ruefully. "I think Greek vases are the only public art to have portrayed the erect penis—not on satyrs or gods or as pornography or as phallus cult objects—but on men and boys, on *people.*"

Oh, well, perhaps she does want to gorge on people after all.

"Can you imagine the rumpus if someone tried to sell those postcards in Oxford Street? And another thing I want to do is find Aleister Crowley's Abbey of Thelema at Cefalù."

"Yes, for that one, you're on," I say.

"Oh, JG! *Cefalù* sounds Hawaiian, doesn't it?"

"Perhaps we're not pronouncing it right."

Throughout the conversation we keep breaking into helpless laughter, accompanied by clinks from the mass of heavy gilt jewelry she's supporting. Great jokes are not being cracked. It must simply be delight in each other's company. There is something ludicrous about our being here.

"Do you think it's a good idea to move into my hotel?"

"No. Because I've fallen in love with the Villa Isadora."

"Try some of this *heavenly* goo," she commands, pushing a spoonful of her pudding into my mouth.

Normally my orientation is good but for the first few days higgledy-piggledy Taormina confounds it. But one morning we do reach the Greek Theatre, which is red brick with plenty of reconstruction, graffiti cut into the cactuses, and hairnets round the rocks. The view through it is one of the world's most celebrated; a number of hills descend from Aetna, on the right to the sea on the left.

Whoever contrives these things has placed a string of small pylons across the center.

At noon there is a terrific racket. Church bells, barking dogs. Not sweet bells but fast furious clangs on two notes only. Cannons go off with a flat boom. In the afternoon a number of carved and painted carts, drawn by fantastically caparisoned horses, parade down the Corso. Tourists gobble their ice-cream cornets in order to take up their cameras. Plumes tremble as the horses, with stiffened front legs, begin to slide on polished lava down the shallow gradient of the street. In each cart is a band of three, four, sometimes five players: accordion, flute, tambourine, boom-boom drum. They wear black trousers and waistcoats, white shirt, red scarves, red cummerbunds. The flutes have an especially tender tone of Peruvian character. We applaud with the other tourists, then visit the town library, which is housed in a deconsecrated church in the main piazza. Having been based on the old British Subscription Library, which existed here until the Second World War, it has mostly English titles. *Through Persia on a Side-Saddle* by Ella C. Sykes, *Kashmir in Sunlight and Shade* by C. E. Tyndale-Biscoe, M.A. Ah, those were the days, when an author might place "M.A." after his name and not be abashed. The British influence was long sustained hereabouts by the Viscounts Bridport, descended from Admiral Nelson's brother. Lord Nelson was given a large estate at Bronte forty minutes west of Taormina by Ferdinand IV, and the family maintained it until 1981, when the current Viscount Bridport, alias Duke of Bronte, sold it to the Italian government for two million pounds. William Sharp, alias Fiona Macleod, is buried at Bronte. Equally surprisingly, Samuel Butler wrote and is remembered at Calatafimi on the other side of the island. Edmund John, the English poet, is buried in Taormina's protestant cemetery. Dylan Thomas's widow, Caitlin, lives somewhere on the east coast here.

Breakfast, which finally I've got the hang of, is brought to me in solitary state in the dining room by Riccardo. He is twenty-four with round dark eyes, semi-circular eyebrows that convey an air of bewilderment, short black curls, and cheeky alertness, which is neither Arab nor Spanish but from the ancient Greeks. He knows he is handsome but is prevented from being cocksure by an underlying anxiety expressed in nervous or aggressive hand movements. He says he is paid very little for this work, "but my wife works so it's not a problem. Did you sleep well?"

"No."

"Neither did I. My little son wouldn't stop crying. So I've learned to sleep with a pillow over my head and now my wife complains, 'But I can't see you, Riccardo!' You have a nice car." They miss nothing. Later he surprises me by telling me my age—it dawns on me that he's memorized every detail in my passport while it was lodged at the desk for registration. "How do you find it, driving on the right-hand side?"

"Fine. Except where a viaduct curves outwards. Then it seems there's nothing between you and the air."

"Yes, I know, because I was a passenger when my friend drove on the viaducts of the Cosenza-Crotone road. I hated it. Do you want breakfast tomorrow?"

"Yes, every day. I'll pay for it even if sometimes I don't sleep here. Do you do laundry?"

"No, but there's one in the Piazza del Duomo. By the fountain. I have to do something downstairs now. See you later."

Return to room for a bowel movement. I'm gradually becoming acquainted with the *vecchia signora*. Occasionally I have to remove the lid and manipulate the innards to precipitate a flushing. And there is a knack to the handle that I'm beginning to comprehend. The bidet, however, functions like a cool dream. All of which is accomplished, with hands washed and toweled, by the time Von arrives.

"I'm falling in love with this room too," she says, spread-eagling on the bed. "It reminds me of Oxford. It is like being in a picture that's on the wall of a room in Oxford. Are you ready for the beach? Guess what."

"What?"

"Aetna's making impressive growlings. God, I'd love a blow-off!"

The beaches beneath Taormina are reached by a funicular and are not very good. The best are at Letoianni where there's also a chiesa Cristiana Evangelica (one sometimes sees them in Italy; they usually look like shops). But all the beaches have a road, a railway, and now a motorway along the back of them. Whereas the beach boys in

France are solicitous, agreeable, and earn plenty of tips, the beach boys here are a gloomy lot. They show you to a deckchair, put up your umbrella, and that's it—they sit all day long ignoring the clients. Even creepier—no fee is charged for the use of these items. So what's the form? To get something for nothing in a tourist town gives one a strange sense of unease. Unalloyed jollity quickly becomes inane and one isn't asking for that, but the sullenness among the beach boys amounts almost to resentment of holidaymakers.

"Oh, don't keep on," says Von. "I'm sure that it's just part of their Sicilian inferiority complex."

"But we didn't pay to come in and we haven't paid to use these things—I'm sure they'll sting us later."

"Your shorts are that grey with a bit of green in it."

"Chewing-gum grey."

"Some grey has blue in it, which is a different sort of grey."

"Then of course there's grey. Black and white mixed."

"Oh, yes, there's always that," she says. "Ennui grey. I haven't done my bikini line. Does it look dreadful?"

"Not absolutely dreadful."

We move on to hair in armpits. She shaves hers. When she came back from Greece it had grown and her mother told her to get rid of it because it looked like dirt. "And another thing—when I press my navel I can feel it right down into my vagina. I told my mother about it and she said she could too. This is the sort of thing that's never mentioned in books. Do you know what's the best for sunburnt skin? Bleach. Heinz dabbed it on me—and I didn't feel a thing. The sun isn't hot enough for me."

"The sea's cold."

"It's a funny color. Ash grey, tin grey, cadaver grey. It's a very *arcane* sea, don't you think?"

But the sky is blue and out of it large heavy drops of rain begin to fall. Where is the rain coming from? Verily a mystery. It falls faster and faster, vertically, and all the Italians stream for cover in the café, aghast at the merest touch of rain. But the weather clears later for the Assumption of the Virgin Festival in Taormina, where a waiter picks up a chair and pushes it up under an awning to shift the water that has collected in a deep sag. A blue virgin is paraded through the streets on a large ball of pink roses to the accompaniment of brass bands. Schoolchildren in black smocks hold gladioli and lilies. At night shells explode in the sky and many firecrackers are thrown sputting down the stepped alleyways. In the Piazza del Duomo I say, "That laundry over there is bloody expensive," and she asks, "When can we go to the Abbey of Thelema?"

I'm up early, having slept well, and surprise Aurora in the dining room desperately screwing the top back on a gin bottle, looking round at me with mouth full and a drop of spirit on her lip. Bosford Extra Dry Gin. Prodotto Italiano.

She swallows—and sings, "*Buon giorno!* I get Riccardo." Cough splutter.

Who saunters in wearing a freshly ironed salmon shirt. "Gin gin gin," he mutters up at the ceiling.

"I hope you slept better."

"No," he replies. "I had terrible toothache. I took many pills but they don't help. I often get it." His beautiful face is creased.

"Why don't you have the tooth out?"

"I'm frightened on the injection. I faint with fear. And the pain has now spread to three teeth. I take Novagin. You mustn't take too much because it's bad for the heart but I took more than twice the maximum dose yesterday."

"But you look marvelous this morning."

"I feel terrible."

"Is there anything round here I should see?"

"The rocks of Alcantara are very beautiful. I show you if you like."

"Let's go tomorrow if the weather doesn't clear up."

Aurora clacks back in, her coughing calmer and more regular, her sweet smile working to perfection and without a trace of irony. She wants to show me her drawing room, the *salone*. It is large and divided from the dining room by a brown wood screen incorporating colored glass panels of flowers in vases. Without this screen the huge pillared *salone* of the original house would be restored. Aurora's half contains bizarre and flimsy ornaments in pewter and silver plate, reproduction antique furniture, and delicate gold lace curtains the height of the room. Against the screen stands a black upright piano in the Art Nouveau style with a pair of candelabra holding four red candles fixed to its front and a faded album of old songs written by her father propped above the open, waiting keyboard. Despite a patterned '50s carpet, the atmosphere is 1920. Pre-Mussolini. I stand there repeating *"bellissimo"* while Aurora purrs.

The sirocco brings stodgy, oppressive weather, with bursts of torrential rain clearing into misty heat. Von has found a cheaper, friendlier laundry, the Lavanderia Primavera, near her hotel. Antonio, who runs it, gave us aperitifs before lunch and Von did the splits on the floor. She says it's the first time she's ever done the splits in a laundry. Antonio can't speak English but his uncle lives in Staffordshire. Another load of banging: dogs, church bells, canon fire. At the beach the steam rising off the lava rocks has a pungent metallic and vegetable smell. A violent storm finally breaks, the sky collapses on to roads made for maximum puddlization and we return to the Villa Isadora where multiple thunderclaps mix with the sound of church bells. The storm-over-the-bay electrifies the blood and irritates the nerves. I play the *Gurrelieder* very loudly on the radio cassette machine and cry. There is something about Sicily that works directly on the emotions. Early impression of Sicilians: they're crazy. This is an enormous relief. They could've been horribly straight and severe. They live closely together, always communicating with each other—but from their surfaces only, rarely committing themselves from their depths. In this, not in a reticence of behavior, lies their reserve. They love to play games and derive a tremendous kick from successfully hoodwinking another.

Riccardo has recommended a restaurant, the Papyrus, run by a friend of his. "You get a special deal if you go." I don't see why we should and am prepared for a dead-end experience but the food is delicious, simple but prepared to perfection, and one recipe is sensational—pasta alla Papyrus: sauce of olives, tomatoes, basil, coriander. The pasta is in the form of large, short tubes known as rigatoni.

"I'm glad it wasn't spaghetti; I can't eat spaghetti," confides Von, who has quite a collection of these little rules. "Go on, tell me how stupid I am, but I think of worms. Have you seen any snakes? I've been dying to see one—but haven't been vouchsafed the pleasure." With inverted commas.

"Is that a serpent's head on your chain?" Von has a number of metal talismans hanging round her neck, as well as heavy bangles on her arm.

"No, it's a penis. Are you hoping to find anything at Noto?"

"One's always hoping. Hoping is a kind of disease. But in a sense, it's just an excuse for this drive, isn't it? Do you know *Ithaca* by Cavafy?"

"Noto is such a weird name."

"There's lots of weird names in Sicily. Gangi for example. One I found on the map the other day—Rampingalotto."

"Oh, I'd love to go there!"

That night Von suffered an excess of vibrations so I gave her an all-over massage, returning to the Villa Isadora very late. Aurora watches endless television in the dining room, plays endless Patience, endlessly smokes cigarettes and endlessly tipples—she's never drunk, only a little high—never moves from the villa but prowls smilingly and dazedly about it, full of the past, sustained by memory. Tonight she has fallen asleep with her head on the dining table and the television set utters an end-of-transmission roar. I have asked for a key but she says it's not a problem. Scop's owl in the vicinity adds its odd whirring call. At least, I've been told by a resident of Fentiman Road, Vauxhall, that this uncanny Mediterranean night noise is attributable to the Scop's owl, but have been unable to verify it.

In the morning there is high-tech luggage in the hall, grips of ribbed rubber, and I say, "I'm not the only guest now."

"It's a couple from Turin," says Riccardo, "but they stay only one night."

"Shall we go to the rocks today?"

The original intention was to go during bad weather but in fact it's a fine day after the storm, and Aetna, whose upper parts are normally concealed by cloud and smoke, exposes her snow-smeared crown. At lunchtime I collect Riccardo, who is scarcely recognizable since the shorts and sunglasses into which he's changed have altered his entire aspect. The rocks line the gorge of the Alcantara River with sculpturesque formations at a location fifteen minutes inland. We bolt a lunch there, buy tickets, choose waders, and take the lift down to the river. The river is high but after a moment's consideration, during which Riccardo worries about the consequences of getting the tummy cold and wet so soon after eating, we pull off our waders and trousers and plunge forward against the stream, barefoot and in underpants. For ten minutes we make slow but creditable headway until the rain-swollen torrent and the rockiness of the riverbed make further advance inadvisable at a point just short of the bend round which the sculpturesque formations begin; and so, having seen nothing phenomenal, though well exercised, we return to the car parked above in a secluded spot and remove all our clothes, setting them to dry in the sun. I notice that Riccardo has slightly fleshy nipples. It is a Sicilian characteristic, he says, for men to put on weight first at the breasts. Sometimes he breast-feeds his son with one to keep him quiet. He shows me his knife, which slides horizontally into his belt and is thus hidden. It has no blade, only a sharp steel point a few inches long.

"You have to be careful in Sicily," he says. "The latest trick in Catania is for some scooter boys to make a little accident in front of your car and when you stop to help they rob you."

We pull over at a café in Giardini Naxos and whenever a girl walks past it's incumbent on Riccardo to cluck or coo or hiss or whistle or yell or make any of a number of other nonverbal noises at her, whereupon he turns back to our conversation as if there'd been no interruption, as if nothing had happened—and of course nothing has happened. He polishes off my flask of whisky and I say, "Let's go."

At the villa, Aurora asks, *"Un buon bagno?"* which is invariably her greeting regardless of where I've been. A wheeze and a cough collide in her fragile torso and while she's involved in a minor paroxysm I notice over her shoulder David Niven's typical expression on the TV, a combination of superciliousness and surprise. His voice is dubbed into Italian with a marked English accent, a form of pronunciation known as "Stan and Olly" (from Laurel and Hardy films, which are immensely popular here) and which causes all Italians to die of mirth.

At night I tell Von of my trip to the rocks and she says, vis-à-vis nothing I can discern, "You have a profound contempt for women."

What have I done now?

First Sunday after Trinity, June first, Corpus Domini Parade. Everyone very dressed up, even the Chief of Police, who wears a cream comic-opera tailcoat with epaulettes, pavement-scraping sword, and all the trimmings. At night Castel Mola explodes with aerial bombs and star shells. My stool was very together when I arrived in Taormina. This is no longer the case.

Riccardo is strange with me too.

"Riccardo?"

"Yes?"

"You know that drug and sex fiend I was telling you about? The Englishman?"

"Yes." He tucks one foot behind the other and nervously rubs the knob of a chairback.

"Well, can you help me find his abbey at Cefalù? My Italian's not up to it."

"Maybe."

"Tomorrow?"

"No."

"Dopo domani?"

"Maybe."

This simple outing grows complicated. When on the following day I explain that I'm bringing Von he looks down in the mouth; and on the day of departure he refuses to come unless he's allowed to bring along a Norwegian piece he's managed to find. "It would be OK the two of us," he explains, "but you have someone, so I must have someone also. Otherwise we are not equal."

Sicilians can make a drama out of anything—this is exciting or draining according to your mood.

Von has discovered from Nicky Hall, her tour operator, that a Professore Pietro Saia has written a book about Aleister Crowley's period in Cefalù and she has his phone number. With much gesticulation and pleading Riccardo is persuaded to try the number but the professore isn't at home—his wife explains he's a schoolmaster at the local school and will be back later. We decide to drive to Cefalù and hunt.

His "Abbey of Thelema" idea (and name) Crowley took from Rabelais, likewise his motto: Do what thou wilt shall be the whole of the law. Is there *anything* original in Crowley? No, he's a genuine charlatan, and a remarkable character. His ostentations are irresistible, indeed courageous, when set against the attitudes of his time. Having dressed up and invoked various gods and goddesses in London, he went to Cefalù, took a cottage overlooking the town, and founded his "abbey" therein in 1919. He wrote a fictional account of it in *The Diary of a Drug Fiend*. The titles of his works are always more promising than their contents are rewarding, e.g., "Of Eroto-Comatose Lucidity." The activities at the abbey, including many varieties of sex-magic and inebriation, became notorious and in 1924 he was expelled by Mussolini.

Riccardo suggests we go to Cefalù via the motorway as this will be quicker, thus affording our first experience of the Sicilian interior, which stuns us with its gyrating beauty. A want of trees is noticeable, as are the peculiar shapes of hills and crags and the absence of inhabitation. Furry heat flows in through the open windows. In the back Riccardo and his Norwegian, Odrun, are snorting powder—he becomes a little loud while she remains red, chubby, and tranquil. "I am a student," she says, "and I begin my studies in October at Oslo University. I am happy to come with you today."

Von turns round and explains with painstaking care why this fun pilgrimage is very much a part of her Sicilian experience, how life is a kind of stenography that only some can read, how Crowley had a lot of things against him but probably even more things going for him, after which Odrun, clearly nonplussed, repeats, "Yes, I am happy to come with you today."

On the outskirts of Cefalù we halt at the Bar Galizzi for coffee and aracini (savory rice balls, a toothsome specialty of the island), and after a double whisky Riccardo once more phones the professore, who is now at home. The professore, not at all convinced of our good intentions, reluctantly explains that the abbey is a small cottage in Portera district up the hill, owned by a woman from Palermo who rarely uses it. Riccardo rapidly absorbs another double whisky and we motor off to the Portera district, drive around in several circles, and stop outside a police station. Riccardo, now quite voluble, chats them up. They are most amused, say yes, they've heard something about this mad and beastly Englishman, and think it's *that* way. Odrun smiles and Von looks aroused. "Yes, I'm *sure* it's *that* way," she affirms, having sniffed the air and checked out the psychic data.

We continue up a hill of modern villas with the great rock to our left and stop the car at a small rudimentary stadium on the edge of town with a view north across the sea.

"I'm sure . . . we're close . . . ," divines Von, after scanning several directions—her voice has acquired a hierophantic tone and she now looks decidedly hormonal. Followed by chubby Odrun, she makes off along a mudpacked path and disappears among wild shrubbery, in search of something, someone, a clue, a revelation, while Riccardo and I lean against the car, staring out to sea.

"Odrun has clearly come to Sicily to lose her virginity," I say. "Many girls don't want to begin university as virgins. It's too much of a weight."

"She won't lose it with me," he says to my surprise. "Last night she begins to suck me, it's OK—then I lose the force. This happens these days. I used to have many girls. Now only with my wife. With her I can always make love. But with other girls I lose it. I wish it wasn't so."

Although he demands fidelity from everyone else, the male finds his own fidelity shocking, upsetting, sinful, a trap to be fought against.

"It sounds as if you really love your wife."

"Is that it?" He looks shy, thoughtful, amazed. "But I'd like to be able to have others. I used to like older women because you can do different things with them, in the ear, in the trees, everything. You know, I am very nervous today. This is the reason I have the whisky and the drug. I wanted it to be only the two of us, you and me."

I'm touched by these confessions and give him a hug.

The girls trudge back. "No luck," says Von. "It would help if we knew what we were looking for."

"That's not a very occult remark. Can't you feel your way by vibration?"

"It's too hot. Is there any water left in the car?"

Odrun says, "We are looking for an old church, yes?" She's very red.

43

Riccardo boldly suggests knocking on the door of a nearby peasant dwelling, but an old woman, bent at the waist, is already shuffling toward us across its garden and she asks, "Why have you come looking for this place? It's terrible. We hear ghosts at night. He took a local virgin and tortured her to death, a dreadful murder in the woods. At night sometimes we hear her screams. He was an *evil* man. Those two girls," and she indicates Von and Odrun, who have their heads cocked to one side, "they could've been killed."

"She says you could've been killed," explains Riccardo.

"Why?"

"Because," continues the crone through her several teeth, "they went up that path. There's a mad dog up there. Very big."

Despite all this discouragement, the hag points an accusing finger at the Abbey of Thelema, which turns out to be a small traditional Sicilian cottage not far away in a large overgrown garden. Only its reddish roof tiles can be seen above the leaves. We turn back to thank her but she is already retreating. Von, flushed and enthralled, throws a loud British "Thank you" after her. The old gammer pauses, half turns as if she might've heard something, then vanishes indoors.

The gate into Crowley's erstwhile garden is locked but the cottage nestles against a low ridge and perimeter wall by which access may be had. "Coming in?" asks Von with a most unnerving leer and slips over the wall and down into undergrowth. Odrun and Riccardo won't follow. They return to the car, perhaps to essay another suck, although by this time Riccardo has very likely been discouraged from everything by the possibility of evil spirits. Like all bright, cynical, grown-up Sicilian boys he's extremely superstitious. But I follow and descending the wall find myself in a thorny thicket that breaks into long grass, rampant vines, and gnarled olive trees. Below is the sea and the old town with the duomo sheltering beneath the great rock on which there is said to be a prehistoric house that the wandering Ulysses would've seen with his own eyes. And then of course the unsightly postwar accretions. If you can subtract these in your mind's eye, you will be able to grasp how sublime it was in 1919—the magic of that.

The cottage is one story with closed green shutters along the garden side, whitewashed walls, terrace with no porch, three steps down from a double front door, pink and red geraniums running wild. In a copse there is a tilted plinth of maroon, blue, and white diamond tiles. Nothing stands on it. A battered suitcase and broken-down gas oven are sunk in grass. By the back entrance is an old door painted with a ghoulish grimace, perhaps one of the survivors of Crowley's invocatory decorations.

"Must have a photo of *that*," declares Von, leveling her camera.

"It's the only Crowleyish relic."

"There may be others. *Inside.*"

"No. Von."

She tries a few shutters but they are secure and impenetrable.

"I don't feel at all threatened by anything, do you?"

"No," she agrees, taking more photographs. "The place has a good feeling."

"Very good."

Indeed it does. We sit in the bee-loud sunshine awhile, enjoying the secret sweetness and solace of the Abbey of Thelema.

Suddenly Von jumps to her feet, clenches her face, shouts, "Io io Pan! Io io Pan!" and laughs long in a high trailing ribbon of heartfelt gold.

We buy cherries and grapes before returning to the motorway and on the drive home the conversation grows ribald. We learn:

1. The different words in Norwegian, English, and Italian for fuck, penis, vagina. Sicilian for cock is *ciolla* or something very like it. I commend the English slang "to shag"—truly pagan and slightly horrible.

2. How in my visits to straight saunas I have noticed that the Italians are less hypocritical than the English and will more freely look at one's body, whereas British men stare rigidly into one's eyes as if saying, "I'm not remotely interested in the rest of you. Not remotely." It's normal, especially in a clothed society, to check out the genitals of a naked human being. Men's sauna in corpore sano. Von says, "They did a test about what women really look at when they see a naked man, as opposed to what they think they look at. They look at the penis first and the face second."

3. That Riccardo has a friend with a very big cock. He was leaving a garage to go and jump on his scooter when the attendant stopped

him because he thought he'd stolen something and stuffed it down his trousers. He wouldn't believe it was his cock until he felt it. "We Sicilians can be very suspicious."

Riccardo is lolling in the back with Odrun, who is feeding him grapes. I notice his face in the rearview mirror. He's swigging from the flask—black curls, he's placed cherries over his ears, Greek ogling eyes, being larky. He IS Dionysus. I catch his eye and he opens in a huge relaxed smile.

"Von, you didn't raise Pan—you raised Dionysus."

She turns round and exclaims, "My God!" Von is also blooming, fulfilled by the day, free to do the next thing.

Odrun remains Odrun, unflappable, heavy-titted, tethered to the earth by her warm wide rump; lovable sanity, Norwegian style. We drop her off at her self-catering flat in Giardini Naxos and she says, "Have a happy voyage!"

We ask Dionysus to join us for a meal but he and his wife are going to the house of Argentine friends for a football dinner. With great approval he describes one of the English footballers as "very bastard."

Back at the villa, Aurora asks, *"Un buon bagno?"*

I give her a peck, have a bath, dress, and walk up to Von's, where at last we open her bottle of champagne, then have during dinner plenty of Corvo red on top of it. I have something to say.

"What does Syracuse convey to you?"

"Nothing," she says.

"Doesn't it convey something fabulous and uncertain to your imagination? It does to mine."

"Yes, that's what I meant. Something fabulous. And uncertain. Look, I know it's your next stop and I've got to go back to London, and shan't be able to see Noto, so don't taunt. Let's have some more wine."

"OK. Now listen, just before I left England I received a freebie in the post from Island Sun—a free fortnight in Sicily, everything paid for. Just like that. Don't ask me why—I don't have to write anything in return. And sheer coincidence that I was coming anyway. But I've been chatting to them and they will commute it to a free week for two in Syracuse at the Grand Hotel Villa Politi, half board, which means breakfast and one other meal per day. So what I'm saying is—come along!"

"But . . . let me think. I was all geared up for being back in the office on Monday morning and someone's just thrown a free week in Syracuse at me and I'm not sure that—but what am I saying, *I'd love it!* Oh, God."

"What?"

"I don't think I can change my ticket."

"Try. Nicky Hall will help you."

"I've gone all doo-lally . . ."

A Wedding
in the Sky

Michael Klein

One night, some members of my tribe and I were sitting at a marble tabletop in a romantic restaurant, which meant that we couldn't see each other. It was dark light, so we talked about love.

Then we were talking about what it is like to have a specific love for someone you haven't met yet. The context was that one of us wanted to adopt a child. I suddenly remembered children, the way they are in my life sometimes like dividers in a notebook. It used to be that you could tell children what the future would be like because so much of what already happened would be in it. The future would just be the next installment of what couldn't stop happening. Then you could teach children what was simply waiting for them. They would join a dance that had been going on for such a long time in the old city. They would just lengthen into what was already, what you knew, what your parents knew. They would just add themselves like beads on a cosmic necklace. The old world.

The world didn't change very much then. Time was still linear. Time was still there, like a quality. Then, a speed. This is the first time in history we are teaching something that won't necessarily go forth. And so we're lost, in that way. We're wired, but not inspired. We're virtual. But still, I love. Or forget that I love, where it comes from, why it's always so fucking moving. I've come to a kind of between place, as hard to gauge as a meadow in the sky.

I still love in the old queer way. But too much about queer life is bereft. I'm not tired of being gay, but I'm tired of everybody else just discovering it. Mainstreaming thinned us out. I miss the margin. I miss fighting. We're like everybody now. We're vain. We emphasize what's popular. We talk about famous people. We're too beautiful on the outside. We flee to ghettos for vacations.

Yesterday in the Provincetown ghetto, J.T. and I were talking about romance. I know J.T. because of some radar we both share. We're connected by an inappropriateness. Sometimes we fall in love with friends. Bobby was a friend I fell in love with once. I fell in love with Bobby in the middle of a New Year's Day kiss. We drove to a beach in Truro. Thomas Merton said Truro sounds like a word that means the loneliness at the edge of the sea. I understood Merton's sentence so fast the day I kissed Bobby because of the idea that a kiss is one stage away from loneliness and one stage toward loneliness. Bobby's kiss was proof of what had been in the air for a year. His kiss happened after it was in the air for so long with the light and the dampness from the sea. I fell for Bobby in a room next to the sea.

And watched Bobby as he wandered into an AA meeting. He looked like the painting of the priest hanging in the middle of the room. The priest was beautiful, but a little haunted like he had seen the wrong death—that the death he saw would not let his life fit into it. Bobby looked broken spirited too. He was a rumpled and beautiful character out of a Dostoyevsky novel. Rogozin, I think it was, from *The Idiot*. It was winter, so Bobby was bundled on the outside. Then his heavy gray wool overcoat gave way to a T-shirt and shorts. He was lean and Mediterranean handsome and looked like summer—which means that, since it was winter, he was some-one dressed for a dream.

I was drawn to Bobby. Badly. There was an obsession percolating, which meant that I was making Bobby up before knowing who Bobby was. I was attracted to what drew Bobby: the sea there and the men and women huddled around the coffeemaker. I was thinking, while I was standing there with the drunks, that I have always been drawn to men who don't dress for the weather—men who are in the world but not wholly of the world. Dreamers. The job of the world where the dreamer is concerned is to interrupt him with proof.

But Bobby fought back. Bobby tried hard to stay in his dream. He was committed to it. Then one day, he sat in a chair next to me with his cock hanging out. He had a very provocative relationship to his body and to sex. And so his body was very beautiful. Every limb had the same amount of conversation in it, which made it more per-sonal than other beautiful bodies.

Once, a long time after this, I saw Bobby driving in a car with a new boyfriend. When they got closer I could see that they were both naked. Jack and Bobby were driving down a crowded street in the middle of summer—a street from a dream. Dream Street. Jack stopped the car and Bobby climbed out through the window and sat on the hood for a minute, for a reaction. Then he climbed back in. It was too funny and out of context to be sexy. But then it was sexy, too, because it was him, and this was the way Bobby liked to be in the world. Before the car and the boyfriend, Bobby sashayed and walked down a dirt road every Monday night, away from AA and all its principles, to me where I lived in a little studio on Atkins Lane in Provincetown. There was a skylight that was flush with the edge of the sea. I could smell the sea on my sheets. And the sun was there, too, mixed up in the sea smell.

Bobby talked about his acting career gone bust in New York City. He went to graduate school and joined a theater company. Then Bobby met an actor/addict whom he loved. Then Bobby drank. Bobby came to Provincetown to find sobriety. Bobby didn't know that the sea wouldn't automatically give him sobriety, but we both knew there are days when the sea can look like being sober.

There, there, there. Calm, with the old terror underneath—like any mirror.

One Monday Bobby and I were wrestling on my bed. We were playing a game, which always lets you know a little more about a person, so the rhythm of who we were was changing into other ways we've come up with to live. The game floated merrily along with the psychological. It was a serious and funny game that started out being a game like the towel snap in the locker-room game. Or the pat-on-the-ass game. It was a game that is never read as sexual, although it could *only* be read as sexual. I touched Bobby's chest and stomach through his inappropriate clothing and named his chest and stomach. I named his arm and inner thigh. And when I casually lay my hand across his crotch, I decided to let him name it. Bobby whispered, "And that's Bobby's penis."

I think this was falling in a heap that comes after roughhousing instead of love. It didn't have the little coma that comes with love. It felt like something that was always there and we were just putting a game next to it. We were tender like wolves. Or accidentally tender, like a tooth loosening. Then in the space between the accident and the tenderness we recognized each other as gay men who were brothers in recovery. The touching game was more like sweetness than a direct invitation into bed, but it stayed with me for a long time. It stayed with me long enough to become rhythmic.

But it was still the troubling theme that never leaves a story. When the opportunity arose every Monday night to go back to that touching place, it would be skipped over because we didn't want to have the wrong idea about each other. So I despaired whenever Bobby left to walk the beach back to the house he was living in, because I knew that to reach my hand deeper down than his crotch and into his love life wasn't something he needed in early recovery. But I wanted Bobby. I wanted my friend. Then the New Year's kiss happened, and so I thought it meant that Bobby and I were sliding away from friendship into the unknown where the little coma happens. Then the thought came to me that we could be lovers, that we were on our way to being lovers. Plus, I loved him during all the stages of loving him.

Two weeks later Bobby went to New York, and I called to tell him that I wanted to be lovers. He was shocked by my desire and suddenly confronted with desire, or whatever amount of it was left after my news neutralized it. Once love was put into a context, it was patented, which was hard for Bobby. The kiss was in a dream, and the boundary between friend and lover wasn't strong enough to stop us. Bobby wanted to remain friends—friends who kissed and had sex every once in a while. Then after that, we had sex every once in a while. But the confusion drained the relationship. I kept showing up for the dream kiss from a man who didn't want me in his dream.

I couldn't see clearly. I knew early on—the way one always knows early on—what was possible and impossible in terms of love and Bobby. I knew that we were both playing a kind of game and that I was accepting love in its constricted form, which it doesn't actually come in. I wanted my friend because, like all obsessives, I couldn't have him. But I wonder how much of myself I wasn't letting *him* have? And how much of *that* was love?

Two years later I found myself in another friendship that turned its head to face the same weak boundaries of friendship or love. We were outside a cabin, on a lake, on a dock, in midsummer. His name was Gabe, and we had spent the early part of the summer in a bearable heat wave at his family retreat, which was a funky cabin right outside Boston. The cabin was a few exits down from an infamous rest area. Gabe called the cabin the Fort. The Fort was hidden by the trees and pitched on the top of a slope that reached down to Spectator Pond. Days circled around the pond, and nights, when the pond was too dark for swimming or boating, circled around a parking lot at the mall. At the mall, we went to the movies with the rest of America. I was falling in love with Gabe during the story on a screen in America.

I tried to keep the love away because he was a friend and had been a friend for too long for everything to change suddenly into the other kind of love. I didn't know how to tell Gabe that my heart had grown specific around him. But what's the rule for such things? Is there an expiration date for romantic love? If you don't make your intention known with someone soon enough, does the friend automatically take over and push the man who wants sex aside? Why don't men ever ask, in the beginning, what kind of relationship we want it to be? How long does being a friend stave off Eros? Why can't you have sex with someone you've known for years?

Every man I meet in the beginning is a potential sex partner until the sense of the erotic is neutralized by a hope for the future. I don't know how to act all the time. I don't know how to seduce or look for clues or ask the right questions. In sobriety, I'm in the same room with intimacy, but I'm never used to the light.

In the beginning of our relationship, Gabe was picking up guys, having sex. I was celibate when I moved to Provincetown. I didn't cruise at night because sex was too much in the air. The air made me disinterested. All I wanted to do with the air was breathe it, not get all sexed up about it. I wasn't pushing romance that summer. But there were feelings *around* romance, *around* possibility, that went toward Gabe. I wound and wound and wound the feelings around Gabe to see how tight they could get. In this way, I was involved with a possibility. I wound and wound, and then I talked. We talked. We talked in his truck and in his kitchen. We talked in his bed and in his garden, where some rabbits were. I came to appreciate Gabe's heartbreak and vulnerability. He had been abused. He was in recovery. His recovery made him financially successful, which surprised me, the way it always surprised me—money enough for more than enough.

And he was fractured, but whole inside that fracture. His fracture kept healing, which gave him an effervescence. And his effervescence made me vibrate. We slept together without having sex, and his effervescence was in the bed with us. Gabe used to shine. Gabe was alive when he shouldn't have been. Because of the recovery, Gabe was alive. Especially in summer.

We lay naked together on the dock and talked. Or we got in the canoe and moved around the lake in slow circles. We sang Joni Mitchell songs, and Gabe turned me on to Tori Amos, whom I liked. Tori Amos sounded good on water. Late lake music. And that lake had a kind of hum that typified summers for me. The lake brought down a drowsy band of sunlight that got interrupted by a smaller summer of crickets or laughter.

Gabe and I had perfected the canoe in Provincetown the summer before, when we used to make Sunday sojourns out to Long Point. There were a lot of dolphins that summer, and after the dolphins, we got out of the canoe and collected sand dollars. There were a lot of sand dollars that summer too: lots of riches right under the surface.

Then an extraordinary hurricane happened. Gabe and I were there on earth simply to look away from it and up at the sky—which was particularly startling, black blue, full of stars. It looked like the sky from Luis Buñuel and Salvador Dali's *Un Chien Andalou*—which dissolves into a woman slicing her own eyeball. But this sky—Gabe's and mine—had been swept clean after a hurricane without rain turned it upside down and knocked out the electricity in Provincetown. The summer business—the heart of economic life in the town—stopped, along with the heart of a photographer in the East End after his house fell in around him.

At night, real night, Gabe and I took our flashlights and cruised Commercial Street in the dark. We kept the flashlights off until someone passed who we intuited might be attractive, and then we turned the flashlights on and seductively asked, "Are you cute?" But it was hard to cruise guys with Gabe, even in the dark, because I wanted to be cruising him.

Hurricane Bob hit the town hard enough for a T-shirt to be written about it: *I was blown by Bob.* And I watched most of the storm through the window of Gabe's house—an intermittently shaking house on a high point of town—reading Patricia Bosworth's biography of Diane Arbus and thinking about the one time I met the photographer and knew, even then, standing outside her oncoming fame, that she was utterly unique. Arbus had just gotten a pair of X-ray glasses—the kind you send away for with a coupon from the back of a comic book. The glasses were supposed to give you X-ray vision, and she was looking *through* her hand as she held it up in front of a table lamp.

As turbulent as it was getting outside, it was also perfect napping weather—or weather for construction paper, scissors, and glue or soup. Before the storm, Gabe cut out the sunflowers from his picture-perfect garden and set them on the kitchen table. The brilliant stalks were bigger than the vase they were standing in, and watching Gabe with the sunflowers, I realized I've always envied men who have been able to navigate those parts of being alive that *only* have to do with remembering how to finish something—daily rituals that keep the *personality* out: baking, planting seeds, raising rabbits, making furniture. I lived with an architect once who used to take my breath away by taking down a wall.

Occasionally we ran outside to feel the storm against our skin, to be *in* something like that—an act of God—to feel an act of God pushing on our minds. The sky had grown so colorless that we were in outer space even more than usual. On another day, there would be nothing in the sky to refer to the fact that we were moving at all—except a cloud or two. But on that day, antennae were moving against the colorless sky and roofs were flying and boats out in the bay were fast going under. And then it became a storm that seemed to have a distinct target in mind: the trees.

In the front lawn, limbs and leaves got mixed up with a fence. A telephone pole at the end of Pearl Street fell into a power line, which suspended its crash and kept it from going through a roof. So many leaves smashed into fronts of houses, windows, and cars that the street looked camouflaged. And the sound of all this: puffing and sucking—the sounds of centrifugal force. The most spectacular sight I saw was in front of the 1807 house in the West End. A huge elm uprooted along with half the right side of the lawn. It pulled the roots up four or five feet, taking the lawn with it, so that hedges were turned almost vertical.

In the week after the hurricane, the sound of the wind and the rain was replaced by the sound of generators and applause from people in the street whenever a Com Electric truck would roll by on its way to restore power to so many powerless houses. Lights finally came on in the studio where I lived, which was situated in back of one of the only houses in Provincetown that had two chimneys. One chimney went when an elm fell on it, the other a few days later when, in a tree-cutting mishap, a huge limb swung out of control, knocked the other chimney over, and sliced through three Georgian columns of the house across the street from where I lived.

The tree company didn't come back until the next morning to finish cutting the whole tree down. Then they cut it in tire-sized sections and stacked them in the garden at my front door. Jackson Lambert, married to Carmen, owner of the property, restacked the sections of the tree late in the afternoon so that it looked like the original. His memorial to the savage hurricane beauty, I suppose. And in front of the house, Carmen left her memorial: a pink rose in a glass jar that sat on top of the three-foot stump—all that was left of the tree that had given the house so much shade. It was mild that day, and the wind blowing through Carmen's flower wasn't strong enough to turn it around.

After the hurricane was finished with Provincetown, Gabe was somewhat finished with me. He found a real lover and disappeared into him, into the country, into his own business, and into what would become our last summer together. And I remembered what I had promised my friend, Michael M., before he died—that I would try and succeed, like Dr. Frankenstein, in making a monster of love out of equal parts: Michael M., of course, and everyone else I loved. Gabe and Bobby were added. Which is what I was telling J.T. There was this certain storm of love: the story about falling in love with friends. Which became *this* story about falling in love with friends.

J.T. and I were standing in the chrome reflective sea of cars in the parking lot at Herring Cove. The air was filled with wet salt and beach roses. The sun was drenching but specific. I was ready for a conversation in which I would really have to pay attention. I've never been much of a beach reader. I'm available. Or I'm in a play. Sometimes my friend Al and I take copies of *Who's Afraid of Virginia Woolf?* to read out loud. We would grab a couple of beautiful boys and force them to read Nick and Honey. As George and Martha, Al and I always up the stakes of the script a little. We flirt with Nick and Honey a lot more than the stage directions call for.

There's a famous old rumor that Edward Albee originally intended the play to be performed by four men. But we can never imagine it. It would make the play sound ridiculous. It would make the play be about men kibitzing over an imaginary child that holds them together from a boarding-school distance. In the all-male production of *Who's Afraid of Virginia Woolf?* it would be hard to believe a child could ever keep two men together.

Who would I marry? I thought about it with J.T. standing there. I thought about it in the sun where I was widening. I was surprised to be thinking about marriage. I'm sexually conservative, but mostly radical in other ways. I didn't think I could ever marry a man again. Officially or not officially. There wasn't a ceremony, per se, to legitimize that first marriage. I was still young enough to feel that any real time away from home was only like running away.

I loved a man named Richard. I told my parents. I moved away from one house into another house. If the family is a cult, the journey out of Brooklyn was leaving the cult for love life. I knew I wasn't going to get the love kit down in Brooklyn. Thomas Woolf said only the dead know Brooklyn.

I'm not much for cults or rituals, but I like the way séances look and feel. The dead rise in a glamour of nostalgia and goofy knowing, all without technique. The mind of the medium is the whole show. Marriage is the séance's opposite. Marriage is too sealed, too poised on the future. Marriage is too much money in the bank. It's strict with the idea of being the right thing. It's a step in logic, rapturous or dreadful. I know two people who got married so they could break up.

Richard and I got married so we could stay glued to the future. We had a strong sense of the future because we were monogamous. We believed in the old idea of romance. We didn't keep a lot of company. We kept money in the kitchen. We stayed off the subculture and out of the pride parades. We weren't proud that we were gay, just happy about it, happy to have met. I met him in the theater district, in a bar, and then the next week I went to see him at the restaurant where he worked. I was sitting at a table and Richard came out with a tablecloth. He threw the tablecloth over my head and starting setting the table on my head. Then I loved him.

I was going to be a dancer, which is what I was doing in the theater district. Studying being a dancer. The jazz dancer, Luigi, said that the source of all movement was the asshole, but I side with Isadora, who said it was the solar plexus. I could feel more life in my solar plexus and more tragedy. If the asshole were really the source, I think we would all be doing a dance about getting out of our own way. I was going to be a dancer because I had fallen in love with a dance teacher at Bennington College who made dancing look like living. He had a glamorous habit of dancing into my dreams every night. And so I woke up wanting to dance. Then I woke up in a studio and played a piano for the dancer I loved, and he was dancing to the music I was playing for him.

I wonder if relationships are best measured when they're understood as a variation of the self making enough room for someone else—dancer for the music? It's harder now to accommodate for the physical fact of *him*. I'm on the next level of being free. The space that was so easy to part inside me has been filled in by who I am without him. Something more, again, about myself. But I don't know what it is. Who will I be when I am finished filling in all the inner space? Am I filling it up with absence or consciousness?

Part of Richard's consciousness was taken by a dream about picture taking. He always wanted to be a photographer. I stayed in New York after we broke up and he went to South Carolina. Richard moved into a house with everything photographic crowded in around him. He moved into a bunker based upon career. The house had very low ceilings and reminded me of the chicken coop my great aunt in Long Island had converted for her and a girlfriend to live in a thousand summers ago. Richard's house was dark.

And Pelion, South Carolina, was dark leading into Columbia, South Carolina, and then into the sky. Some of Richard's photographs were of young boys he had met at the university. Gorgeous boys—a glamorous fact that was hard to put alongside the other fact that Richard had stopped having sex. He told me he had stopped having sex because there would never be someone like me again in his life in the South and how dark it was there now and why bother having sex when there was nobody like me. I told him to get a real life. I told him to go have sex. I told him about how I went and had sex whether it meant anything or not. Life or not. Love or not. I had sex to work the muscle, to open a door made of people. To connect. I told Richard why I had to go and have sex. Then I was alone and Richard was alone, which meant that we couldn't be together.

And because he was celibate, there was something wrong about all the pictures. They were noisy. And sneaky. They were taken by someone leering, someone who had forgotten the body, someone who wanted to steal sex. They were erotic pictures taken by someone who wanted to erase the erotic. I began to think of my ex-lover as someone I didn't know at all. Or was he turning into his anti-self? It was a different self there in South Carolina reflected in the rest of the domestic surroundings. Nothing about Richard, exclusive of our relationship, ever made it into the room, settled on the feel of clean sheets, or added to the toughness of old silk that got pulled taut enough so it could be nailed to the frame of a couch he probably found on the street.

After I left South Carolina, I wasn't in touch with Richard until a few years later. We had one of those phone conversations you might have with an old relative with whom you haven't kept up your end of the bargain nobody signed. You love them, but you've stopped telling them you love them. Or in some cases, you can't remember why you do, apart from the fact of blood. Which isn't love, but the rhythm of someone coming back, leaving, coming back again into the other person's life they don't quite know how to stay put in.

Richard told me that he runs every day, stopped smoking, and still loves me. And still has no sex. He hasn't met the man. I haven't met the man either. And I wonder if my—what still feels like *new*—independence has put me in a country of dreams and actualizations I couldn't possibly inhabit with another person, couldn't ask of another person. I am so fiercely about one life. I can't call one life what I used to call it. I can't call it loneliness anymore. I don't know what to call this thing I have.

At Home with James Herriot

Raphael Kadushin

I took the first job I was offered in London, as an editorial assistant for a publisher that specialized in memoirs. All the manuscripts I had to read were tragedies, but some were more tragic than others.

"I was abused as a child, by a man who wore sort of a cone hat," a nurse from Shropshire wrote in her proposal. "My father had Asperger's and my mother, who stuffed mattresses for a living, was bent double with colitis. They both barked like dogs. In the course of my travels I was mistaken for a spy and arrested in Majorca; in Pakistan I almost died of cholera. Whilst in Paraguay a drunk with a loaded pistol took my eye out, but only the left one."

"Sorry to extend your run of bad luck," I wrote back, picturing a glass eye popping out of its socket and careening sadly across a Shropshire cottage floor, "but our list is full for the foreseeable future."

"Be tough," my boss told me. "People have to brand their own sad bits."

In London that was hard. Every sad bit had already been claimed a long time ago and the city, though it was supposed to be happy now, could still seem as slumped as all the old writers promised it would be, and as leaky. Poets would say it was quietly keening, in a winsome, elegiac way, but really it was just having a big blubbery cry for itself, shoulders heaving, everything dripping and puddling: the daily drizzle; the weeping women on the tube; all the rheumy eyes and panting, long-tongued dogs, their drool mixed up in their fur balls; the wool jumpers that seemed to steam. And the boiled candy drops, which left their own little thumbprint of a wet spot behind and which the British still called sweeties, like a twee in-joke.

My own tragedy seemed, at first, just slapdash and prosaic, because it couldn't compete with a city full of practiced bloodletters, people who were smart enough to load their pockets with stones before they went in for a swim. It was just loneliness. My South Kensington bedsit was London's signature deathtrap, the one Jean Rhys could never escape, with the sprung mattress and dead space heater and cracked window that rattled in its oversized frame and added its own taunt; you could lift the glass and flee but you'd only pass out into a scrub-brush yard that belonged in Durango. The dustbowl garden was so dry that some British version of tumbleweed blew through, dragging along the flintiest trash, washed out things, as colorless as fish scales.

I tried to focus on work, where the memoirs kept piling up.

"My grandfather," a Japanese man pitched, "survived Hiroshima but died on a mountain top. Wild boars ate his clothes."

"Wild boars are the worst," I scrawled, at the bottom of our standard rejection letter, like someone used to fighting off feral animals.

At night I went to clubs in Soho where British men danced in mirrored rooms, glancing shyly up at their own reflected faces, waiting for an introduction. That's where I met Marcus. He was English, but his genes had crossed somewhere with something else—a Norman invader or the last of the Neanderthals, desperately passing on one last gentle seed—because his skin had a golden olive tint and his long eyes were almost black. His chestnut hair fell in the British way, an Eton swoop, onto his forehead, and when he'd push the bangs from his eyes, with his big hand, the muscles in his arms jumped, so he was both the schoolboy and the headmaster, together at last.

"I was something of a junkie at uni," he said in a guileless way, as if he were offering me a sweetie, but it didn't matter.

"I like to see some tracks on a person," I offered, pretending I was talking to one of my industrious memoirists. "It shows spirit."

When he undressed he was a surprise. His loose, heavy sweaters hid a disciplined torso and his nipples were like his eyes; long and nut brown.

He was a travel writer so when he would disappear I was blithe about it. I wasn't going to add to London's sorrows and I was casual even as the little disasters started happening, like an homage to my bedsit. These were homey misfortunes, I thought, the kind that deceptively add up, more Stevie Smith than the one who put her head in the oven, beside the dinner roast.

In pieces, though, parts of me started falling off or exploding. First came my hair, torched by the space heater that stayed cold to the touch, except for the thirty seconds each week when it would inexplicably burst into flames. Once it fired up I would quickly shampoo and drop my head over the side of the bed, willing the heater to dry my layered fringe, though I only had a good ten minutes outside; that's how doggedly my flattened bangs would revert to their difficult Jewish roots and start their slow, demented curl, even though I would move my head very slowly, like a geisha, or a Las Vegas showgirl, inching my way through the London drizzle. The afternoon I fell asleep on the bed and woke up to the smell of a bad British breakfast I knew what had happened even before my fingers found the crusty tangle on top of my head, the hair crisped, like English toast, by a lick of my suddenly raging heater. In an instant I was half bald, though Marcus said nothing when he came back from one of his trips, eyeing my head calmly the way an anthropologist, or a travel writer, would when confronted with a tribal headdress made of birds' nests and dung, sizing up the kind of lavish comb-over you don't usually see on twenty-year-old boys.

Most people, I thought, wouldn't notice the deep side part or the stumps of blackened, crazy hair poking out under the remains of my shell-shocked bangs. No, no one would sense anything amiss.

But of course they did. The drunks on Wardour Street were suddenly itching for a fight, especially all the drunk beauticians. Marcus stayed willfully oblivious, full of fragments from his recent trips, but he never seemed to have any useful travel tips.

"Romanians," he suggested, "are the kind of affable people who are open to things, like posing in funny undergear."

"An entire country devoted to comic relief," I said.

But sometimes he would unbutton his shirt slowly, and he would put my fingers in his mouth and lick them slowly. He would smooth back my ruined hair with his own fingers, which were long. His wrists were thick and the leather band of his watch circled the soft brown hair, which you could only see in certain lights, when the veins running down the underside of his arms suddenly surfaced too. He could, I thought, kill me. When he was there, in my bedsit, it filled up; the heater would boil and the window would settle submissively into its frame. The bed would stop wobbling on its broken legs.

South Kensington's indifference, though, was more abiding. Its cracked sidewalks tipped me onto the cement, so my nose wore a long tribal scab; its puddles sent me skidding into a sprain, so I walked with a rolling sailor's limp. "I don't really look like this," I told sales clerks, seeing my reflection, the strip down my nose, the charred coils of hair. "I don't really look like this," I told Marcus. "I don't really look like this," I wrote on a card, sending a photo of me standing beside my space heater—cold as an igloo and refusing to pose—to the nurses back home in Minnesota, where my mother had sat up in her hospital bed, before I left, before I put her ashes in the cloisonné vase, on a bookshelf, beside the little leather pumps she always wore.

"Let's get cooking," she would say, holding her fragile arm out, trying to see the numbers on her watch, and then, after the nurses took her watch away, just staring at the bones of her wrist. When she yawned her whole mouth slid over to one side and she looked like a little girl.

"Wait now," she would say, remembering something, and forgetting to tell it, though you could see the lost story in her rapt face.

"Eat, Mom," I would say.

"I'm eating with my eyes now," she said, but she didn't sound sad; she said it in an earnest way, because she was guileless.

Then London got sunny for a bit. The dark skies, always whining about something, finally bored themselves and brightened and the newspapers ran photos of girls streaking, giddy, through Hyde Park in floaty dresses, under boiling headlines—"Midsummer Night's Dream," "Summer Madness," "Hotcha"—as one improbably warm week stretched to two and then three.

To fill the flat I bought a pair of mice. "We usually sell them as feeders," the pet store owner told me, so I figured every day the girls—Mrs. Fishman and Tovuh—survived was a whole salvaged world, a reprieve from the big reptilian tumble. They cost two pounds each and the double-decker cage cost another forty but I thought it was worth it. They slept curled together, looking like a little fur rug, or a hamster's toupee, but when they woke up they were different. Mrs. Fishman was bug-eyed and brassy; she raced on the wheel that cost another ten pounds and when she heard me open the bag of sunflower seeds, and later the box of imported Belgian biscuits, she would leap on the side of the cage, so that her whole brown body was splayed out against the bars, her head bobbing. I named her for my high school French teacher, who was just as jumpy and tenacious. "You are Jean Claude," Mrs. Fishman would say, in her own odd midwestern rendition of Gallic, "not John Clod," but her anger never enticed me. I only learned, in the end, three words—comme ci, comme ça—though they did seem to constitute the entire foundation of French culture.

Tovuh was different. She did everything in a thoughtful, considered way, as if she were a philosopher, or an aesthete, and she had a delicacy about her. There was a little bald patch on her gray back. She would hold each single sunflower seed up to her mouth, in her tiny hands, and she would tuck tissue paper around the walls of her coconut, and make macramé out of her bedding. When I talked to her at night she would cough up a low, guttural, Flemish chirp, and her head would spring back with the effort. Sometimes she would raise one tiny hand and hold it, speculating. If you looked closely you could see the delicate spray of whiskers shooting out from her nose in a perfect arc, like fireworks.

When Mrs. Fishman was too manic, and they couldn't sleep, I would read to them. I began with *To the Lighthouse* but Mrs. Fishman, considering things for a minute, jumped on her wheel and started racing anxiously. I tried J. R. Ackerley and Barbara Pym: Tovuh looked wide eyed and chewed the edges of her coconut. Then I got a copy of a James Herriot book from the library, because the cover shot of grazing sheep reminded me of the painting I liked at the National Gallery; it was a big canvas of a girl, in a pink dress, and there was a lamb curled up in her satin lap, one of its paws resting in her open palm. Herriot, a Yorkshire farmer or ranch hand or vet—it wasn't clear to me because someone had ripped out the bio on the back cover—held everything in his lap too; calves and goats, rabbits and chickens. The beauty of the meek didn't scare him, and every time I read them one of his stories, about a pregnant cow or a feverish lamb, the girls would crouch for a minute, their heads arching up.

A playdate with Squeaky down the hall, an addled lug of a mouse who gnawed on any old seed, confirmed what I knew; mine were big-brained rodents, and I thought they didn't just deserve a reprieve but also some revenge. I wanted to grind up a garter snake and maybe a beady old tabby, drunk on its life of dismemberment, its ugly teeth used to crunching through the beauty of fur and feathers, puncturing something soft so it collapsed with a sigh. I wanted to grind the toothy carnivores into a paste and feed them to the girls, smeared on top of their biscuits; who's eating who now? "It's all a trial run," I told Marcus. "If things work out I'll jump species."

"Yeah," he said, "stick to your own kind." And then, because he was back for a while, he decided we should take a trip together. So one weekend, when the British sun was still surfacing each morning, stuck now and surprising itself, I left the bag of finest grade rodent feed, and some tuille cookies, with Squeaky's owner, locked the bed-sit door, and met Marcus at the big townhouse in Chelsea where he lived with a rich man I never met named Mr. Wooster. I went into one of their bathrooms and sprayed myself with berry cologne.

"I wanted to smell fruity for the trip," I said, waving my hands and limping to the car, which was also owned by the rich man, but Marcus grimaced when he sniffed. "That's the room deodorizer," he said. "Best to avoid the urinal cakes, as tempting as they may seem, when we stop for a piss."

"Tee hee," I said. I didn't care where we went but Marcus said Yorkshire so we got in the shiny car and drove north. Marcus packed a wooden suitcase, so quaint it looked like chickens would come flying out, and he wore a straw hat that sat poetically on the back of his dark head.

"Is that what you wear when you go travel writing?" I asked.

"Writers," he said, "have to be photogenic these days."

In Whitby there was an old ruined abbey. "This," a guide told us, "is where Bram Stoker's own Dracula first went stalking." The guide had one of those wrecked Celtic faces, all piano-key teeth, and it was easy to see why people offered up their necks, to the whitest fangs they had ever seen. But it was hard to guess what drew Dracula to shore. Most of the people crowding the streets were pink-skinned Brits who seemed gorged on a pedestrian kind of blood, chips, and curry, nothing a count would find interesting, because he always seemed to choose the anorexic, at least in his movies. Maybe he felt, charitably, that the job of sucking was already half finished.

Then we drove across the Dales, past a manor house where Byron got married, and then to Hilltop, where Beatrix Potter lived. In the photos that hung in the hallway she looked blousy and pie-faced, her padded body as soft as one of her groundhogs, but her husband was surprisingly handsome, his hair slicked down. Marcus only poked a head inside and then left for a smoke. "Will you be alright?" he asked, oddly solicitous.

"It's Beatrix Potter's cottage," I noted. "Just me, Squirrel Nutkin, and Jemima Puddle-Duck. Though Mrs. Tiggy-Winkle could be trouble." From the window of her bedroom—did she and her husband sleep together in that narrow bed?—I could see Marcus throwing butts and then a plastic baggie into the garden. Dilly Duck, if she waddled through, would end up with a beak full of speed. In the gift shop I bought a little figurine of Mrs. Rabbit and Peter. Mrs. Rabbit's right ear flopped but the other one was cocked and her black eyes were intent; she was tying a scarf around Peter's neck and her little hands were working, nuzzling her bunny as she wrapped him up. The inside of Peter's ears were painted a soft pink and he was alert too, a rabbit intent on remembering the moment.

"It looks sort of like Mr. Wooster with one of his protégés," Marcus laughed. Mr. Wooster was an uncertain thing. I pictured a fleshy queen in pastel sweaters, flapping his wrists, singing along to opera tapes. Maybe I limped a little now but my pupils were dilated all the time and I could bang my hips like a drum.

In Thirsk there was a big, open, market square and a hotel called the Golden Fleece, where we took a room. A statue of a gilded lamb dangling from a loose harness hung outside, though it was hard to tell if it was being dragged up dead, after some muttony lynching, or if it was being gently lowered to safety.

"All seasoned travelers know this," Marcus said. "When selecting a hotel for the night, look for the corpse suspended over the front door."

The town, I thought, seemed familiar and then I remembered why. It was where James Herriot lived, laying hands on animals. "I'll wait in the bar," Marcus said, because he hadn't read the books, or because the bartender serving afternoon tea was a boy with long, furry sideburns, and I went to the Herriot house, off the market square, that they had turned into a museum. I paid five pounds for the audio guide.

"James Herriot," the guide said in my ear, "or Alf, which was his nickname, stayed in Thirsk all his life. Even when he was famous he preferred not to leave Yorkshire."

The house was preserved the way Alf had left it and there was a wax dummy of Herriot in his parlor, sitting on a chintz couch, reading a newspaper, looking very content. No London or even Liverpool for him, just this chintz couch and the Yorkshire livestock and the town square and the inelegant Thirsk bakeries that sold blocks of sponge stuffed with cream and studded with any old raisiny bits, stuck on in a slaphappy way, and a cake log called, simply, lardy. "Sorry, we're open," read the sign propped in one grocer's window. Alf would buy a fat rascal and sit on the couch; his bald forehead, at least the wax one, was high, like a rising soufflé, and the garden outside the parlor window was green, fed maybe by animal bones and botched surgeries.

"Comfortably furnished," the audiotape said in an androgynous, Wedgewood English accent that seemed as mysterious and arcane as Old English now, "the parlour was the place to relax, surrounded by books and music. Here Alf would listen to the radiogram. Mrs. Herriot would sit and mend. The children, Jim and Rosie, would play with homemade toys." They never, apparently, were savaged by animals with distemper. Not in Thirsk, in the parlor. In the breakfast room there was a long, wooden table. "It was not unusual for Alf to perform small operations here," my new friend said, with what sounded, for a split second, like a sinister shudder, so there was a passing suggestion that Alf was grafting lamb's tails onto calves, or gutting bunnies. In the library there was a display of Herriot books translated into other languages. "Todas las cosas brillantes y hermosas," the Spanish title read.

"Alf," the voice in my ear said, rambling now, maybe a little drunk, "was a pipe smoker. He didn't like his son, Jimmy, to wear long trousers in the house." There was a catch in the voice and I wondered, for a minute, if that was Rosie speaking. "He didn't like it at all." Or Jim. At the exit I turned around and went back through the hall, so I could see Alf's head again, comfortably resting against the chintz couch with his newspaper. The logs were in the fire, and Rosie and Jim were tucked in, and the mending animals were settling down on their straw bedding, and Alf was still happily going nowhere after all these years, plopped there, immobile and waxy, for good.

Our hotel room sat above the market and at night Marcus and I looked down on the long, cobbled square where the town drunks were doing a crazy jig. "Look at the two toffs," one of the men said, staring back up at us. He took a big swig of his bottle and then he pushed his wobbly friend into a lamppost.

"I thought the limit was one idiot per village," Marcus said, loudly, but the drunks kept reeling. He pulled me over to the big bed and kissed the scar on my nose.

"You look like Franz Liszt," he said.

"Could you hold me like a little boy?" I asked. I pictured Franz Liszt wearing a baby bonnet, his mouth plugged with a pacifier. Marcus stretched his whole weight on top of me, so I couldn't move. When he fell asleep his hair fell down into his eyes. "My toff," I said. I dreamt about my mom. She was walking through rain, wearing a little brown slicker, staring down at her wet feet.

"Where is your yellow coat?" I asked, in the dream.

"I don't wear it now," she said. "I'm not so happy here."

In the morning Marcus dumped a pile of tapes on the bed. There was *Rugby Rump Boys, Scalliwag Cottage Lads, Rudeboiz: Council Trash,* and *Interview with My Arse.* Marcus chose his own favorite. The DVD cover featured a boy flopped onto his belly, his eyes covered with a blindfold, under the title *What I Can't See.* I wondered if this was part of Mr. Wooster's oeuvre, because I'd seen the big room with the floodlights, in the Chelsea townhouse, and I thought maybe Marcus had played the part of a scallywag or two, the way any junkie at uni would, but I didn't ask. The boy never took his blindfold off until the end of the movie, when a big chocolate lab walked up to the bed, and the boy draped a limp arm around the dog's head and lazily scratched behind its ear.

"Alf," I said, "would have liked that."

When we got back to London we ate at a new restaurant. Marcus ordered a mousse made from sheep's milk, served with a sorrel foam, infused with the sorrel the sheep grazed on. "We want to offer a whole ecosystem on the plate," the waitress said though they didn't include the sheep's bones, or a drop of the rain that fell on her bowed head, or a little fleecy curl from the lamb that ran after her.

"Where do you travel next?" I asked Marcus when we got back to the townhouse, but he didn't answer. We stood in the elevator that shot straight to the top floor of Mr. Wooster's tall building.

"Are there elevators in St. Paul?" Marcus asked.

"Yes," I said. "It's a city of elevators. Nothing's too good for us."

He held the back of my head when we kissed, as if it were a fragile thing. I pictured him taking his big, cultivated fist and slamming it into my mouth, over and over again, until every tooth, one by one, had dropped out of my head. It would, I thought, seeing myself in Mr. Wooster's bedroom mirror—the stumps of hair, my red nose—complete the look.

"Maybe I'm going to Taormina, the place where that old German shot all those Sicilian boys in togas that look like their mamas' wash. Or it could sort of be France," he said. "On assignment."

It was hard to know what that meant.

"I bet he's a head-turner, that Wooster," I said, picturing a tree trunk.

"That's for certain," Marcus said.

At work there was a little excitement when the *Times* reviewed one of our memoirs. It was the story of a man who kept a chronicle of his own flesh-eating disease, writing each day as his body whittled down to nothing, until he was just a hand holding a pen, and then a disembodied voice gasping into a tape recorder, coughing up every last word—I see leaves outside the hospital window, the nurse in her starched apron—as if that would save him from what he became, just a trace of ashes on the white bedsheets.

"We may well be only the second-longest-running insolvent business in Britain now," my boss said. But the success just invited more manuscripts.

"My great aunt," Sheila the Shropshire nurse wrote in hopefully, "had something of a similar wasting disease; she might work as my sort of doppelgänger. I have a metal plate in my head and blood in my stool." Mostly the new memoirs were sent in by agents representing the merely depressed ("Josey Clark has suffered just about every personal indignity, from marriages that just wouldn't stick to the unfortunate night of the hammer attack"). We also received a lot of diaries written by refugees racing over borders; I thought of them slipping their proposals into mailboxes as they barreled toward another crossing.

"Doesn't anyone stay home any longer?" my boss asked, as if all those panting people were merely restless. He was deciding what might sell: there was the story of an Afghani cosmetologist chased all the way to Canada by an angry mob; and a Nigerian girl fleeing mercenaries; and an old Italian Jew, retired in Atlanta, who chronicled his childhood in Naples, before the war, before everyone disappeared and only the smoking volcano was left, waiting for another disaster. He didn't remember a mafia or any Neapolitan drug-runners and whores; he only remembered the courtyard of his family home, where the citrus trees were so ripe the oranges landed, in the flower beds, with a thud, like little bombs.

"Why don't you ask your friend, the travel writer, to send in a manuscript?" my boss asked, but I had only seen random pages of Marcus's work and I wasn't sure.

And it didn't matter, really, because suddenly Mrs. Fishman stopped racing around the cage. She stayed rooted in one place and wheezed. Her little head bobbed each time she took a breath and every day she got smaller, and more hunched, so she seemed to be returning to the fluff of a baby she had been when she arrived. And then, toward the end, I realized the rattling I sometimes heard, lying on my bed, wasn't the window or the tree branches; it was the sound of Mrs. Fishman's teeth, clacking together, grinding with the awful pressure of each painful breath. Tovuh sat near her at night, guarding her, or maybe trying to absorb her, and she brought small bits of cookies to Mrs. Fishman and dropped them by her heaving head. But Mrs. Fishman kept shrinking and then, one evening, in an instant, she convulsed. Her legs shot up to her chest and her mouth jerked open, like a dummy's mouth clanked wide by a string, and she deflated; all the softness passed out of her and she went as dry and stiff as a fritter.

Marcus sent a message from France. "I'm in the Dordogne, doing the truffle hunt story every food writer does; it's like a matador with his first bull. Though you can't actually hunt truffles, as it turns out. You just follow the old farmer around, with his pig, and after hours of scratching at dirt the pig, not the farmer, gets excited and starts burrowing, until she comes up with a clump of fungus. Here is what I wrote. 'Fat as a baby's fist, the black diamond gives off a sweetly nauseating whiff. On market day, in towns like Martel, the entire village can go dizzy and suffer migraines, inhaling the dense, musky perfume, though that doesn't stop the local housewives from slicing disks of the velvety morel over everything. Small slippers of potatoes come slathered with knobs of truffle butter, chestnut risotto is tossed with truffles, pan-fried foie gras gets bundled up in cabbage leaves lined with slivered truffles. It's a seduction and everything here looks gorged. The ripe livers of the geese and ducks seem ready to split in half. The walnuts are as big as a milkweed. And the truffles, all over-sized, reveal a lacey whorl of ropey veins when you cut them down the middle.'"

"You didn't know I could feign enthusiasm, did you?" he wrote. "I love all the innards, the livers and kidneys they toss in everything, even the salads. But the Frenchmen here are all little weasels, poncey and a bit dodgy. It's why people prefer the simpler migraine of the truffles. I may stop in Paris after I finish with the fungus so it will be sort of another week, I think."

What, I thought, would Jean Rhys do? I circled the squares of South Kensington, passing the posters of missing cats tacked on telephone poles. I visited all the museums I had ignored, and I called in sick and stayed in bed, thinking of Mrs. Fishman, flattened into a tiny curl, and Marcus eating truffles; I watched the heater, waiting for it to glow, and I listened to Tovuh scuttling around the cage, looking for something. The rain started again, like everyone knew it would. I called a psychic. Bring a photo of your loved one, she said, but I only had the one photo and I thought it was too blurry for a reading; my mother was walking fast toward the camera, smiling, and I was behind her, holding her hand. I picked at the last month's newspapers, stacked by my bed because I couldn't read after work, and then I saw what I knew I would. "Fat as a baby's fist, the black diamond gives off a sweetly nauseating whiff," Clara Wilkins wrote in her "Bones over My Shoulder" column, in an old issue of the *Guardian*. "On market day, in towns like Martel, the entire village can go dizzy."

I had to wait all afternoon but when I saw him finally come down the steps of Mr. Wooster's townhouse I was too tired for my big surprise. "Are you over the migraine?" I asked. He squinted at me, as if I were standing a long way off. The little straw hat sat on the back of his sarcastic head, a scratchy tiara, and there was a filmy green scarf wrapped around his neck. "I was," he said, "but it's starting up again."

"Of course," I said, turning and walking, without looking back, watching the iron rails of the gate that surrounded the square in Chelsea, hearing a child scream and maybe Marcus's voice, but maybe not.

I thought of getting another pair of mice and turning the cage into a weekend pile. I'd fill it with little teacups and name the girls after the Mitford sisters—though not the crazy Nazi one—so they could trail some kind of madcap legacy: Debo, Decca, Hen, Honks, Cheeky, Dropsey. But then I realized it was too late for Tovuh to start over. I watched her trying to settle. She moved from the spot where she would lie every night with Mrs. Fishman, under a dome of bedding, and she roamed like an insomniac, curling up in different corners. And then she moved into an empty coconut and wouldn't leave. She propped her thoughtful head on a cushion of tissue, gathered along the lip of her coconut, and looked out. Each night I fed her sunflower seeds, one by one, stroking the soft nape of her neck, and scratching behind the left ear she would hold up. And then I packed my suitcase and banged the space heater over and over again, with a hammer I bought, until it buckled into one big dent.

"Good-bye little Tovuh," I said, holding the last of the seeds out to her. She held it in her paw and looked at me while she ate, and the last thing I remember is the soft fur of her head, framed, like a cameo, in the round door of her coconut. Her little hands were tucked under her chin, clasped together tightly, so it looked, when I shut the door, like she was just starting to pray.

The Heart
of Paris

Douglas A. Martin

I departed alone. I arrived from Luxembourg by train in Paris. Again, I had to change my money. The different currencies went through my hands as I tried to ask for directions. The train I was looking for, to London, the one that goes under the sea, departs from Gare de l'Est. I finally made this out in the French I don't quite speak.

I'm told I need to get on the local subway where I am at Gare du Nord, take it one stop to Gare de l'Est where I should be.

Sliding into the silver train, I shoot forward to the next pause, before the train goes on again. I carry all of my baggage with me.

Eyes occasionally look me up and down.

At Gare de l'Est, I run up the stairs. From Luxembourg there's been a time change, and I'm too late to make the last train to London tonight. The next train is at six in the morning. That leaves me with ten hours to stand around in the cold. I have a hundred-franc note left to my name, and nowhere to go tonight. I was going to go to my sister's in London, call her whenever I got there. I never have any money, but I'm not going to let that stop me. It will be an adventure, that's what I originally thought. I said I'd be fine until I got there.

Gare de l'Est is an open-air train station.

The November winds make the cement floor ice black.

Cold steam seems to pour out of my mouth. I'm scared of spending my last bit of money trying to figure out somewhere to possibly go on the subway. At least in London there would be someone I could ask for help, if I was lost, further directions I could understand. I can't figure out how to call my sister or anyone from here, how to make the phones work. The French speak their French. I'm stuck here for tonight.

More and more families run off to the street lit with neon outside. I eye expensive cheese sandwiches, and finally I break my bill for a late croissant and coffee for dinner, before the concession stands call it quits. The platforms keep emptying out, thinning to a few lost souls. Trains stand still. Fewer bodies walk around fewer bodies. Movement dwindles to the occasional man walking the station from one end to the other.

The toilets here require coins. Hot showers are also available there on the lower level, if you have money for the slots that open them. I have no credit card, nothing, in case of some emergency.

I thought I'd be fine, that I'd just get to London and take it from there, call my sister once I got there.

I shove my hands deep down into the worn pockets of my jeans. The few men left in the station are gathering around a glowing pillar of sorts, a column of electricity that emits heat. Their mouths mumble in this or that language I don't really know, but I understand at least how their bodies are drawn to the radiation of warmth in the center of the station's body. We all understand what it's like to be cold.

I walk over and stand around with them for a couple of hours, alternating between sitting down on my suitcase and standing up to stretch my legs, letting the blood course downward.

A few more men warm their hands around the pillar, reaching out as far as they dare before pulling back, voicing half-hearted observations, like it's only four more hours.

Before the station opens back up properly, they mean, and the trains start running again. People will flood the gates, push against these entries to the veins of the city.

Only four more hours to wait, like this.

When I could take no more of just standing there like I was, I figured it would cost nothing to wander the streets until the sun rose. It couldn't be any colder.

I started to walk out toward the street, and that's when he followed me, beyond the arches, through the western wing. Why else would I have been here in the middle of the night, this late? He must have been able to see I had nowhere to go. He began to converse with me in broken English. I used versions of my few French phrases. He knew I didn't understand much more than his hand on my arm.

He followed me down rue Saint-Martin, further into the city that was closing in around itself. He looked like any other unattractive man. Only a few lights still shined in windows without shades like open eyes watching us wander. Paris did sleep.

He was following me.

He was trying to find a way to phrase desire to find a bed with me. The streets watched. The other men warmed their hands as they watched him come after me. They did nothing. It was the district of the working class. I wondered if he thought I lived here. He kept following me, trying to translate a desire. It was hard to understand exactly what he wanted. I didn't know where I was going, not really. I was just walking.

I just kept walking. I'd never been with a man before in Paris.

I don't know what he thinks of me, if he thinks I come here, sneak out in the middle of the nights, to wander down around the train platforms, despite the baggage, looking for someone like he does. I stare at him, thinking at first maybe he's just trying to ask me for money.

D'argent.

He could be offering it to me. That could be it, part of it. Or is he just cold, homeless, his desire simple? Does he think I have a floor to offer him, anything?

Taxis yawn by us. I don't know how to ask him what he wants. Does he live close by? He has greater access to my body in this weather. I have nowhere to sleep tonight. The thin coat of my racing jacket is so beside the point.

I'd been standing around outside in the air of that station so long, desiring more warmth the later it got, waiting for the night to finally end. That's it. I was turning more tolerant toward any and all company the longer I stood in it.

He's saying he'll buy a room for me tonight, for us.

That's what he's saying. All I have to do is go with him. I don't like him but he'll help. He rubs up and down the length of my racing jacket, black, with the red stripe up the sleeve, while the buildings watch and promise their privacy.

He could push me up against one of the many locked doors up and down the street. He leads me down an alley, and I follow, thinking he must have some cheap hotel in mind, something. He fondles my biceps as he leads me, smiling. I weakly smile back. He offers to help me carry my luggage. It's heavy. I'm a little afraid he's going to run off with it. I don't know why I have a hard-on, but now I do. I'm sure he can see it. He reaches down to touch it then, running his fingers up and down the vein of my jeans. The gold teeth of my zipper strain a little more under his fingers prying.

He's anyone, French. My mouth knows how he's about to get to me, as soon as he finds a place dark enough in me, for me. The situation is suddenly deep enough to go ahead and concede.

The first hotel won't give him a single rate for us, even if there is only one bed we'd sleep on top of each other in.

There are two of you, a desk clerk clicks, wanting more francs.

The man decides to take me someplace cheaper.

Going from one run-down hotel to another in the vicinity, I lug my suitcase behind him holding out this promise of the small comfort of a bed. He might give me some money, which I need. I had just enough money to get to London. It's been a day since I've slept. Maybe I won't really have to do anything, just be allowed to sleep, share the bed with him. He could be nice to me. It's been two days straight now I've been traveling, trying to sleep sitting up on trains.

Once he gets us far enough away from the station, tracks, I'm aware that he could do whatever he wants. There must have been other boys like me he's followed before, trying to read their thoughts, their wants, their needs, standing around the station.

I look like another.

Gare de l'Est is the name of the street.

Another desk clerk in another hotel looks at us. Another desk clerk makes an assessment, quotes some price reasonable enough for the man to pay. There's our room key.

Up the stairs and inside, the bed in the chamber is no larger than a padded bench. He touches my knee on it when I sit down. I smile like it's a pleasant day.

He motions for me to get naked. Get up and get naked. He is undressing, standing there wanting me up against the wall in the room we've parked in.

Now that it's started, I don't know how not to do it.

Outside, Paris breathes through all its cells.

There's no shade on the window. Here's the night's warmth, criminal. The lights from the street break through the window as he huddles with me behind it, turning him toward something more golden.

Later, he unwraps a candy bar he's brought along, and he starts feeding me the foreign chocolate. It might be something they do here I don't know about. The chocolate has been wrapped up by him in a piece of newspaper colored like Monopoly money.

He sucks on my bottom lip while I chew, tells me to touch him here and here. I want to sleep now, but I'm not going anywhere that fast. He wants me to eat more chocolate. He keeps shoving it in my mouth.

He wants me to be a plane on top of him, a ship under him.

He pretends like he's strangling me and I don't say anything, just lie still and pretend he's just pretending. I try to drift away from him in my mind, here, now, and forever.

Someone's touching me. It's nobody.

He looks like nothing.

Chemicals flood my brain, beat out memories of every mouth I've ever encountered like this. He is none of them. He's nothing.

This is nothing.

All of them, I thought I loved all of them before him.

He is something else, something new, and something nothing. I have to tell myself this is still me, here.

He lights his cigarette, and though it strikes me as odd, it's happening. He begins to ash the cigarette into my hair. He sticks his tongue into my mouth now, and his skin smells like suffocation, feels smooth like nothing but a rock, a rubbed blank subway token.

It's Paris, and we are here for only one night.

In London I'll see my sister. That's where she lives. It is almost Christmas. She will be surprised to see me, finally.

He wants me to swallow him in my mouth, now, like coal.

I can feel my body again, but he is putting his hands around my neck. He is putting more of the chocolate in my mouth again.

In a flash, he holds his big hands around my neck. He's just playing like he's strangling me. He says something about me in French. He tastes the chocolate in my mouth, melting.

The room is warm.

Outside, it was so cold I was turning purple. He wants me again, awake. He shakes me, lights another cigarette, reminds me he's still in the room with me, reminds me where I am.

I'm in Paris, waiting for the train in the morning.

Later, he starts to snore, and I do get to sleep finally, up against the wall I could crawl into, like I could crawl inside the building's foundation.

In the morning, he won't let me walk back to the train station alone.

I want him to let me go. He won't let me leave. We stumble back while the sky is still mostly dark around its edges, bruised in its own way.

Some of the men from last night are still there in the station, still waiting on their missed trains. He offers to buy me a coffee. I think that's what he asks me if I want. I nod, but then I'm more reluctant, realizing that means we have to go back across the street together. Nothing is open yet at the station but the doors.

There's an all-hours café across the street. It was there all along.

I was distracted. I was scared I was going to miss my train if I didn't just stand right there and wait for it. I was planning to sleep the whole way under the sea, through the Chunnel.

We cross the street together, and there inside the café is a boy who nods his head coyly at me, points out the waiter while the door comes to rest closed behind me, telling me to have a seat, explaining with his hands that I could join him.

To
the Miraculous
Land of Beauty

Philip Gambone

I am eleven years old, in the sixth grade at the Lincoln School in Wakefield, Massachusetts, and Mr. Rizza, the town's itinerant music teacher, who shows up once a month, has decided that we should be exposed to some of the great classical composers. Our room is furnished with an upright piano, at which Mr. Rizza can plunk out a tune and a simple accompaniment tolerably well. Each month, under the stony watch of Miss Doran, our classroom teacher, Mr. Rizza introduces us to a new composer, telling us a little something about his life: Bach had twenty children, Beethoven went deaf, Handel wrote music that was played on a barge in the river. After each story, he plays us a bit of music, a simple, catchy theme to represent the composer of the month. The signature piece for Bach is a jaunty little bourrée; Schumann's is "The Happy Farmer" from his *Album for the Young.* The hushed, ticktocking slow theme from the *Surprise Symphony* stands for Haydn, and whenever he plays it, Mr. Rizza makes sure to get softer and softer until the very end, when he lets rip with a crashing *Wake up!* chord. At that, we gleefully jump out of our seats, the one raucous moment that sour-faced Miss Doran ever allows us.

Sometime that winter, Mr. Rizza gets to Schubert. For the characteristic piece, he has chosen the "Marche Militaire," or rather, the first theme from it. The opening salvo, like a military reveille, outlines a D major chord. It's bright and snappy—just the kind of thing to make us sit up and listen—and I, who six years later will become the drum major of our high school marching band, just love it. But what really captures my attention is the melody that grows out of that trumpet call. It combines the martial spirit of the opening fanfare and the inexhaustible tunefulness of Schubert's consummate art as a melodist. At the time, I can't put any of this into words, of course, but I feel it—the brio, the lyricism, the generous and genial nature of the music. That and something else: the way, toward the end of the opening tune, the harmony takes a slight detour into another key, a little surprise modulation that turns a charming melody into something absolutely marvelous, indeed mysterious.

I walk home after school that day, humming the tune to myself over and over again. And every time I recall it, I hear once more, in a niche of my aural memory that I've never experienced before, that beguiling change of harmonic color, right where the melody reaches its highest note. I can't get enough of it. It makes me so happy, so oblivious to every little pain and disappointment that my eleven-year-old psyche is heir to. For the rest of the year, whenever Mr. Rizza returns to our classroom and asks for requests, I squeal for Schubert's "Marche Militaire."

That early memory came back to me a few years ago, one hot July afternoon on Vienna's Schwartzenbergplatz, where I was waiting for a streetcar with some friends. There were ten of us in the group, united by a common experience and a common objective. Our destination was the Central Cemetery, Zentralfriedhof, the largest and most famous burial ground in Vienna, where several of the composers that Mr. Rizza had introduced me to, over forty years ago, are now buried.

I had arrived in Vienna two weeks earlier, one of a group of thirty U.S. teachers under the sponsorship of the National Endowment for the Humanities. We were participants in a month-long institute on the operas of Mozart, perhaps the composer most famously associated with Vienna. It was a dream study tour: the chance to look closely at a few masterpieces (we were examining the "Abduction" and "The Magic Flute"), to attend performances at one of the greatest opera houses in the world, to live and breathe magnificent music in the very city where it was created. Mornings we attended classes in a lecture hall at the Schottenhof, an eighteenth-century monastery on the Freyung market square. Afternoons we explored the city, sometimes in formal outings, sometimes at our own leisure. Our pilgrimage to the Zentralfriedhof was one of the many optional excursions our professors had planned for us.

When our tram arrived, we climbed aboard and settled in. The trip was slow and stuffy, a lumbering journey out along the Simmeringer Hauptstrasse. By the time we got off at the main entrance—the Central Cemetery is so large one has a choice of three different tram stops—we were listless and drowsy. It was the summer of 2003, one of Europe's hottest. I noticed that we were practically the only visitors that afternoon. As we ambled toward the gates, the sight of flower stalls overflowing with profusions of fresh, colorful blossoms perked me up. Vendors dressed in neat smocks were going about their business in a restrained, unobtrusive manner—no hawking or shouting, no raucous competing with each other for business—the understated decorum that is so much the spirit of Viennese life.

We had been previously informed about the flower stalls. "No need to bring flowers from the city," our professor had told us. "If you want to decorate the graves, you can buy flowers there." We headed toward the booths to make our purchases. I knew exactly what I wanted: three red roses.

In keeping with the focus of the seminar, our outing was intended as a kind of pilgrimage to Mozart's grave, or rather, to one of two Mozart "graves," neither of them definitively the composer's final resting place. The actual burial, on a cold, stormy day in December 1791, took place in an unmarked, third-class grave (the "pauper's grave" of legend) in the St. Marx Cemetery. Today a simple monument in a quiet, unobtrusive corner of that shabby burial ground commemorates the event if not the actual location, which remains unknown. Later that afternoon, we'd visit the St. Marx site, too; but for now, we wanted the other Mozart grave, the far more elaborate one at the Zentralfriedhof. For four and a half euros, I bought my three red roses, then followed my friends through the gates.

When I applied to the seminar the previous winter, I had expected that lots of gay men would be attracted to a month-long immersion in opera. As it turned out, I was one of only a few gay men among the thirty of us. Initially, this state of affairs disappointed me. At fifty-five, I had recently broken up with a man whom I had considered to be the love of my life, a man I had literally traveled halfway around the world to be with. Minh had made me ecstatically happy, as blissful as the miller's apprentice in Schubert's great song cycle *Schöne Müllerin.* Now, single once more, I had hoped to make some new gay friends, perhaps even fall into a gay romance, among my opera-loving comrades. In fact, I did make friends, both gay and straight, but as to the prospect of a love affair, things seemed pretty dim. So dim that a field trip to a cemetery was turning out to be the highlight of my week.

It was a green, shady world that we entered—leafy trees, elegant landscaping, the whole place immaculately manicured. For size, beauty, and the impressive array of its illustrious inhabitants and their monuments, the Zentralfriedhof, my guidebook told me, rivals the Père-Lachaise cemetery in Paris. It was easy to see why. We followed Central Avenue to the *Ehrengräber,* or Groves of Honor, where Austria's most renowned artists and politicians are buried. We were looking for Sector 32A, the section for composers.

"Oh, my gosh," someone suddenly whispered. "There they are!"

A respectful hush fell over the group. As corny as it might sound, I felt—I think we all did—as if we were entering hallowed ground, the final resting place of some of the greatest gods of music. We easily spotted Mozart's monument and assembled around it, acolytes at the sacred altar. As a former Roman Catholic, my initial impulse was to do what Roman Catholics do at gravesites—kneel, or make the sign of the cross, or say a prayer—something to mark the solemnity of the occasion. Instead, as did the rest of my colleagues, I merely stood there in silence. Eventually, someone broke the stillness by moving forward and laying her flowers at the base of the statue. The others followed suit. I did not leave a rose. I had three other composers in mind, three favorites who had not been topics of discussion during our seminar.

Breaking away from the group, I wandered over to the first, Beethoven's grave. A grand, metronome-shaped pillar decorated with a bronze lyre, it's clearly a monument to a hero. Beethoven—the consummate Romantic artist; the angst-ridden, triumphant revolutionary in whose hands the old classical forms of the symphony, string quartet, and piano sonata reached new heights of expressiveness; the promoter of the brotherhood of mankind. Once again, I felt inadequate. All I could do was stand quietly, trying to grasp what it meant to be there. Then I leaned over the low, wrought-iron enclosure and left my rose on the ground.

Brahms was a few steps away. Here, too, I was acutely aware of being in the presence of something great. Brahms is traditionally considered the heir to Beethoven's legacy, the third of the three great "B's." Brahms was an exquisite craftsman who achieved a perfect fusion of intellect and emotion, the voice of elegiac pathos and autumnal serenity. I had promised a friend of mine in Tokyo that I would take a photo of the grave for him. I left the second rose, stepped back, and composed the shot.

One rose was left. I'd saved the best for last. My colleagues must have sensed that I wanted to be alone, because no one followed me as I slowly made my way over to Schubert's grave. I had brought along my Walkman and a CD of his dances for piano that I'd picked up at Caruso, one of Vienna's many classical record shops. I pushed the play button. A *Ländler*, a slow country waltz, came on, its lilting melodies and bittersweet harmonies drifting through my head. I was glad the sun was so bright, a perfect excuse to wear sunglasses, because tears were welling up in my eyes.

Beethoven and Schubert each died before the Zentralfriedhof was opened in 1874, Beethoven in March of 1827, Schubert a year and a half later. Both were buried in the local cemetery of Währing, Schubert near the grave of Beethoven, whom he had idolized. In 1888, their remains were transferred to the Central Cemetery, an occasion marked by festivities that included thousands of amateur choral singers.

Given how high-pitched my expectations were, the monument itself was a bit of a disappointment. The architect had opted for a Greco-Roman style, one modified by late nineteenth-century German romanticism. It's a tall slab of white marble surmounted by an ornate triangular pediment and flanked by two graceful, though slightly effete, Ionic columns decorated with a pair of winged cherubs at the bases. The relief sculpture in the slab depicts one of the Muses holding a lyre and crowning a bust of Schubert with a laurel wreath. One reference refers to "the delicate images in stone, reflective of Schubert's sense for beautiful melody." But the whole thing, as sincere as it was, struck me as an example of Vienna's ever-so-tasteful flirtation with kitsch.

As I stood there, listening to the music, memories of my long history with Schubert filled my head: Mr. Rizza playing the "Marche Militaire"; a few years later, discovering my mother's scratchy 78 recordings of the *Unfinished Symphony* and the *Rosamunde* ballet music; sophomore year in high school when I played the fourth French horn part in the *Great C major Symphony*; taking voice lessons in college, frustrated that I couldn't recreate the beautiful sounds I heard on Fischer-Dieskau recordings of Schubert. Frustrated, too, because I was in love with my voice teacher's accompanist. He was a thin man with effeminate mannerisms—delicate, pliant wrists, a studied toss of the head, an overall swish to the way he moved. Actually, I wasn't in love with him as much as I just wanted him to notice me, to look at me (his head was always in the score!), to let me know that he knew I was a gay man, too. Except for a love affair the previous summer, I had not come out to a soul. It was the seventies.

Over the years, without my realizing it at first, Schubert became my hero. After college, I discovered his other symphonies, then the chamber music—the glorious F major octet and the late, haunting string quartets—the Masses, the men's choruses, the piano sonatas. And the songs, hundreds of songs, many of them small masterpieces. (Brahms himself called one of Schubert's songs "the loveliest song ever written.") The sheer volume of his music is staggering—close to a thousand compositions in all, and each one a delight, a surprise, an astonishing journey into colors and textures, ideas and moods, that I have found in no other composer.

By now, the sun was lowering on the horizon, casting long shadows onto the green-and-golden lawns. When the CD finished, I popped in another one. My friends looked ready to leave—we still had the St. Marx Cemetery to visit—but I wanted to stay longer, listening to this lovely music, music as delicious and delicate as the description of eating an apple that Rilke makes in his *Sonnets to Orpheus:* "something / indescribable slowly happening in your mouth."

I thought about other aspects of Schubert's life, too—about his painful battle with syphilis; his bouts of despondency; his death at age thirty-one. I thought about the courage and good cheer with which he faced all this sorrow. And, of course, as a gay man, I thought about his sexuality. Whom did he love?—this charming young man with his coterie of male friends, "playing and singing as if they were one," as one of Schubert's biographers has put it.

As far as we know, Schubert courted only one woman, Therese Grob, a childhood neighbor and the soprano soloist in his first Mass. "She was not exactly pretty," Schubert once recollected to his friend Anselm Hüttenbrenner, "and her face had pockmarks; but she had a heart, a heart of gold." Schubert asserted that for three years Therese "hoped I would marry her; but I could not find a position which would have provided for us both." Little is known about the actual nature of their relationship, which ended in 1816, when Schubert was nineteen. In his diary entry of September 8, 1816, the composer noted, "To a free man matrimony is a terrifying thought in these days; he exchanges [that freedom] either for melancholy or for crude sensuality."

Whatever the reasons behind Schubert's reluctance to marry, Therese finally "bowed to her parents' wishes and married someone else." With that, Schubert seems to have given up the courtship of women. Hüttenbrenner noted that Schubert was "cold and unforthcoming toward the fair sex at parties" and, indeed, seemed to have "a dominating aversion for the daughters of Eve." Moreover, while there exist many affectionate letters between Schubert and his male friends, not a single such letter to a woman has survived.

Whether or not Schubert had other ladyloves, what is certain is that he was hardly celibate. The memoirs left by Schubert's friends strongly suggest that the composer was not only sexually promiscuous (he contracted syphilis around 1822) but also, as musicologist Maynard Solomon puts it, "his promiscuity was of an unorthodox character." Prostitution, rampant in Schubert's Vienna, is the standard understanding of what was behind this alleged promiscuity. But some scholars have looked elsewhere. In a famous and controversial 1989 essay, "Franz Schubert and the Peacocks of Benvenuto Cellini," Solomon concluded, "That the young men of the Schubert circle loved each other seems amply clear." He went on to say that it is "reasonably probable that their primary sexual orientation was a homosexual one. By finding sexual release with anonymous partners in Vienna's *Halbwelt* they apparently were able to maintain idealized passionate friendships with each other."

What might Vienna's homosexual *Halbwelt* have been like in Schubert's time? In 1782 an Austrian officer who had spent several months in Berlin published a series of notes on the city's "gallantries," a euphemism for extramarital sexual life. Among his observations, the officer described the homosexual demimonde he encountered there. At a party one evening, he saw men who "embraced with the warmest tenderness, kissed each other, squeezed hands, and said such sweet things to each other as a fop might say to a lady." At first, the officer takes "these displays for merely a friendly tone, for true male sympathy or spirits," until it is explained to him that the affectionate gentlemen are "warm brothers," that is, men who engage in "Socratic love."

The host continues this unorthodox educational tour by taking the officer to a *Knabentabagie,* a "boy establishment," or male bordello. There the soldier observes "a gathering of ten to twelve boys of various ages, men of various character at their sides." (This is James D. Steakley's translation in his article in *Male Homosexuality in Renaissance and Enlightenment Europe.*) "With astonishment I watched the embraces with which the older rams met the younger ones. There a foursquare Bacchant toasted his Ganymede with a full wine glass, there a second one cuddled against his boy with the warmest feelings of delight; here on the other hand a loose lad played with the belt of his Zeus, and there a victor disappeared with his Thracian booty."

Did similar boy establishments exist in Vienna during Schubert's life? Were there cruising areas? No explicit documentation has yet surfaced, but there is plenty of evidence to suggest that assignations were easily arranged under the pretext of various kinds of male clubs. Another traveler, writing shortly after Schubert's death, noted that the Viennese had "no great need of streetwalkers or stews, in a city where every liaison which a stranger may choose to form, can be carried on, without offense to morals, even in his hotel or lodgings."

Maynard's article was soundly denounced in many circles, as have been other attempts to address the possibility of Schubert's homosexuality. Such scholars have been deemed crackpots, "determined to drag our Schubert through the mud," as one particularly hostile Schubert-lover once put it. This "closeting of Schubert," to use the phrase of musicologist Philip Brett, is supposedly justified on two fronts. The evidence is scanty and inconclusive, the naysayers attest. Moreover, they deny the relevance that Schubert's sexuality could possibly have on any appreciation or understanding of his music. During my month in Vienna, I had a lot of time to wonder about that.

Evenings, after the opera or dinner, my colleagues and I would often go out for drinks—the soft, pleasant Austrian wine, Grüner Velt-liner, was our beverage of choice that summer—talking shop until the wee hours. But sometimes, I'd make my excuses and disappear alone into the night. Armed with a map and a guidebook, I'd wan-der the streets, scouting out gay venues: the restaurants, bars and cafés, saunas, bookstores, and cruising areas of the modern-day city.

Early on, I discovered the Theseus Temple in the Volksgarten. Despite the fact that it was not listed in any of the gay guides I consulted, it seemed like a perfect place for cruising. Built in 1823, the temple was a copy of one in Athens. Schubert's contemporaries deemed it a handsome structure, worthy enough to house another Greek-inspired work of art, the gorgeous, and utterly sexy, statue of Theseus and the Centaur by Antonio Canova, which the sculptor had completed a few years earlier.

Schubert's friend, the poet Grillparzer, described how he paced the streets of Vienna one night, anxious and lonely, until he came to the Volksgarten, where he threw himself down, sobbing, on the steps of the Theseus Temple. It was easy for me to imagine lots of romantic young men of the day prostrating themselves at luscious Theseus's feet. Canova's statue has been moved to the main staircase of the city's Museum of Fine Arts, though nowadays there's an equally fetching statue, "The Winner," that stands on a pedestal just outside the temple. Sculpted by Josef Müllner in 1922, it's of a naked bronze youth, all hearty, healthy Aryan masculinity, one of the most homoerotic pieces of sculpture I'd ever seen.

As it turned out, I never saw any cruising in the Volksgarten, though I quickly learned that the nearby park in front of the Rathaus more than made up for that. It was there, and at the Kaiserbrundl, a sauna in the shadows of the Franziskanerkirche, a sweet baroque church run by the Franciscans, that I began to hook up with gay men. The Kaiserbrundl soon became a regular nighttime destination for me. Large, clean, and affordable, the place was tricked out in faux-Moorish decor, though it also sported all the more modern amenities of other European bathhouses I'd visited—steam room, sauna, showers, dark room, private cabins, a bar, and a small swimming pool, again *à la turca*. Sometimes I'd stay all night, enjoying the twenty-first-century equivalent of those "liaisons which a stranger may choose to form." My strangers were a cross-section of gay Mitteleuropa: Austrians, Poles, Germans, Bulgarians.

One night at Kaiserbrundl, I got to talking to a guy in the sauna. A few years younger than I, Sandor had a lovely smile, a nice body, and a beautiful cock. His English was excellent and we quickly fell into easy, friendly conversation. We talked about our jobs, about Vienna, about his name, which I said didn't sound Austrian. No, it was Hungarian, he told me, from his grandfather's side, a legacy of the multi-national Austro-Hungarian Empire.

After a while, I invited Sandor to join me in one of the private cabins. At first, he seemed reluctant. I took his hesitation as a sign that, although he wasn't interested, he didn't want to hurt my feelings, one more example of the sweetness that I liked in him. But then he surprised me by changing his mind. "Sure, let's go," he agreed. When I suggested that we take a shower first, Sandor told me to go ahead but that he wanted a few more minutes in the sauna. I made my way to the shower room, figuring this was another one of his strategies to let me off gently, but when I returned to fetch him, there he was waiting for me.

The first cabin we tried was equipped with a TV blaring a porno film. I'd hoped for something a bit more intimate, so I suggested we find another, quieter cabin. For the next two hours we made love. Sandor's kisses were more passionate and loving than I'd expected. I began to get it into my head that his hesitation had just been a case of shyness. Between lovemaking, we talked. He told me that he used to live in Vienna but now had a house in the Austrian countryside. He had come into the city that evening to attend a dinner party at his brother and sister-in-law's. Eventually it came out that he'd had a lover for eleven years, but that they had recently broken up. The ex-lover was living in Vienna with a new boyfriend now, a much younger man, Sandor emphasized, "only twenty-five years old."

I scanned his face, trying to pick up how Sandor felt about men our age taking up with much younger lovers. Was he jealous, disdainful, ridiculing? And what was his attraction to me? Was I just the stranger of the moment, distracting him from his heartache? I knew I shouldn't hope for too much—does anyone ever find a long-term romance in a bathhouse?—but at one point in our lovemaking, when Sandor stopped, looked up at me, and said, "You in Boston, me in Vienna—why?" my heart just melted.

We nestled into each other's arms again. Except for the occasional tread of someone walking by or the muffled sound of a TV, the whole place, as far as I could tell, had taken on the peaceful, sleepy atmosphere of post-sex languor. I knew I couldn't invite him back to my hotel, where the front desk was guarded by a clerk as strict and unforgiving as old Miss Doran back in my sixth-grade days. Instead, nuzzling into Sandor, I gingerly suggested we should get together again soon, perhaps for dinner. Suddenly, he was full of excuses—a business trip to Cologne, just one day back in town, another trip . . .

"Well," I ventured, not wanting to be pushy, "I could give you the telephone number of my hotel and you can call me if you'd like to get together."

At first, this seemed acceptable to him. Then, all of a sudden, Sandor disengaged from my embrace. "I can't see you again." A moment of silence passed between us before he added, "Look, I think I'll just spend another hour here and then drive home."

I nodded my understanding, though I didn't understand at all. Not a half hour before, we had been making passionate love. What had happened to upset the mood so quickly? What had I said or done? What story wasn't he telling me? He gave me a final, chaste kiss, one that felt completely different from those he'd lavished on me earlier, the brush-off kiss, the consolation prize.

It was five in the morning when I left Kaiserbrundl. Though a blue sky was dawning over Vienna, the little baroque church across the way was still in shadows. As I walked the narrow, empty streets back to my hotel, Schubert came into my head—this time, the cantabile theme from the slow movement of the *Great C major Symphony*, one of the saddest, most tender, most valedictory melodies that I know—another kind of consolation prize.

Consolation, and more, much more. Schubert's music engages me in ways that no other composer's music does. Whenever I listen to one of his compositions, I'm drawn into a world where light and shadow, surface and depth, sweetness and pain, clarity and mystery are held in transcendental balance. Listen, for example, to a song like "Wiedersehn" (D. 855), a deceptively simple two-strophe composition about the anticipation of love's return. In gorgeously calm but radiant music, Schubert perfectly captures the exquisiteness of suspense, "sweet bearer of rapture." You don't really need to know what the German means to catch the hushed ecstasy of love's greeting, like "the sound of the pole star thundering down through night and remote distance."

Musicologist Susan McClary notes that Schubert "was producing constructions of male subjectivity that differed markedly from most of those that surrounded him." She points to several features of Schubert's work—especially his "deviance" from the compositional practices and formal tonal conventions of his day—as evidence of an essentially "effeminate" character to his music. "Schubert," she goes on to say, "tends to disdain goal-oriented desire per se for the sake of a sustained image of pleasure and an open, flexible sense of self—both of which are quite alien to the constructions of masculinity then being adopted as natural."

"An open, flexible sense of self"—I've often wondered whether we homosexuals engage the world with a sense of self that is more fluid, flexible, and unfinished than do straight people, to whom the prevailing culture offers nicely prepackaged images of who they are and how they should behave. For most of us queer folk, the dominant paradigm holds out none of that—no reassuring roles and clearly defined identities. By and large, we're left to make it up as we go along, improvising the bittersweet impromptus of our lives, always a little bit aware that we're deviating from the norm. Is that what I respond to in Schubert, the effeminate, flexible, exploratory character of his music? The pilgrim soul? The night wanderer?

Schubert's friends affectionately called him "Schwammerl," which means "little mushroom," though "tubby" would not be an inaccurate translation. In fact, Schubert was quite short, not much over five feet one inch, and quite pudgy. But, for the life of me, I simply can't find the "ugliness" that one historian sees in Schubert's appearance. On the contrary, for the longest time I've thought of him as rather "cute," the Matt Damon of Biedermeier Vienna. An 1825 watercolor drawing by Wilhelm August Rieder captures the twenty-eight-year-old Schubert in all his sweet-faced loveliness—the head of curly brown hair, the full lips and delicately sloping nose, the dark sensitive eyes beneath a pair of wire-rimmed spectacles, the dimpled chin. I feel embarrassed even describing the painting. What possible relevance could Schubert's looks—handsome or not—have on any serious assessment of him as an artist? Is my enthusiasm for Schubert's music merely an extrapolation of the warm, fuzzy, adolescent charge I used to get—still do get, in fact—over his pretty face? Shouldn't I keep those feelings under wraps, in the closet, as it were?

Whatever the source of my pleasure in Schubert, it's not simple. It encompasses the complexity and mystery of a love affair. For me, Schubert is inexhaustible. Attempts to categorize him—"divinely frivolous," says one critic; "apocalyptic classicism," says another—can only suggest the full spectrum of his music's richness. Say it is happy music, and you soon recall the heaven-storming anguish of the *Unfinished Symphony* or the terrifying fury of *Erlkönig*. Say it is bittersweet music, and the raucous jollity of the Octet comes to mind. Say it is sober, and there's the will-o'-the-wisp sprightliness of the G major quartet (D. 887). Delicate? How about the soaring majesty of the *Mass in A-flat Major* (D. 678)? Naïve? Listen to the virtuosic complexity of the *Wanderer Fantasy* (D. 760). Perhaps the only conclusion to make about Schubert's music is that it is generous: it does not skimp or hold back. It gives unsparingly, openheartedly, yard after yard, bolt after bolt, of radiant sonic fabric.

Do I have a favorite piece? How can I when there is so much, and it is so good, and so astonishingly varied?—the liquid, rippling outpourings of the *Impromptu in A-flat Major* (D. 899); the easy, expansive gladness of the *Piano Sonata in A major* (D. 664); the heartbreaking tenderness of *Lob der Tränen* (D. 711); the haunting and sweet robustness of the music for male chorus; even the schmaltzy romanticism of some of his waltzes, those pieces I played on my CD at Schubert's grave. It is all, as Schubert's biographer Alfred Einstein once put it, music that has "fallen from heaven."

—╀—

On my final Sunday morning in Vienna, I visited Schubert's birth house. You can get there on another streetcar line, the one that runs up the Nussdorfer Strasse. It's a modest apartment, one room and a kitchen, 25 square meters in size. Maintained by the city, the reconstruction approximates the state of the dwelling as it was in 1797, the year Schubert was born. While almost all the Schubert family furniture has disappeared, the curators have deliberately not sought to refurnish the house in similar, period pieces. Instead, there's a simple exhibit of memorabilia: manuscripts, published scores, paintings and drawings of Schubert and other members of his family and circle of friends, a piano once owned by Schubert's brother Ignaz, a concert program, and, of course, those wire-rimmed spectacles, now cracked.

Various stations around the apartment provide headphones and channels for listening to recordings of Schubert's music. For an hour that sunny morning, I had the place to myself. I spent most of the time moving from headphone to headphone, just listening to the music, again fighting back tears. Tears over what? The beauty of the music, certainly. But so much else, too. The sense of Schubert's greatness cut so short. The joy of being in the very room where, as a boy, he lived and made music. The sadness of my magical summer coming to an end. The sense of my own mortality, of my smallness, of my chances—for love, for achievement, for leaving something beautiful in the world—dwindling away. But tears of gratefulness as well. For the life of this man, for his inestimable musical legacy.

Nine days before he died, in the last letter he ever wrote—it was to his friend Schober—Schubert mentioned that he was reading the novels of James Fenimore Cooper. He tells Schober that he has already read *The Last of the Mohicans, The Spy, The Pilot,* and *The Pioneers,* adding "If you have anything else by him I beg you to leave it for me."

What was Schubert's fascination with Cooper? And why, of all people, did he communicate this fascination to Schober, the most decadent member of the Schubert Circle and the one who "lured [him] into loose living"? What did he find so compelling in these German translations of *The Leatherstocking Tales?* Was it the unbounded American landscapes? The bumptious fledgling democracy? The homoerotic friendship between Natty Bumppo and Chingachgook? The Vienna of Schubert's time was a repressive police state. Surveillance, arrest, and persecution were common. Metternich, the Austrian foreign minister, was suspicious of any kind of liberalism; peace and quiet were his watchwords. "The head and heart of immature persons must be protected . . . from the dangerous phantoms of perverted minds" ran the Censorship Edict of 1810. Indeed, Schubert himself was once hauled in for questioning by the police because of his association with student activists. And our poet friend Grillparzer, whom we have already met weeping on the steps of the Theseus Temple, once recorded, "The censor has broken me down—One must emigrate to North America in order to give his ideas free expression."

What would Schubert have thought of the America of the 1820s? What would he think of the America of today? Would he be delighted or appalled? What would he think of the insipid mediocrity that passes for "music"? What would he think of the frenetic pace of life? Of the degradation of nature? Of our obsession with wealth? Of a government that more and more seems strikingly like Metternich's? On the other hand, what would he think of the freedoms we still enjoy? What would he say of the freedom that people have—at least in some places—to express same-sex affection openly? What would he think of the advances in medical science that created penicillin to treat syphilis? What would he think of gay marriage? Would such gorgeous, "effeminate" music have poured forth from his pen had he been more sexually fulfilled? To what extent is the art of a homosexual artist an art born of what Edmund White once identified as the *blessure,* the wound?

One last memory: It is the summer of 1979 and my boyfriend and I are touring the Iberian peninsula. We've come to Mafra, a nondescript town 40 kilometers northwest of Lisbon, to see the one attraction that the guidebooks say is worth a visit, the Convento-Palácio de Mafra. A combined palace and monastery, it's one of the largest and most sumptuous (some would say kitschy) baroque complexes in Europe. We've toured the church and some of the apartments, and are now taking a rest in one of the courtyards. Suddenly, blaring from a row of huge, open windows on the second floor of the building across the way is a loud, scratchy recording of Schubert's "Marche Militaire"—in an arrangement for wind band!

Checking the guidebook, we discover that part of the complex is now a military barracks. I look up at those second-story windows again. Inside whatever enormous room they penetrate—a baroque ballroom converted into an indoor parade ground?—the soldiers of the barracks are drilling. I can't see them, but I can hear the heavy tread of their boots on the floor and the commandant calling out the steps, the rhythms of Portuguese totally out of synch with Schubert's music: *direito! esquerda!* Framed in one of the windows, two soldiers in fatigues and berets are relaxing, smoking cigarettes. The whole scene strikes me as incongruous, more charming than serious—the sleepy Sunday morning ambiance in the courtyard, the use of Schubert's music for a military drill, the casual way that these two soldiers seem to have dropped out of the exercises. But this is Portugal, a few years after the Carnation Revolution toppled a military dictatorship. The sun is shining; everyone is happy.

It's also the summer I have turned thirty-one, and I am feeling old. And not quite sure about this man I call my boyfriend. We've been together about three years. Something isn't quite right, though it will be several more years before I figure it out—that we're not suited for each other, that our dreams run in different directions. For now, I just allow myself to fantasize about these beautiful, olive-skinned Portuguese boys playing at being soldiers to tunes by my beloved Franz Schubert.

Now, twenty-nine years and three boyfriends later, I wonder about "dreams that go in different directions." Do they really? I'd like to think that Schubert's music has taught me that we all ultimately dream the same dream, though to say what that dream is would be to diminish it. In 1821, Schubert set Schiller's wonderful poem "Sehnsucht" (D. 636)—the word means "longing"—to some of his most impassioned music. It is a poem, and a song, about the soul's search for a way out of *dieses Tales Gründen,* the valley's depths. Beyond the cold mists, the poet can discern lovely hills, harmonious sounds, golden fruits, eternal sunshine, but the madness of a raging storm separates him from this heavenly place, and the boat that might take him across has no boatman. The final stanza, in Richard Wigmore's translation, concludes:

> Jump in without hesitation!
> The sails are billowing.
> You must trust, and you must dare.
> For the gods grant no pledge;
> Only a miracle can convey you
> To the miraculous land of beauty.

Schubert is one of those miracles in my life. He makes me glad to be alive. In his company, I trust and I dare. I can't imagine traveling without him.

The Law of Diminishing Returns

Dale Peck

Someone told me they were more careful in England. He said they were more careful in Europe actually, because of all the wars. He said as a result of centuries of conflict they had less to spare over there, less to waste, and so, dutifully, but not, like the environmentalists in the States, piously, they collected their cans and plastic and paper, their dead batteries, bald tires, and scrap metal and turned it all in for recycling, they built energy-efficient appliances, took shorter showers, swaddled their children in cloth rather than disposable diapers. On account of the wars? I remember asking. They bombed the *shit* out of that place, my informant told me. Trenches, he said. Mines. Mustard gas. It all had its effect, and they're still feeling it today. Blood, he said. Blood is a poison. On some battlefields it was years before anything would grow. He had said they were more careful in Europe but I had to settle, when I left, for England—the language thing—and I guess I just hoped that the English would follow the European example because I liked the idea of living among a careful people: I liked not just the idea of frugality but of return, of re-use, of, to put it bluntly, second chances, and it seemed at first that England, that London, where I settled, did offer that. Within a week I had a flat in a terrace house, in Bethnal Green admittedly, but it was cheap and clean, two large barren rooms with a view over my downstairs neighbor's vegetable garden, I had an umbrella, a TravelCard, an adapter cable for my computer, a phone number even, and I had Derek. That's *my* name, I said, when he told me his. It wasn't actually, but I would have used the line no matter what his name had been. I was a new man in a new country and I had decided that a new name—not a new name, but a borrowed name, a recycled one—suited the occasion, if only for a night. Your name's Derek? he said, fancy that, and then he grinned and he said, Fancy a walk in the park, Derek? I thought he was joking, and brought him instead to my place—I'd gone, on a Sunday night, and on the advice of a gay guide I'd bought, to a loud little club just down Mile End Road—and in the morning I woke up with a large bruise on my tailbone, because I had blankets but no bed. No bed and no Derek: he'd slipped out in the middle of the night, leaving only the bruise and a note next to the phone. *I took the liberty of taking your number,* he wrote. *You're a sound sleeper.* He had, in fact, peeled off the tiny piece of paper affixed to the phone which B.T. had provided me, and thus he didn't just take my number, he deprived me of the ability to give it to anyone else, because I hadn't yet memorized it. I think that's how he got me. The sex had been great but it had also just been sex; it was the peculiar piracy of peeling off a sticky phone label and pocketing it, so odd, so determined in securing its goal, which led me to believe that Derek must have felt something more than mere lust for me. At that time I believed emotion flowed from motion, from action, that love was a feeling emanating from a certain routine—sex, shared meals, shopping for Christmas presents—and it seemed to me that Derek's little theft was the first step in such a routine. Now, as I look back on it, it seems to me that I was thinking about love as if it were some kind of byproduct. Love is like trash: it's not something you hoard, it's merely something you don't waste, like heat, or water, or paper. Or words, for that matter, for what is more recycled than the language of love? The language of hate, perhaps, or the language of disinterest: *Let's be friends.* Which is what Derek said when he called a few days later. He said Let's be friends, shall we? and I assented innocuously, because I was trying to think of a way to ask him what number he'd just dialed. I never did, and as a result didn't know what my phone number was until the bill came three weeks later, by which point Derek had called several more times, always during the day, and once or twice a week he stopped by on his way home from work. In the meantime I acquired a bed, a sofa, a table and two chairs, enough dishes to feed as many as four people at the same time, and my flat absorbed all of these new acquisitions and still somehow seemed empty, and so, as an exercise, I typed up every single thing in the flat that wasn't attached to it by nails or glue, starting with myself and ending with three loose paper clips I found in the bottom of my computer case, and the entire list, single-spaced, a single entry per line, stretched to seven pages, and I felt a little better then, and reminded myself how deceptive appearances can be. The list went with me on my first trip to the local recycling center, but the pages I left there were just as quickly replaced by an office supply store I'd found which sold unbleached stock made from 100 percent postconsumer waste. I had, as they say, gotten my break, and I was working on a screenplay, and also several treatments, and the amount of paper I went through was unconscionable. I wrote at home, all day, every day; the words barely trickled out of me but even so the pages seemed to flow from my printer, the spool of fax paper spewed forth a cataract of queries and comments and suggestions for cutting which seemed to require twice as much new material to fill the gap, and the stacks of paper I took regularly to the recycling center were embarrassingly large. I'd been . . . what, not careful, not in the manner of Europeans, but concerned about waste since I was a child. People think I'm lying when I say that my earliest memory is of Jimmy Carter appearing on television during the OPEC crisis, but it's true. He sat, as I recall, in front of a fireplace in which burned a few small logs, and in a quiet drawl I still consider the very voice of reasonableness, if not reason itself, he urged Americans to turn their thermostats down to sixty-eight degrees. Put on a sweater, he said, pulling on the placket of the gray cardigan that, along with two destroyed helicopters and seven dead bodies in the middle of the Iranian desert, would become a symbol of his political folly. The cardigan might have been light blue actually, the number of bodies in the desert higher or lower than seven, but the one detail I've never forgotten is the temperature, sixty-eight, if only because it happened to be the year of my birth. Sixty-eight degrees and a sweater—not sixty-seven and thermal underwear, not sixty-nine and a T-shirt. Perhaps the only thing that bothered me about my flat in London was that the thermostat was scored in Celsius, and several months into my stay, in my own sweater—and scarf sometimes, and open-fingered gloves—I still worried that I was wasting energy, that ir-retrievable kilowatts were pushing through the warped glass and wind-rattled frame of my living room's big bay window and evapo-rating into the gray gray *gray* winter sky that hung above London like a shroud, but all I did was buy a set of heavy curtains to help retain the heat. By then I was more worried about Derek, about, I should say, my relationship with him, which had taken on a pattern that seemed a little too familiar for comfort: the phone call from work, the quick fuck between five-thirty and six, the occasional drink at Benjy's, the club where we'd met, or some gay venue in Brixton or Islington or Shepherd's Bush—places, as my guidebook told me, distinctly not on the beaten gay track—and finally I just asked him if there was someone else. Not exactly, he said. Not exactly? I repeated. Well, he said, the truth is that there is someone. *You're* someone else. He didn't call for a week after that, but he did call eventually, and he said he had an extra ticket for a play on the South Bank, Friday, he said, eight sharp. Did I want to go? In the end I was early; he was late. I'd wanted to ask him how he came to possess an "extra" ticket for a play, but immediately he said Derek's ill, meaning, I realized with a start, the someone measured against whom I was someone else. He grinned sardonically when he said it, and I wondered if he were on to my ruse, if he'd found something with my real name on it in my flat, or if he was merely perpetuating a ruse of his own, but before I could question him we were rushed into the theater by the usher, just as the curtain lifted. Coffee? Derek said afterward, and I assented, picturing some dark firelit café where jazz would be playing softly, more West Village than West London, really, but it didn't matter, really, since what I got was one of the garishly bright antiseptic eateries at the theater complex itself. One espresso later—served in an unbelievably over-designed demitasse made of bleached white paper complete with a glued-on handle whose wings folded open and shut like a butterfly's—and Derek said, I have to be off, and I started to protest but he said, My patient calls, and then he shook my hand with mock formality, winked, and told me to be a good boy and use the loo before I got on the tube. He nodded at a door behind me. Another espresso—the countergirl looked at me strangely when I presented my paper cup to be refilled, They're not free you know, she said, to which I replied, I *know*— and I headed for the door Derek had indicated. It led to a hallway which led to a long narrow descending staircase which led in turn to another hallway, this one dim, dirty, and smelling of subterranean damp, at the end of which was a door marked Gentlemen. There was no Ladies to be seen. I went through the loudly protesting door, and then, three feet farther on, another, just as loud, and found finally a small room containing three sinks and three stalls. No urinals. I almost turned around but by then I really did have to go, so I settled for a stall. What a waste, I thought, addressing Derek in my head, 5.0 litres per flush as the Armitage Shanks commode dutifully indicated in faint periwinkle stencil, all for a thin piddle that would hardly fill one of those ridiculously wasteful paper demitasses used upstairs, and almost at the same time as I noticed the hole chiseled into the wall next to the toilet roll dispenser I heard the delayed double whine of the outer doors, and I knew why Derek had sent me down here. The stalls were partitioned by what looked like granite, a brown stone mottled with black and white and flecked here and there with purple, their doors were oak and heavy—solid, I mean, not mere veneer—and brightly varnished, and they reached all the way to the floor; the toilet was, in fact, rather more grand than the poured concrete structure twenty or thirty feet overhead, a structure which just happened to be the preeminent theatrical venue in the country, by which I mean that it wasn't exactly the place one would expect to find a glory hole, let alone one so laboriously, even lovingly constructed: perfectly round, its edges invitingly soft, and placed at an appropriately average height. The door to the stall next to mine opened, shut, its lock clicked. For a moment I heard only the hum of fluorescent lights, then, distinctly, the sound of a zipper opening, but nothing else, no plash of liquid into the bowl, no jingle of coins and car keys as pants slid down thighs, and so, after a moment, I bent over and risked a peek. All I saw at first was another hole in the wall opposite mine, and then, almost on cue, into the circular frame stepped a pair of dark trousers from whose open fly protruded an erect uncircumcised penis. A brown hand was stroking the penis, which was a slightly darker brown, and when it seemed to me that my own silence had grown conspicuously long my neighbor also bent forward, and our eyes met. I could see just one—it was dark and bright—and a large nose, and a full-lipped mouth which smiled almost immediately, revealing the inevitability of tea-stained teeth. He stood up, and a moment later his penis poked through the hole in the granite partition, but before I could decide what to do with it, or about it, the entrance doors whined in warning and the penis was gone like a mouse retreating into its hole. Faint footsteps, then silence. Then the water began running in the sink and I knew instinctively that we were fine: who washes their hands before they use the toilet? Well, the British probably do, but I wasn't thinking that then. The water ran; the penis reappeared; for some reason the sound was the license I needed, and without hesitating I took it, first in my hand and then in my mouth. The water continued to run. I closed my eyes against the kaleidoscopic spangles of the granite wall so close to my face. The thing in my mouth seemed to have no odor, no taste even: it simply felt. Warm. Living. Not even human really, just . . . alive. The granite was cold against my forehead when I let it rest there, and my urine in the bowl gave off a faint stink, making me wish I'd flushed. When the man twitched a bit, a warning or an invitation depending on your point of view, I moved aside; when he came his semen shot straight into the bowl and I couldn't quite suppress a chuckle; when, a moment later, I stepped out of the stall, unconsciously wiping my lips with the back of my hand, I saw a dainty little thing, tight pants, tight shirt, both black and shiny, crowned by a bleached-blond Caesar, standing at the sink where the water was still running down the drain at the rate of one gallon, one British gallon, per minute. I went right up to him and turned off the tap. That's very wasteful, I said, especially given the fact that we're in the middle of a drought. A moment later the man from the other stall joined us. He was Indian, about my age, more handsome than I would have expected from this sort of encounter, and taller than I'd realized; he must have had to bend his knees awkwardly to make it through the hole. As we walked out together the queen at the sink said, Greedy, greedy, greedy, in what I think was a Brummie accent, *Grey*-dy, *grey*-dy, *grey*-dy, and then he turned the water back on. My trick's name was Nigel. He carried a briefcase, wore a loosened tie; he was on his way home from an incredibly late day at the office, he said, and thought he'd check out the cottages on the South Bank before catching the tube at Embankment. My good luck, I said. It's usually busier, he said, but the play got bad notices. The play? I said, barely able to remember it. You're American? he said. I assumed he'd noticed my accent, but instead he squeezed my shoulder. Americans are just so big, he said, all that conspicuous consumption, and then, before we'd made it up the long flight of stairs, he'd told me about a few other places, Russell Square, the second floor toilets at Harvey Nicks, Mile End Park on Sunday nights, but the place which caught my ear was the Stoke Newington cemetery. People have sex in a cemetery? I said. What else are they going to do there? Nigel said, and then he made me hold back for a minute so we weren't seen leaving together. He kissed me first, said he was sorry he hadn't returned the favor but the boyfriend was waiting at home, and then he grabbed my crotch. Damn, he said. What a waste, and then, with an all-purpose Cheers mate, he was gone. Upstaged then, by not one but two boyfriends, I made my way home. Mile End, as it happened, was the next tube stop past mine, and I decided to ride the extra distance to take a look at the thin spit of trees at the north end of the park across from the station, a tiny copse which, according to Nigel, held as many as two dozen men each Sunday after Benjy's let out. I wasn't looking for another trick, but between Derek and Nigel I felt all worked up and there wasn't anything in particular to rush home to, and it was only a little before midnight when I spilled out of the tube with a large loud number of kids on their way to Benjy's— straight kids, because Benjy's only catered to a gay crowd on Sundays, and then only surreptitiously—and I let myself ride their swell for half a dozen steps until I saw the trees across the street, low scrubby evergreens fleshing out the trunks of some kind of short deciduous with pale shiny bark. Stick skinny girls in short skirts shivered in the cold October wind while boys with acne on their foreheads tossed their keys up in the air and looked around to see if anyone was watching, and measured against their camaraderie the little grove looked cold and inhospitable, but still, I decided to check it out. The nearest entrance to the park was a ways in on Burdett Road, past Benjy's and a busy chip shop and the back of a darkened dingy council block, and after I'd made it through all that—I was sure that everyone I passed knew exactly what I was up to, and walking through them felt like running a gauntlet—I had to walk back up to the trees across a lawn whose grass was so dry it broke audibly under my feet. The papers said it had been, literally, the driest summer in recorded history, and though fall had brought the relief of coolness the gray skies had not yet delivered any rain. Still, the drought had been some kind of vague comfort to me during my several months here. At first I thought it was simply because it reinforced my natural urge to conserve resources and ration them appropriately. Each evening as I washed my handful of dishes with a barely dampened sponge I watched the news on Channel 4 and felt joined with like-minded people all over England. The lawns of Hyde Park browned like toast, black cabs withered beneath a never-washed patina of dust, and swimming pools—said to be in Oxfordshire, although I had a hard time imagining something as American as a swimming pool anywhere in England—filled at summer's start, were by now nothing more than puddles at the bottom of dirt-encrusted concrete holes, and, as I said, I felt a kinship with these people which had comforted me, or at least I thought it had. I would watch the news and give the taps an extra twist to make sure they were fully closed and imagine my downstairs neighbor doing exactly the same thing, but as I walked across the open lawn of Mile End Park I remembered that New York, like London now, had been in the midst of a drought when I'd moved there a decade earlier, and I realized that it was probably only memory which assuaged my loneliness, not recycled water but recycled thoughts, recycled habits: letting laundry accumulate, showering every other day, putting a brick in the toilet tank to save a quart of water—an American quart—with each flush. The moon was the single light in the night sky bright enough to push through the clouds, and I felt its beam focused on me as I crunched my way across the wide open lawn. When I was on the street the trees had seemed slightly sinister but now they cast friendly sheltering shadows, and as I got closer I could make out several gaps in the low evergreens. I headed for the nearest, pushed aside a few scaly branches, and suddenly found myself on a well-worn path. A mulch of last year's needles and leaves softened my footsteps, which only three or four paces further on brought me to a small oblong clearing, where, like socks on a laundry line, a row of more than a dozen condoms hung over a couple of thin branches. Or flags, I thought. The condoms hung there like a row of welcoming banners in front of a swanky hotel, although that night the clearing was without any guests. It was surprisingly bright though. The branches overhead did little more than filter the moon's glow, and plastic wrappers from condoms and candy glittered like something more precious than mere trash while patiently waiting out their millennia on earth. A flash on a tree trunk caught my eye: a shred of red cloth. I tried to imagine the man who had leaned up against this trunk and what had caused him to tear his shirt, perhaps a startled twitch as a pair of headlights shone through the leaves, or the inevitable shudder as he came, or perhaps the grove had simply held on to a piece of him when he walked away, unwilling to take the tryst as lightly as he had, as had the men who'd draped the condoms across its branches. A pair of voices disturbed me then, and, peering through the trees, I could make out a couple of stout men passing by on the sidewalk, which couldn't have been twenty feet away. Their blond crewcuts reflected the moon like mirror balls—almost all the white men in this neighborhood were blond and crewcut, just as almost all their Asian neighbors wore their hair long, either beneath turbans or, on the younger men, in neatly dressed ponytails—and their East London accent was so pronounced I could hardly make out a word, but the tone was loud and boisterous, drunken but not particularly so, and I imagined they were making their way home from the pub to their wives, and as their voices faded away they were replaced by the memory of another disembodied voice, this one also loud, but angry, shouting actually, I was only taking a *piss,* is what the voice had shouted. Can't someone take a piss without you shutting the light off behind them? and I remembered shouting back, I piss in the dark all the time, even though the light I had shut off had been in the living room. Some people, I shouted, don't need to look at their dicks to make them work, and a moment later the voice and the body from which it emanated appeared in my door. Well, some of us should clean up the mess we make beside the toilet in the middle of the night, is what he said. I'm just trying to do my part, I said then, to which he replied, This isn't a play. There are no parts, there isn't a script. There are only lights, which we leave on so we can see where we're *going*—and just then a car's headlights splintered the grove of trees, dancing a chorus line of skeletal shadows across the clearing where I stood, and I shook myself and pretended I was shivering. As a memory, it was simply a piece of trash, and, dutifully, I shoved it back in the bin and slammed the lid down on it. I pocketed the scrap of red cloth and headed for home, and when I got there I showered off the coating of dust I seemed to have acquired on my foray into the woods. I felt guilty that I couldn't bring myself to shower as someone told me they did in Germany—a quick spray, a lather with soap that congealed perceptibly as the water evaporated from one's body, and then a second splash to rinse. I'd tried it only once, on what seemed like a hot summer morning, and when I stepped out of the shower my teeth were chattering and my skin slimy with soap scum, and as I toweled off I looked longingly at the spume of steam which, along with a falsetto caterwaul, rose up from my downstairs neighbor's bathroom window. That night I indulged myself, lingering in the shower for nearly ten minutes, but afterward I turned the heat all the way down and wrapped myself in a comforter I'd bought when I'd bought my bed, and I said, out loud, defiantly, I *am* doing my part. In the morning I saw that Derek had called the night before, while I'd been in the park, and he came by later that afternoon to make it up to me. It's fucking freezing, he said when he arrived, and with a carelessness, an insouciance really, that I envied, he rotated the dial on the thermostat without even looking at it. By the time he left the sun had gone down and my flat was so hot my eyes watered in their sockets. I turned the thermostat down, blindly, as Derek had turned it up, but it wasn't until I woke up shivering that I realized my place was, once again, freezing cold, and empty, and life went on that way, it got even colder but still neither rain nor snow would fall, I saw Derek once a week on average, a quick meal usually, followed by a quick fuck, although sometimes he sneaked out on a weekend and we would go shopping, Oxford Street, Covent Garden and Soho, South Ken, and I blew hundreds of pounds on those occasions but it didn't really matter because in between days with Derek I was writing the most puerile sorts of advertising copy masking itself as cinematic entertainment, for which money was simply being thrown at me, and even at an unfavorable exchange rate I had cash to burn. And so it happened that I woke up one morning after Derek had been there the night before and saw that, Derek or no Derek, my flat was hardly empty. I looked around my bedroom, through the doors to the front room. There were things everywhere. Electronics equipment especially: television, VCR, stereo, computer, printer, fax, phone, the answering machine with its unblinking red eye. Stacks of books grew from the mantel up the chimney, flanked by a pair of candleless candlesticks I'd picked up in the market on Brick Lane, and in the grate itself was a chest I'd bought the same day to hold the British linens I'd bought to cover my British mattress, which, like British paper and British men, was longer and skinnier than the American variety. I remembered then the list of my possessions which I'd made in my first week here, and draped by my comforter I made my way to my desk and sat in my chair and turned on my computer—so many things!—and tried to recreate it. I stopped after thirty pages. I hadn't looked in the closet yet, or pulled open a single drawer, but I didn't need to: it was clear I had somehow managed to stuff my flat as fat as a turkey on Thanksgiving, and I remembered then what Nigel had said about Americans and their conspicuous consumption. For the first time I wondered what would happen to all of my possessions when I left. I tripped on that for a moment, I wasn't sure why, until I realized it was the first time I'd acknowledged that just as surely as I'd come to London I'd leave it one day, I wasn't sure when and I wasn't sure why, but then I wasn't exactly sure why I'd come to London either. I'd thought I wanted to live unburdened by the things which had weighed me down in New York, but as I scrolled through the list on my computer—I couldn't bring myself to waste the paper it would take to print it out—it seemed to me that life was nothing more than a process of accumulation. The only thing you lost was time. But I refused to accept this conclusion, and I resolved, again, to divest myself of as much extraneous matter as possible, months of newspapers that had accumulated and needed to be recycled, the books I'd read, which I sold to a used bookstore for a few pounds, also a nested stack of electronics boxes that took up almost all the space in my closet. Why did I save this stuff?, I asked myself as I snapped the boxes' styrofoam packing sleeves into tiny pieces, why did I think a minor act of conservation could repair the damage already perpetrated by the manufacturing process that had belched forth all this shit? Also in my closet were a couple of shirts that had come from New York with me, shirts which I'd rarely worn there and never worn here, and I decided I would give them to the Salvation Army. The nearest one I could find was in Camden, which required a formidably complex tube journey, but I negotiated it successfully, and handed over the two shirts plus a couple more which I'd bought for Derek and which he'd said he couldn't accept, and a pair of pants he'd bought me which I liked but still shucked out of spite, and as I handed my package over I told myself that I was becoming one of those faceless people who provide all the great finds that I'd been adept at sniffing out in my first years in New York. It was an image of myself I liked, and so the circuitous route between Bethnal Green and Camden became a regular sojourn for me. I only went when I had bought something, a jacket or a pair of pants or shoes, and all I did was weed out a similar older item to make room for the new thing, and I hadn't realized how frequent a visitor I was until one day when I went in armed with a single pair of green cotton chinos, and, because I felt silly going in to surrender one item, a white button-down shirt that I would have had to replace sooner or later, and the old woman whom I saw most regularly smiled at me and said Simon will be glad you've been in. Simon? I said, and the old woman beamed. He works at the weekend. He's just your size—he usually snatches up whatever you bring in before it makes it to the floor. Says you keep him in clothes, you do. Even shoes. I mumbled something incoherently then, I wasn't even sure what I'd meant my mumbling to sound like, and quickly left the store, but that weekend, after an early meeting with Derek, I found myself in front of the Salvation Army. There was the thinnest coat of frost on the ground—the weatherman tried to call it snow, but no one was fooled—and I'd worn sunglasses to protect my eyes from the glare. I kept them on when I went into the store, thinking they would serve as some sort of disguise, but when I realized that Simon would have no idea who I was I took them off quickly. There was no mistaking him though. The green and brown plaid shirt he wore had come from my closet, as well as the brown corduroy pants, and although I couldn't see Simon's feet I guessed he was wearing a pair of suede boots I'd dropped off on the same day I dropped off the plaid shirt and corduroys. Excuse me, I said then. I was in here earlier this week and I saw a pair of pants I liked. They were green. Canvas, no pleats. Simon looked up from the book he'd been reading. Sorry? Despite myself, I was surprised. He was young—I mean, much younger than I was—and a part of me had expected my own face to look at me from out of my own clothes. Green pants, I said quickly, stammering slightly. I saw them earlier—I don't work during the week, Simon interrupted me. Wouldn't know what was here, but I don't remember no green *pants* in, what was it, *can*vas? He stressed the words slightly, and I wasn't sure if he was mocking the words themselves, or just the way I'd said them, but then he laughed lightly, waved an arm, said, We've got loads of polyester to choose from, and as he spoke he turned his book over and placed it open-faced on the counter, a college text-book, economics. He didn't even look like a younger version of me. His hair was floppy and brown and darkened by a tinge of grease, whereas my hair was crewed like the men in my neighborhood. Derek had teased me when I first cut it off, asked me if I was trying to score with the skinheads down at the local, but then he'd grown serious and run his hand over my downy head and said, It suits you. It suits you, I guess, though I think you deserve the luxury of hair, but still, I continued to buzz it: I'd bought the clippers after all, and couldn't let them go to waste. I shook my head then, to clear it. I'm sure I saw them, I insisted. I even remember the size: thirty-two in the waist and inseam both. Simon's expression was puzzled and un-comfortable. He shrugged thin shoulders inside the green and brown plaid shirt. Maybe they sold. The collar of the shirt had darkened from the grease in his hair, and he pulled at it now, nervously, and I felt sweat filming my own neck, beneath my scarf. I placed my hands flat on the counter. Could you check in the back? Maybe they were taken off the rack for some reason. Look, Simon said, we don't take stuff off the floor unless we're holding it for—That's it! I said. I asked her to hold it for me. What's her name, the old woman. Trudy, Simon said. His voice was suddenly suspicious. That's right, Trudy. I could feel the sweat coursing down my neck now, wetting my shirt inside my winter coat. I could feel the redness of my face and the pounding of my heart. Trudy put it back for me, along with a white shirt. A button-down. Simon stared at me now, disbelief written plainly on his face. Trudy's holding a pair of green trousers for you, and a white shirt? I just nodded my head then. I couldn't bring my-self to speak, nor even to meet his gaze. My eyes caught the cracked spine of his textbook, saw a yellow sticker, itself creased into near il-legibility: *USED.* Just a minute, I heard Simon say, and as he walked from the counter I watched for his feet. There were the boots. I felt a thrill up and down my spine when I saw them, and a knot in my stomach as well, and then Simon was back with the same brown bag in which I'd delivered the clothes. It was stapled closed now, and the word *Simon* was written on it in black magic marker, and the man who bore that name, and my clothes as well, dropped the bag on the counter. Here you go. I still couldn't look at him. I grabbed the bag and turned for the door, but Simon's voice stopped me. All right, hold on. I turned slowly. Yes? Simon's face and voice were flat when he spoke, but his knuckles were white where his hands gripped the counter's edge. That'll be a fiver, he said, and I said, I'm sorry? That's five for the pants, Simon said again. He paused. And five for the shirt. I thought of protesting, but didn't. What could I say: But they're mine? I thought of running out of the store then, even jerked a little toward the door, and Simon jerked when I jerked, not as if to follow, not even in imitation: it was as if his body was attached to mine by the threads woven into the clothes he wore. Slowly, I returned to the counter. I pulled two fives from my wallet and fingered them for a moment. They were fresh from a cash machine, crisp, sharp-edged. You could cut your finger on these, I thought. I thought, This is how much it costs. It wasn't very much, even if I was buying something that already belonged to me. I gave the boy called Simon the money. Brazen now, Simon put the money in the pocket of the corduroy pants. I looked at him a moment longer. They all fit you. Even the shoes. Something changed in Simon's face then. Disgust gave way momentarily to shame, and then, quickly, anger rose up again. Aw, go on, get out of here before I call a copper. His voice—young, high-pitched, almost cracking under the strain— wasn't convincing, but I nodded once and left. Outside it was cold and bright and I squinted against the glare until I remembered my sunglasses and covered my eyes. The bag with Simon's name on it dangled loosely in one hand, and as I walked toward the tube station I remembered something else Derek had said not so long ago, when I'd tried to tell him that my name wasn't actually Derek. I'd stuttered my way around the subject until, eventually, I realized that he'd figured it out long ago, and that he hadn't cared. What he'd said was that some things, like names, can be used over and over again— or bodies for that matter. But then he went on. He said, Some things *can't* be used twice. There are some things, he said, that are used up on the first go-round, and whatever's left behind, if anything, is just pollution. There's no point in saving it, he said, or re-using it, it's just left over, and as he spoke his hands were on my shoulders and he was looking me straight in the eye and, although I knew it wasn't his intention, I still felt as though he were telling me *I* was one of those things that can be used only once. People like Derek, I thought, people like Nigel, they were able to have boyfriends and still find the time for tricks on the side, and trysts, whereas it was all I could manage to be someone's someone else. They renewed themselves endlessly, shed the days like skin cells and grew new ones without even thinking about it, while all I could do was fade away slowly as though I were simply semibiodegradeable packaging whose contents had long since been consumed, and suddenly I felt the bag with someone else's name on it hanging from my arm like a dead weight. Why did you keep coming back then? is what I'd said to Derek—it was what I had said in New York—and what Derek had said was I never left, and the more I thought of his words the less I could make of them. In New York it had been worse. In New York it had been: I was never really here, and what can you say to that? I stopped walk-ing then; I'd gone far past the tube station; I looked around and saw, in fact, that I had no idea where I was. But even the strangeness was familiar from my first days here, it brought with it a familiar elation and a familiar dejection, but I threw all these old feelings away, and threw away my old clothes as well, dropped them in the first bin I came across, and then I turned toward what I thought was the east and set out on foot for my flat. I got lost, of course. Of course I got lost: for London is laid out as haphazardly as a warren. It is a myriad of Streets High and Low, of Courts and Cloisters and Crescents and full Circles, Paths and Parks and Parkways, and Yards, and Mews, and Quays, Palaces and Castles and Mansions and Halls and mere Houses (never so mere in reality), and Drives (which sounds creep-ingly American to my ears, and suburban at that), there are Ways to go and Ends to be arrived at, Barrows and Buries—or would it be Burys?—Moats to be crossed and Bridges to cross them, also Brydges, which don't seem to cross anything, and Squares, which rarely are, and all of this (and much, much more) is further compli-cated by a strange feud between lexicography and cartography, so that what is here a Road becomes, a few feet farther on, a Terrace; a

Vale might become a Walk or broaden suddenly into a Mall; Groves are treeless, Gardens without plants, Gates nowhere to be found. London is, in other words, a maze, but I was simply amazed, surprised that it had taken me so long to realize I was lost. But it was why I'd come here after all, to lose myself in a foreign place. That seems, now, just another way of saying that I wanted to throw myself away, and if I didn't actually succeed it's probably only because it's against my nature to litter.

Skinned Alive

Edmund White

I first saw him at a reading in Paris. An American writer, whom everyone had supposed dead, had come to France to launch a new translation of his classic book, originally published twenty-five years earlier. The young man in the crowd who caught my eye had short red-blond hair and broad shoulders (bodyguard broad, commando broad) and an unsmiling gravity. When he spoke English, he was very serious; when he spoke French, he looked amused.

He was seated on the other side of the semicircle surrounding the author, who was slowly, sweetly, suicidally disappointing the young members of his audience. They had come expecting to meet Satan, for hadn't he summoned up in his pages a brutish vision of gang rape in burned-out lots, of drug betrayals and teenage murders? But who they were meeting now was a reformed drunk given to optimism, offering us brief recipes for recovery and serenity—not at all what the spiky-haired kids had had in mind.

I was charmed by the writer's hearty laugh and pleased that he'd been able to trade in his large bacchanalian genius for a bit of happiness. But his new writings were painful to listen to and my eyes wandered restlessly over the bookshelves. I was searching out interesting new titles, saluting familiar ones, reproaching a few.

And then I had the young man to look at. He had on black trousers full in the calf and narrow in the thighs, his compact waist cinched in by a thick black belt and a gold buckle. His torso was concealed by an extremely ample, long-sleeved black shirt, but despite its fullness I could still see the broad, powerful chest, the massive shoulders and biceps—the body of a professional killer. His neck was thick, like cambered marble.

My French friend Hélène nudged me and whispered, "There's one for you." Maybe she said that later, during the discussion period after the young man had asked a question that revealed his complete familiarity with the text. He had a tenor voice I was sure that he'd worked to lower or perhaps his voice sounded strange because he was just shy—a voice, in any event, that made me think of those low notes a cellist draws out of his instrument by slowly sawing the bow back and forth while fingering a tremolo with the other hand.

From his accent I couldn't be certain he was American; he might be German, a nationality that seemed to accommodate his contradictions better—young but dignified, athletic but intellectual. There was nothing about him of the brash American college kid, the joker who has been encouraged to express all his opinions, including those that have just popped into his head. The young man respected the author's classic novel so much that he made me want to take it more seriously. I liked the way he referred to specific scenes as though there were literary sites known to everyone. This grave young man was probably right, the scandalous books always turn out to be the good ones.

Yes, Hélène must have nudged me after his question, because she's attracted to men only if they're intelligent. If they're literary, all the better, since, when she's not reading, she's talking about books. I'll phone her toward noon and she'll say, "I'm in China" or "Today, it's the Palais-Royal" or "Another unhappy American childhood," depending on whether the book is a guide, a memoir, or a novel. She worries about me and wants me to find someone, preferably a Parisian, so I won't get any funny ideas about moving back to New York. She and I always speak in English. If I trick her into continuing in French after an evening with friends, she'll suddenly catch herself and say indignantly, "But why in earth are we speaking French!" She claims to be bilingual, but she speaks French to her cats. People dream in the language they use on their cats.

She is too discreet, even with me, her closest friend, to solicit any details about my intimate life. Once, when she could sense Jean-Loup was making me unhappy, I said to her, "But you know I do have two other . . . people I see from time to time," and she smiled, patted my hand and said, "Good. Very good. I am delighted." Another time she shocked me. I asked her what I should say to a jealous lover, and she replied, "The answer to the question, 'Are you faithful, *chéri?*' is always 'Yes.'" She made vague efforts to meet and even charm the different men who passed through my life (her Japanese clothes, low voice, and blue-tinted glasses impressed them all). But I could tell she disapproved of most of them. "It's Saturday," she would say. "Jean-Loup must be rounding you up for your afternoon shopping spree." If ever I said anything against him, she would dramatically bite her lip, look me in the eye, and nod.

But I liked to please Jean-Loup. And if I bought him his clothes every Saturday morning, that afternoon he would let me take them off again, piece by piece, to expose his boyish body, a lean-hipped and priapic body. On one hip, the color of wedding-gown satin, he had a mole, which the French more accurately call a *grain de beauté.*

Jean-Loup came from a solid middle-class family but had climbed a social rung. He had the most rigid code of etiquette, and I owe him the slight improvements I've made in my impressionistic American table manners, learned thirty years ago among boarding-school savages. Whereas Americans are taught to keep their unused hand in their lap at the table, the French are so filthy-minded they assume hidden hands are the devil's workshop. Whereas Americans clear each plate as soon as it's finished, the French wait for everyone to complete the course. That's the sort of thing he taught me. To light a match after one has smelled up a toilet. To greet the most bizarre story with the comment, "But that's perfectly normal." To be careful to serve oneself from the cheese tray no more than once ("Cheese is the only course a guest has the right to refuse," he told me, "and the only dish that should never be passed twice").

Also not to ask so many questions or volunteer so many answers. After a two-hour train ride he'd ask me if I had had enough time to confide to the stranger at my side all the details of my unhappy American childhood. Like most Frenchmen who have affairs with Americans, he was attracted by my "niceness" and "simplicity" (ambiguous compliments at best), but had set out to reform those very qualities, which became weaknesses once I was granted the high status of honorary Frenchman. "Not Frenchman," he would say. "You'll never be French. But you are a Parisian. No one can deny that." Then to flatter me he would add, *"Plus parisien tu meurs,"* though just then I felt that I'd die if I were less, not more, Parisian.

But if Jean-Loup was always "correct" in the salon, he was "vicious" and "perverse" (high compliments in France) in the *chambre.* The problem was that he didn't like to see me very often. He loved me but wasn't in love with me, that depressing (and all too translatable) distinction (*"Je t'aime mais je ne suis pas amoureux d'amour"*). He was always on the train to Bordeaux, where his parents lived and where he'd been admitted to several châteaux, including some familiar even to me because they were on wine labels. He'd come back with stories of weekend country parties at which the boys got drunk and tore off the girls' designer dresses and then everyone went riding bareback at dawn. He had a set of phrases for describing these routs (*"On s'éclatait"; "On se marrait"; "On était fou, mais vraiment fou et on a bien rigolé"*), which all meant they had behaved disreputably with the right people within decorous limits. After all, they were in their own "milieu." He slept with a few of the girls and was looking to marry one who would be intelligent, not ugly, distinguished, a good sport, and a slut in bed. He even asked me to help him. "You go everywhere, you meet everyone," he said, "you've fixed up so many of your friends, find me someone like Brigitte but better groomed, a good slut who likes men. Of course, even if I married that would never affect our relationship." Recently he'd decided that he would inform his bride-to-be that he was a homosexual; he just knew she'd be worldly about it.

With friends Jean-Loup was jolly and impertinent, quick to trot out his "horrors," as he called them, things that would make the girls scream and the boys blush. Twice he showed his penis at mixed dinner parties. Even so, his horrors were, while shocking, kind-hearted and astute. He never asked about money or class, questions that might really embarrass a Frenchman. He would sooner ask about blowjobs than job prospects, cock size than the size of a raise. In our funny makeshift circle—which I had cobbled together to amuse him and which fell apart when he left me—the girls were witty, uncomplicated, and heterosexual, and the boys handsome and homo. We were resolutely silly and made enormous occasions out of each other's birthdays and saint's days. Our serious, intimate conversations took place only between two people, usually over the phone.

I neglected friends my own age. I never spoke English or talked about books except with Hélène. A friend from New York said, after staying with me for a week, that I was living in a fool's paradise, a gilded playpen filled with enchanting, radiant nymphs and satyrs who offered me "no challenge." He disapproved of the way I was willing to take just crumbs from Jean-Loup.

Brioche crumbs, I thought.

I didn't know how to explain that now that so many of my old friends in New York had died—my best friend, and also my editor, who was a real friend as well—I preferred my playpen, where I could be twenty-five again but French this time. When reminded of my real age and nationality, I then played at being older and American. Youth and age seemed equally theatrical. Maybe the unreality was the effect of living in another language, of worrying about how many slices of *chèvre* one could take, and of buying pretty clothes for a bisexual Bordelais. At about this time a punk interviewed me on television and asked, "You are known as a homosexual, a writer, and an American. When did you first realize you were an American?"

"When I moved to France," I said.

That Jean-Loup was elusive could not be held against him. He warned me from the first he was in full flight. What I didn't grasp was that he was running toward someone even he couldn't name yet. Despite his lucid way of making distinctions about other people ("She's not a liar but a mythomaniac; her lying serves no purpose") he was indecisive about everything in his own future: Would he marry or become completely gay? Would he stay in business or develop his talent, drawing adult comic strips? Would he remain in Paris or continue shuttling between it and Bordeaux? I teased him, calling him Monsieur Charnière (Mr. Hinge).

Where he could be decisive was in bed. He had precise and highly colored fantasies, which I deduced from his paces and those he put me through. He never talked about his desires until the last few times we had sex, just before the end of our "story," as the French call an affair; his new talkativeness I took as a sign that he'd lost interest in me or at least respect for me, and I was right. Earlier he had never talked about his desire, but hurled it against me: he needed me here not there, like this not that. I felt desired for the first time in years.

My friends, especially Hélène, but even the other children in the playpen, assumed Jean-Loup was genteelly fleecing me with my worldly, cheerful complicity, but I knew I had too little money to warrant such a speculation. He'd even told me that if it was money he was after he could find a man far richer than me. In fact I knew I excited him. That's why I had to find him a distinguished slut for a wife. I had corrupted him, he told me, by habituating him to sex that was "hard," which the French pronounce "ard" as in "ardent" and, out of a certain deference, never elide with the preceding word.

He didn't mind if I talked during sex, telling him who he was, where we were, and why I had to do all this to him. I was used to sex raps from the drug-taking 1970s. Now, of course, there were no drugs and I had to find French words for my obsessions, and when I sometimes made a mistake in gender or verb form Jean-Loup would wince. He wouldn't mention it later; he didn't want to talk anything over later. Only once, after he'd done something very strange to me, he asked, laughing as he emerged from the shower, "Are you the crazy one or am I? I think we're both crazy." He seemed very pleased.

For the first year we'd struggled to be "lovers" officially, but he devoted more of his energy to warding me off than embracing me. He had a rule that he could never stay on after a dinner at my place; he would always leave with the other members of the playpen. To stay behind would look too domestic, he thought, too queer, too *pédé*. After a year of such partial intimacy I got fed up. More likely I became frightened that Jean-Loup, who was growing increasingly remote, would suddenly drop me. I broke up with him over dinner in a restaurant. He seemed relieved and said, "I would never have dared to take the first step." He was shaken for two or three days, then recovered nicely. As he put it, he "supported celibacy" quite effortlessly. It felt natural to him, it was his natural condition.

I went to New York for a week. By chance he went there after I returned. When we saw each other again in Paris we were as awkward as adolescents. His allergies were acting up; American food had made him put on two kilos; a New York barber had thrown his meaty ears into high relief. "It's terrible," Jean-Loup said. "I wanted my independence, but now that I have it . . . Undress me." I did so, triumphant while registering his admission that he was the one after all who had wanted to be free.

After that we seldom saw each other but when we did it was always passionate. The more people we told that we were no longer lovers, the more violent our desire for each other became. I found his heavy balls, which he liked me to hold in my mouth while I looked up at him. I found the mole on his smooth haunch. Because of his allergies he couldn't tolerate colognes or deodorants; I was left with his natural kid-brother smell. We had long since passed through the stage of smoking marijuana together or using sex toys or dressing each other up in bits of finery. Other couples I knew became kinkier and kinkier over the years if they continued having sex or else re-signed themselves to the most routine, suburban relief. We were de-vouring each other with a desire that was ever purer and sharper. Of course such a desire is seldom linked to love. It can be powerful when solicited but quickly forgotten when absent.

Perhaps the threat of ending things altogether, which we'd just averted, had made us keener. More likely, Jean-Loup, now that he thought he'd become less homosexual by shedding a male lover, me, felt freer to indulge drives that had become more urgent precisely because they were less well defined. Or perhaps I'm exaggerating my importance in his eyes; as he once said, he didn't like to wank his head over things like that (*"Je ne m'en branle pas trop la tête"*).

I was in love with him and, during sex, thought of that love, but I tried to conceal it from him.

I tried to expect nothing, see him when I saw him, pursue other men, as though I were strictly alone in the world. For the first time when he asked me if I had other lovers I said I did and even dis-cussed them with him. He said he was relieved, explaining that my adventures exonerated him from feeling responsible for me and my happiness. He was a lousy lover, he said, famous for being elusive; even his girlfriends complained about his slipperiness. That elusive-ness, I would discover, was his protest against his own passivity, his longing to be owned.

Things changed day by day between us. He said he wasn't searching for other sexual partners; he preferred to wait until he fell in love, revealing that he didn't imagine that we'd become lovers again. Nor was he in such a hurry to find a distinguished and sympathetic slut for a wife. When I asked him about his marital plans, he said that he was still looking forward to settling down with a wife and children someday but that now he recognized that when he thought of rough sex, of *la baise harde,* he thought of men. And again he flatteringly blamed me for having corrupted him even while he admitted he was looking for someone else, another man, to love.

Once in a very great while he referred to me playfully as his "husband," despite his revulsion against camp. I think he was trying to come up with a way that would let our friendship continue while giving each of us permission to pursue other people. Once he somberly spoke of me as his *mécène* (or "patron") but I winced and he quickly withdrew the description. I wouldn't have minded playing his father, but that never occurred to him.

I'm afraid I'm making him sound too cold. He had that sweet kid-brother charm, especially around women. All those former debutantes from Bordeaux living in Paris felt free to ask him to run an errand or install a bookcase, which he did with unreflecting devotion. He was careful (far more careful than any American would have been) to distinguish between a pal and a friend, but the true friends exercised an almost limitless power over him. Jean-Loup was quite proud of his capacity for friendship. When he would say that he was a rotten lover—elusive, unsure of his direction—he'd also assure me that he'd always remain my faithful friend, and I believed him. I knew that he was, in fact, waiting for our passion to wear itself out so that a more decent friendship could declare itself.

He wasn't a friend during sex or just afterward; he'd always shower, dress, and leave as quickly as possible. Once, when he glanced back at the rubble we had made of the bedroom, he said all that evidence of our bestiality disgusted him. Nor was he especially kind to me around our playmates. To them, paradoxically, he enjoyed demonstrating how thoroughly he was at home in my apartment. He was the little lord of the manor. Yet he'd compliment me on how well I "received" people and assure me I could always open a restaurant in New York someday if my career as a writer petered out. He didn't take my writing too seriously. It had shocked him the few times he dipped into it. He preferred the lucidity and humanism of Milan Kundera, his favorite writer. In fact, none of our playmates read me, and their indifference pleased me. It left me alone with my wet sand.

He took a reserved interest in my health. He was relieved that my blood tests every six months suggested the virus was still dormant. He was pleased I no longer smoked or drank (though like most French people he didn't consider champagne alcoholic). During one of our sex games he poured half a bottle of red Sancerre down my throat; the etiquette of the situation forbade my refusal, but it was the only time I had tasted alcohol in nearly ten years. We were convinced that the sort of sex we practiced might be demented but was surely safe; in fact we had made it demented since it had to stay safe.

He was negative. While he waited for his results, he said that if they turned out positive his greatest regret would be that he wouldn't be able to father children. A future without a family seemed unbearable. As long as his boy's body with its beautifully shaped man's penis remained unmarked, without a sign of its past or a curse over its future, he was happy to lend himself to our games.

Sometimes his laugh was like a shout—boyish, the sound, but the significance, knowing and Parisian. He laughed to show that he hadn't been taken in or that he had caught the wicked allusion. When I was in the kitchen preparing the next course, I'd smile if I heard his whoop. I liked it that he was my husband, so at home, so sociable, so lighthearted, but our marriage was just a poor invention of my fancy.

It reassured me that his sexuality was profoundly, not modishly, violent. He told me that when he had been a child, just seven or eight, he had built a little town out of cardboard and plywood, painted every shutter and peopled every house, and then set the whole construction afire and watched the conflagration with a bone-hard, inch-long erection. Is that why just touching me made him hard now (bone-hard, foot-long)? Could he see I was ablaze with ardor for him (ardor with a silent *h*)?

The violence showed up again in the comic strips he was always drawing. He had invented a sort of Frankenstein monster in good French clothes, a creature disturbed by his own half-human sentiments in a world otherwise populated by robots. When I related his comics to the history of art, he'd smile a gay, humiliated smile, the premonitory form of his whooping, disabused Parisian laugh. He was ashamed I made so much of his talent, though his talent was real enough.

He didn't know what to do with his life. He was living as ambitious, healthy young men live who have long vistas of time before them: despairingly. I, who had already outlived my friends and had fulfilled some of my hopes but few of my desires (desire won't stay satisfied), lived each day with joy and anguish. Jean-Loup expected his life to be perfect: there was apparently going to be so much of it.

Have I mentioned that Jean-Loup had such high arches that walking hurt him? He had one of his feet broken, lowered, and screwed shut in metal vices that were removed six months later. His main reason for this operation was to take a break from the bank for a few weeks. His clinic room was soon snowed under with comic strip adventures. After that he walked with a bit of a Chaplinesque limp when he was tired.

I often wondered what his life was like with the other young Bordelais counts and countesses at Saint-Jean-de-Luz every August. I was excluded from that world—the chance of my being introduced to his childhood friends had never even once entered his head—which made me feel like a demimondaine listening avidly to her titled young lover's accounts of his exploits in the great world. Although I presented Jean-Loup to my literary friends in London, he had few opinions about them beyond his admiration for the men's clothes and the women's beauty and apparent intelligence. "It was all so fast and brilliant," he said, "I scarcely understood a word." He blamed me for not helping him with his English, though he hated the sounds I made when I spoke my native language. "You don't have an accent in French—oh, you have your little accent but it's nothing, very charming. But in American you sound like a duck, it's frightful!"

I suppose my English friends thought it was a sentimental autumn-and-spring affair. One friend, who lent us her London house for a few days, said, "Don't let the char see you and Jean-Loup nude." The warning seemed bizarre until I understood it as an acknowledgement of our potential for sensual mischief. Perhaps she was particularly alive to sensual possibilities, since she was so proud of her own handsome, artistic husband.

After I returned to Paris, I spent my days alone reading and writing, and in fair weather I'd eat a sandwich on the quay. That January the Seine overflowed and flooded the highway on the Right Bank. Sea gulls flew upstream and wheeled above the turbulent river, crying, as though mistaking Notre Dame for Mont Saint-Michel. The floodlights trained on the church's façade projected ghostly shadows of the two square towers up into the foggy night sky, as though spirits were doing axonometric drawings of a cathedral I had always thought of as malign. The gargoyles were supposed to ward off evil, but to me they looked like dogs straining to leap away from the devil comfortably lodged within.

I went to Australia and New Zealand for five weeks. I wrote Jean-Loup many letters, in French, believing that the French language tolerated love better than English, but when I returned to Paris Jean-Loup complained of my style. He found it *mièvre*, "wimpy" or "wet."

He said I should write about his ass one day, but in a style that was neither pornographic nor wimpy. He wanted me to describe his ass as Francis Ponge describes soap: an objective, exhaustive, whimsical catalog of its properties.

I wanted someone else, but I distrusted that impulse, because it seemed, if I looked back, I could see that I had never been happy in love and that with Jean-Loup I was happier than usual. As he pointed out, we were still having sex after two years, and he ascribed the intensity to the very infrequency that I deplored. Even so, I thought there was something all wrong, fundamentally wrong, with me: I set up a lover as a god, then burned with rage when he proved mortal. I lay awake, next to one lover after another, in a rage, dreaming of someone who'd appreciate me, give me the simple affection I imagined I wanted.

When I broke off with Jean-Loup over dinner he said, "You deserve someone better, someone who will love you completely." Yet the few times I had been loved "completely" I'd felt suffocated. Nor could I imagine a less aristocratic lover, one who'd sit beside me on the couch, hand in hand, and discuss the loft bed, the "mezzanine," we should buy with the cunning little chair and matching desk underneath.

But when I was alone night after night, I resented Jean-Loup's independence. He said I deserved something better, and I knew I merited less but needed more.

It was then I saw the redhead at the reading. Although I stared holes through him, he never looked at me once. It occurred to me that he might not be homosexual, except that his grave military bearing was something only homosexuals could (or would bother to) contrive if they weren't actually soldiers. His whole look and manner were studied. Let's say he was the sort of homosexual other homosexuals recognize but that heterosexuals never suspect.

The next day I asked the owner of the bookstore if she knew the redhead. "He comes into the shop every so often," she said, with a quick laugh to acknowledge the character of my curiosity, "but I don't know his name. He bought one of your books. Perhaps he'll come to your reading next week."

I told her to be sure to get his name if he returned. "You were a diplomat once," I reminded her. She promised but when I phoned a few days later she said he hadn't been in. Then on the night of my reading I saw him sitting in the same chair as before and I went up to him with absolute confidence and said, "I'm so glad you came to-night. I saw you at the last reading, and my *copine* and I thought you looked so interesting we wished we knew you." He looked so blank that I was afraid he hadn't understood and I almost started again in French. I introduced myself and shook his hand. He went white and said, "I'm sorry for not standing up," and then stood up and shook my hand, and I was afraid he'd address me as "sir."

Now that I could look at his hair closely I noticed that it was blond, if shavings of gold are blond, only on the closely cropped sides but that it was red on top—the reverse of the sun-bleached strawberry blond. He gave me his phone number, and I thought this was someone I could spend the rest of my life with, however brief that might be. His name was Paul.

131

I phoned him the next day to invite him to dinner, and he said that he had a rather strange schedule, since he worked four nights a week at a disco.

"What do you do?" I asked.

"I'm the physiognomist. The person who recognizes the regulars and the celebrities. I have to know what Brigitte Bardot looks like *now*. I decide who comes in, who stays out, who pays, who doesn't. We have a house rule to let all models in free." He told me people called him Cerberus.

"But how do you recognize everyone?"

"I've been on the door since the club opened seven years ago. So I have ten thousand faces stored in my memory." He laughed. "That's why I could never move back to America. I'd never find a job that paid so well for just twenty hours' work a week. And in America I couldn't do the same job, since I don't know any faces there."

We arranged an evening and he arrived dressed in clothes by one of the designers he knew from the club. Not even my reactionary father, however, would have considered him a popinjay. He did nothing that would risk his considerable dignity. He had white tulips in his surprisingly small, elegant hand.

All evening we talked literature, and, as two good Americans, we also exchanged confidences. Sometimes his shyness brought all the laughter and words to a queasy halt, and it made me think of that becalmed moment when a sailboat comes around and the mainsail luffs before it catches the wind again. I watched the silence play over his features.

He was from a small town in Georgia. His older brother and he had each achieved the highest score in the statewide scholastic aptitude test. They had not pulled down good grades, however; they read Plato and *Naked Lunch,* staged *No Exit* and brawls with the boys in the next town, experimented with hallucinogens and conceptual art. Paul's brother made an "artwork" out of his plans to assassinate President Ford and was arrested by the FBI.

"I just received the invitation to my tenth high school reunion," Paul said.

"I'll go with you," I said. "I'll go as your spouse."

He looked at me and breathed a laugh, save it was voiced just at the end, the moving bow finally touching the bass string and waking sound in it.

Paul's older brother had started a rock band, gone off to New York where he died of AIDS—another musician punished. He had been one of the first heterosexual male victims, dead already in 1981. He contracted the disease from a shared needle. Their mother, a Scottish immigrant, preferred to think he had been infected by another man. Love seemed a nobler cause of death than drugs.

"Then I came to Paris," Paul said. He sighed and looked out of my open window at the roofs of the Ille Saint-Louis. Like other brilliant young men and women he dissolved every solid in a solvent of irony, but even he had certain articles of faith, and the first was Paris. He liked French manners, French clothes, French food, French education. He said things like "France still maintains cultural hegemony over the whole world," and pronounced "hegemony" as *hégémonie*. He had done all his studies as an adult in France and in French. He asked me what the name of Platon's *Le Banquet* was in English (that's what they call *The Symposium,* for some reason). He had a lively, but somewhat vain, sense of what made him interesting, which struck me only because he seemed so worthy of respect that any attempt he made to serve himself up appeared irrelevant.

He was wearing a white shirt and dark tie and military shoes and a beautiful dark jacket that was cut to his Herculean chest and shoulders. He had clear eyes, pale blue eyes. The white tulips he brought were waxen and pulsing like lit candles, and his skin, that rich hairless skin, was tawny-colored. His manners were formal and French, a nice Georgia boy but Europeanized, someone who'd let me lazily finish my sentences in French (*"Quand même,"* we'd say, *"rien à voir avec..."*). His teeth were so chalky white that the red wine stained them a faint blue. His face was at once open and unreadable, as imposing as the globe. He nodded slowly as he thought out what I said, so slowly that I doubted the truth or seriousness of what I was saying. He hesitated and his gaze was noncommittal, making me wonder if he was pondering his own response or simply panicking. I wouldn't have thought of him panicking except he mentioned it. He said he was always on the edge of panic (the sort of thing Americans say to each other with big grins). Points of sweat danced on the bridge of his nose, and I thought I saw in his eye something frightened, even unpleasant and unreachable. I kept thinking we were too much alike, as though at any moment our American heartiness and our French *politesse* would break down and we'd look at each other with the sour familiarity of brothers. Did he sense it, too? Is that why our formality was so important to him? I was sure he hadn't liked himself in America.

Speaking French so long had made me simplify my thoughts— whether expressed in French or English—and I was pleased I could say now what I felt, since the intelligence I was imputing to him would never have tolerated my old vagueness. Whereas Jean-Loup had insisted I use the right fork, I felt Paul would insist on the correct emotion.

Sometimes before he spoke Paul made a faint humming sound— perhaps only voiced shyness—but it gave the impression of muted deference. It made me think of a student half raising his hand to speak in a seminar too small and egalitarian to require the teacher's recognition. But I also found myself imagining that his thought was so varied, occurring on so many levels at once, that the hum was a strictly mechanical downshift into the compromise (and invention) of speech. After a while the hum disappeared, and I fancied he felt more at ease with me, although the danger is always to read too much into what handsome men say and do. Although he was twenty years younger, he seemed much older than I.

"Would you like to go to Morocco with me?" I asked him suddenly. "For a week? A magazine will pay our fares. It's the south of Morocco. It should be amusing. I don't know it at all, but I think it's better to go somewhere brand new—" ("with a lover" were the words I suppressed).

"Sure."

He said he hadn't traveled anywhere in Europe or Africa except for two trips to Italy.

Although I knew things can't be rushed, that intimacy follows its own sequence, I found myself saying, "We should be lovers—you have everything, beauty and intelligence." Then I added: "And we get on so well." My reasoning was absurd: his beauty and intelligence were precisely what made him unavailable.

I scarcely wanted him to reply. As long as he didn't I could nurse my illusions. "That would depend," he said, "on our being compatible sexually, don't you think?" Then he asked, with his unblinking gravity, "What's your sexuality like?" For the first time I could hear a faint Georgia accent in the way the syllables of "sexuality" got stretched out.

"It depends on the person," I said, stalling. Then, finding my answer lamentable, I pushed all my chips forward on one number: "I like pain."

"So do I," he said. "And my penis has never—no man has ever touched it."

He had had only three lovers and they had all been heterosexuals or fancied they were. In any event they had had his sort of *pudeur* about uttering endearments to another man. He had a lover now, Thierry, someone he met two years before at the club. The first time they saw each other, Paul had been tanked up on booze, smack, and steroids, a murderous cocktail, and they had had a fistfight that had dissolved into a night of violent passion.

Every moment must have been haloed in his memory, for he remembered key phrases Thierry had used. For the last two years they had eaten every meal together. Thierry dressed him in the evening before Paul left for work and corrected his French and table manners. These interventions were often nasty, sometimes violent. "What language are you speaking now?" he would demand if Paul made the slightest error. When Paul asked for a little tenderness in bed, Thierry would say, "Oh-ho, like Mama and Papa now, is it?" and then leave the room. Paul fought back—he broke his hand once because he hit Thierry so hard. "Of course he'd say that it was all my fault," Paul said, "that all he wants is peace, blue skies." He smiled. "Thierry is a businessman, very dignified. He has never owned a piece of leather in his life. I despise leather. It robs violence of all the"—his smile now radiant, the mainsail creaking as it comes around—"the *sacramental.*" He laughed, and emitted a strange chortle that I didn't really understand. It came out of a sensibility I hadn't glimpsed in him before.

Paul longed for us to reach the desert; he had never seen it before.

We started out at Agadir and took a taxi to the mud-walled town of Taroudant. There we hired a car and drove to Ouarzazate, which had been spoiled by organized tourism: it had become Anywhere Sunny. Then we drove south to Zagora. It was just twenty kilometers beyond Zagora, people said, that the desert started. I warned Paul the desert could be disappointing: "You're never alone. There's always someone spying on you from over the next dune. And it rains. I saw the rain pour over Syria."

Paul loved maps. Sometimes I could see in him the solitary Georgia genius in love with his best friend's father, the sheriff, a kid lurking around home in the hot, shuttered afternoons, daydreaming over the globe that his head so resembled, his mind racing on homemade LSD. He knew how to refold maps, but when they were open he would press his palms over their creases as though opening his own eyes wider and wider.

I did all the driving, through adobe cities built along narrow, palm-lined roads. In every town boys wanted to be our guides, sell us trinkets or carpets or their own bodies. They hissed at us at night from the shadows of town walls: lean and finely muscled adolescents hissing to attract our attention, their brown hands massaging a lump beneath the flowing blue acrylic jellabas mass-produced in China. To pass them up with a smile was a new experience for me. I had Paul beside me, this noble pacing lion. I remembered a Paris friend calling me just before we left for Morocco, saying he had written a letter to a friend, "telling him I'd seen you walking down the boulevard Saint-Germain beside the young Hercules with hair the color of copper." In Morocco there was no one big enough, powerful enough, or cruel enough to interest Paul.

Perhaps it was due to the clear, memorable way Paul had defined his sexual nature, but during our cold nights together I lay in his great arms and never once felt excited, just an immense surge of peace and gratitude. Our predicament, we felt, was like a Greek myth. "Two people love each other," I said, "but the gods have cursed them by giving them identical passions." I was being presumptuous sneaking in the phrase "Two people love each other," because it wasn't at all clear that he loved me.

One night we went to the movies and saw an Italian adventure film starring American weightlifters and dubbed in French, a story set in a back-lot castle with a perfunctory princess in hot pants. There was an evil prince whose handsome face melted to reveal the devil's underneath. His victim ("All heroes are masochists," Paul declared) was an awkward bodybuilder not yet comfortable in his newly acquired bulk, who had challenged the evil prince's supremacy and now had to be flayed alive. Paul clapped and chortled and, during the tense scenes, physically braced himself. This was the Paul who had explained what Derrida had said of Heidegger's interpretation of Trakl's last poems, who claimed that literature could be studied only through rhetoric, grammar, and genre, and who considered Ronsard a greater poet than Shakespeare (because of Ronsard's combination of passion and logic, satyr and god, in place of the mere conversational fluency that Paul regarded as the flaw and genius of English): this was the same Paul who booed and cheered as the villain smote the hero before a respectful audience, the air thick with smoke and the flickers of flashlights. It was a movie in which big men were hurting each other.

Jean-Loup would have snorted, his worst prejudices about Americans confirmed, for as we traveled, drawing closer and closer to the desert, we confided more and more in each other. As we drove through the "valley of a thousand Casbahs," Paul told me about threats to his life. "When someone at the club pulls a gun on me, and it's happened three times, I say, 'I'm sorry but guns are not permitted on the premises,' and it works, they go away, but mine is a suicidal response." Paul was someone on whom nothing was wasted; nevertheless he was not always alive to all possibilities, at least not instantly. I told him I was positive, but he didn't react. Behind the extremely dark sunglasses, there was this presence, breathing and thinking but not reacting.

Our hotel, the Hesperides, had been built into the sunbaked mud ramparts in the ruins of the pasha's palace. We stared into an octagonal, palm-shaded pool glistening with black rocks that then slid and clicked—ah, tortoises! There couldn't have been more than five guests, and the porters, bored and curious, tripped over themselves serving us. We slept in each other's arms night after night and I stroked his great body as though he were a prize animal, *la belle bête.* My own sense of who I was in this story was highly unstable. I flickered back and forth, wanting to be the blond warrior's fleshy, pale concubine or then the bearded pasha himself, feeding drugged sherbets to the beautiful Circassian slave I had bought. I thought seriously that I wouldn't mind buying and owning another human being—if it was Paul.

The next day we picked up some hitchhikers, who, when we reached their destination, asked us in for mint tea, which we sipped barefoot in a richly carpeted room. A baby and a chicken watched us through the doorway from the sun-white courtyard. Every one of our encounters seemed to end with a carpet, usually one we were supposed to buy. In a village called Wodz, I remember both of us smiling as we observed how long and devious the path to the carpet could become: there was first a tourist excursion through miles of Casbahs, nearly abandoned except for an old veiled woman poking a fire in a now roofless harem; then we took a stroll through an irrigated palm plantation, where a woman leading a donkey took off her turban, a blue bath towel, and filled it with dates, which she gave us with a golden grin; and finally we paid a "surprise visit" to the guide's "brother," the carpet merchant who happened to have just returned from the desert with exotic Tuareg rugs. Their prices, to emphasize their exoticism, he pretended to translate from Tuareg dollars into dirham.

We laughed, bargained, bought, happy anytime our shoulders touched or eyes met. We told everyone we were Danes, since Danish was the one language even the most resourceful carpet merchants didn't know. ("But wait, I have a cousin in the next village who once lived in Copenhagen.")

Later, when I returned to Paris, I would discover that Jean-Loup had left me for Régis, one of the richest men in France. For the first time in his life he was in love, he would say. He would be wearing Régis's wedding ring, my Jean-Loup, who had refused to stay behind at my apartment after the other guests had left lest he appear too *pédé.* People would suspect him of being interested in the limousine, the town house, the château, but Jean-Loup would insist it was all love.

When he told me, on my return, that he would never sleep with me again—that he had found the man with whom he wanted to spend the rest of his life—my response surprised him. *"Ça tombe bien,"* I said ("That suits me fine").

Jean-Loup blurted out: "But you're supposed to be furious." It wasn't that he wanted me to fight to get him back, though he might have enjoyed it, but that his vanity demanded that I protest; my own vanity made me concede him with a smile. Feverishly I filled him in on my recent passion for Paul and the strategies I had devised for unloading him, Jean-Loup. It's true I had thought of fixing him up with a well-heeled, handsome young American.

Jean-Loup's eyes widened. "I had no idea," he said, "that things had gone so far." Perhaps in revenge he told me how he had met Régis. It seems that, while I was away, a dear friend of mine had fixed them up.

I was suddenly furious and couldn't drop the subject. I railed and railed against the dear friend: "When I think he ate my food, drank my drink, all the while plotting to marry you off to a millionaire in order to advance his own miserable little interests. . . ."

"Let me remind you that Régis's money means nothing to me. No, what I like is his good humor, his sincerity, his discretion. It was hard for me to be known as your lover—your homosexuality is too evident. Régis is very discreet."

"What rubbish," I would say a few days later when Jean-Loup repeated the remark about Régis's discretion. "He's famous for surrounding himself with aunties who discuss the price of lace the livelong day."

"Ah," Jean-Loup replied, reassured, "you've been filled in, I see" (*"Tu t'en renseignes"*).

All sparkling and droll, except a terrible sickness, like an infection caused by the prick of a diamond brooch, had set in. When I realized that I would never be able to abandon myself again to Jean-Loup's perverse needs, when I thought that Régis was enjoying the marriage with him I'd reconciled myself never to know, when I saw the serenity with which Jean-Loup now "assumed" his homosexuality, I felt myself sinking, but genuinely sinking, as though I really were falling, and my face had a permanently hot blush. I described this feeling of falling and heat to Paul. "That's jealousy," he said. "You're jealous." That must be it, I thought, I who had never been jealous before. If I had behaved so generously with earlier loves lost it was because I had never before been consumed by a passion this feverish.

Jealousy, yes, it was jealousy, and never before had I so wanted to hurt someone I loved, and that humiliated me further. A member of the playpen dined at Régis's *hôtel particulier.* "They hold hands all the time," she said. "I was agreeably surprised by Régis, a charming man. The house is more a museum than a house. Jean-Loup kept calling the butler for more champagne, and we almost burst out laughing. It was like a dream."

Every detail fed my rancor—Régis's charm, wealth, looks ("Not handsome but attractive").

Everything.

Paul had a photographic memory, and, during the hours spent together in the car in Morocco, he recited page after page of Racine or Ronsard or Sir Philip Sidney. He also continued the story of his life. I wanted to know every detail—the bloody scenes on the steps of the disco, the recourse to dangerous drugs, so despised by the clenched-jaw cocaine set. I wanted to hear that he credited his lover with saving him from being a junkie, a drunk, and a thug. "He was the one who got me back into school."

"A master, I see," I thought. "*School* master."

"Now I study Cicéron and prepare my *maîtrise,* but then I was just an animal, a disoriented bull—I'd even gotten into beating up fags down by the Seine at dawn when I was really drunk."

He gave me a story he had written. It was Hellenistic in tone, precious and edgy, flirting with the diffuse lushness of a Pre-Raphaelite prose, rich but bleached, like a tapestry left out in the sun. I suppose he must have had in mind Mallarmé's "Afternoon of a Faun," but Paul's story was more touching, less cold, more comprehensible. That such a story could never be published in the minimalist, plain-speaking 1980s seemed never to have occurred to him. Could it be that housed in such a massive body he had no need for indirect proofs of power and accomplishment? Or was he so sure of his taste that recognition scarcely interested him at all?

The story is slow to name its characters, but begins with a woman who turns out to be Athena. She discovers a flute and how to get music out of it, but her sisters, seeing her puffing away, laugh at the face she's making. Athena throws the flute down and in a rage places a curse on it: "Whoever would make use of it next must die." Her humiliation would cost a life.

The next user is a cheerful satyr named Marsyas. He cleverly learns how to imitate people with his tunes: "Prancing along behind them he could do their walk, fast or slow, lurching or clipped, just as he could render their tics or trace their contours: a low swell for a belly, shrill fifing for fluttering hands, held high notes for the adagio of soft speech. At first no one understood. But once they caught on they slapped their thighs: his songs were sketches."

Apollo is furious, since he's the god of music and his own art is pure and abstract. He challenges Marsyas to a musical duel:

Marsyas cringed before him like a dog when it walks through a ghost, bares its teeth, and pulls back its ears. Anguished, he had slept in the hot breath of his flock; his animals had pressed up against him, holding him between their wooly flanks, as though to warm him. The ribbon his jolly and jiggling woman had tied around one horn flapped listlessly against his low, hairy brow, like a royal banner flown by a worker's barge.

To the gods, as young as the morning, Marsyas seemed a twilight creature; he smelled of leaf mold and wolf-lair. His glance was as serious as a deer's when it emerges from the forest at dusk to drink at the calm pool collecting below a steaming cataract.

And to Marsyas his rival was cold and regular as cambered marble.

Since Marsyas knew to play only what was in front of him, he "rendered" Apollo—not the god's thoughts but the faults he wedged into the air around him. The sisters watched the goatman breathe into the reeds, saw him draw and lose breath, saw his eyes bulge, brown and brilliant as honey, and that made them laugh. What they heard, however, was music that copied sacred lines, for Marsyas could imitate a god as easily as a bawd. The only trick was to have his model there, in front of him.

If Marsyas gave them the god's form, the god himself revealed the contents of his mind. His broad hand swept the lyre, and immediately the air was tuned and the planets tempered. Everything sympathetic trembled in response to a song that took no one into account, that moved without moving, that polished crystal with its breath alone, clouding then cleansing every transparency without touching it. Marsyas shuddered when he came to and realized that the god's hand was now motionless but that the music continued to devolve, creaking like a finger turning and tracing the fragile rim of the spheres.

The satyr was astonished that the muses didn't decide instantly in their brother's favor but shrugged and smiled and said they found each contestant appealing in different ways. The sun brightened a fraction with Apollo's anger, but then the god suggested they each play their music backwards. The universe shuddered as it stopped and reversed its rotations; the sun started to descend toward dawn as Apollo unstrung the planets. Cocks re-crowed and bats re-awakened, the frightened shepherd guided his flock backward down the hill as the dew fell again.

Even the muses were frightened. It was night and stormy when Marsyas began to play. He had improvised his music strophe by strophe as a portrait; now he couldn't remember it all. The descending figures, so languishing when played correctly the first time, made him queasy when he inverted them. Nor could he see his subject.

The muses decided in the god's favor. Apollo told Marsyas he'd be flayed alive. There was no tenderness but great solicitude in the way the god tied the rope around the satyr's withers, cast the slack over a high branch of a pine, and then hoisted his kill high, upside down, inverted as the winning melody. Marsyas saw that he'd won the god's full attention by becoming his victim.

The blood ran to Marsyas's head, then spurted over his chest as Apollo sliced into his belly and neatly peeled back the flesh and fat and hair. The light shone in rays from Apollo's sapphire eyes and locked with Marsyas's eyes, which were wavering, losing grip—he could feel his eyes lose grip, just as a child falling asleep will finally relax its hold on its father's finger. A little dog beside his head was lapping up the fresh blood. Now the god knelt to continue his task. Marsyas could hear the quick sharp breaths, for killing him was hard work. The god's white skin glowed and the satyr believed he was inspiring the very breath Apollo expired.

As I read his story I stupidly wondered which character Paul was—the Apollo he so resembled and whose abstract ideal of art appeared to be his own, or the satyr who embodies the vital principle of mimesis and who, after all, submitted to the god's cruel, concentrated attention. The usual motive for the story, Apollo's jealousy, was left out altogether. His story was dedicated to me, and for a moment I wondered if it was also addressed to me—as a reproach for having abandoned the Apollonian abstractness of my first two novels or, on the contrary, as an endorsement for undertaking my later satires and sketches. It was unsettling dealing with this young man so brilliant and handsome, so violent and so reflective.

At night Paul let me into his bed and held me in his arms, just as he sometimes rested his hand on my leg as I drove the car. He told me that although Thierry often petted him, Paul was never allowed to stroke him. "We've never once kissed each other on the lips."

We talked skittishly about the curse the gods had put on us. I pathetically attempted to persuade Paul he was really a sadist. "Your invariable rage after sex with your lover," I declared melodramatically, "your indignation, your disgusting excursions into fag bashing, your primitive, literalist belief that only the biggest man with the biggest penis has the right to dominate all the others, whereas the sole glory of sadism is its strictly cerebral capacity for imposing new values, your obvious attraction to my fundamentally docile nature—" and at that point my charlatanism would make me burst out laughing, even as I glanced sideways to see how I was doing.

In fact my masochism sickened him. It reminded him of his own longing to recapture Thierry's love. "He's leaving me," he would say. "When calls come in he turns the sound off on the answering machine and he never replays his messages when I'm around. His pockets bulge with condoms. He spends every weekend with purely fictive 'German businessmen' in Normandy; he pretends he's going to visit a factory in Nice, but he's back in Paris four hours later; he stood me up for the Mr. Europe Bodybuilding contest at the Parc de Vincennes, then was seen there with a famous Brazilian model . . . He says I should see a psychiatrist, and you know how loony you have to be before someone French will suggest that."

When a thoughtful silence had reestablished itself in the car I added, "That's why you want to reach the desert. Only its vast sterility can calm your violent soul."

"If you could be in my head," he said, not smiling, "you'd see I'm in a constant panic."

To be companionable I said, "Me too."

Paul quickly contradicted me: "But you're the calmest person I know."

Then I understood that was how he wanted me to be—masterful, confident, smiling, sure. Even if he would someday dominate, even hurt me, as I wished, he would never give me permission to suffer in any way except heroically.

I drove a few miles in silence through the lunar valley, mountains on both sides, not yet the desert but a coarse-grained prelude to it—dry, gently rolling, the boulders the color of eggplants. "You're right, except so many of the people I've known have died. I used to talk this way with my best friend, but that was in America and now he is dead." That night, in Paul's arms, I said, "It's sacrilegious to say it, especially for an atheist, but I feel God sent you not to replace my friend, since he's irreplaceable, but . . ."

A carpet salesman assured us the desert was about to begin. We had been following a river through the valley and at last it had run dry, and the date palms had vanished, and the mountains knelt like camels just before setting out on a long journey. In Zagora we saw the famous sign, "Timbuctoo: 54 days." In a village we stopped to visit the seventeenth-century library of a saint, Abu Abdallah Mohammed Bennacer, a small room of varnished wood cases beside a walled-in herbal garden. The old guide in his white robes opened for us—his hands were wood-hard—some of the illustrated volumes, including a Koran written on gazelle skin. Paul's red hair and massive body made him rarer than a gazelle in this dusty village. That night a village boy asked me if I had a "gazelle" back in Paris, and I figured out he meant a girlfriend and nodded because that was the most efficient way to stanch a carpet-tending spiel.

Paul continued with his stories. The one about the French woman he had loved and married off to the paratrooper who had already become his lover. The one about the Los Angeles sadist he ridiculed and who then committed suicide. About his second date with Thierry, when he'd been gagged and chained upside down in a dungeon after being stuffed with acid, then made to face a huge poster of the dead L.A. lover. The one about the paratrooper scaling the mountain at the French-Italian border while cops in circling helicopters ordered him to descend immediately—"and applauded in spite of themselves when he reached the top barehanded," Paul exulted, "without a rope or pick or anything to scale the sheer rock face but balls and brawn."

We're too alike, I thought again, despairing, to love each other, and Paul is different only in his attraction to cartoon images of male violence and aggression. Unlike him, I couldn't submit to a psychopath; what I want is Paul, with all his tenderness and quizzical, hesitating intelligence, his delicacy, to hit me. To be hurt by an enraged bull on steroids doesn't excite me. What I want is to belong to this grave, divided, philosophical man.

It occurred to me that if I thought only now, at this moment in my life, of belonging to someone, it was because my hold on life itself was endangered. Did I want him to tattoo his initials on a body I might soon have to give up? Did I want to become his slave just before I embraced that lasting solitude?

The beginning of the desert was a dune that had drifted through the pass between two mountains and had started to fill up the scrubland. A camel with bald spots on its elbows and starlet eyelashes was tethered to a dark felt tent in which a dirty man was sprawling, half asleep. Another man, beaming and freshly shaved, bustled out of a cement bunker. With a flourish he invited us in for a glass of mint tea. His house turned out to be a major carpet showroom, buzzing with air-conditioning and neon lamps. "English?"

"No. Danish."

That was the last night of our holiday. The hotel served us a feast of sugared pigeon pie and mutton couscous, and Paul had a lot to drink. We sat in the dark beside the pool, which was lit from within like a philosopher's stone. He told me he thought of me as gay in the Nietzschean, not the West Hollywood, sense, but since I insisted that I needed him, he would love me and protect me and spend his life with me. Later in bed he pounded me in the face with his fists, shouting at me in a stuttering, broken explosion of French and English, the alternatively choked and released patois of scalding indignation.

If the great pleasure of the poor is, as they say, making love, then the great suffering of the rich is loving in vain. The troubadours, who spoke for their rich masters, are constantly reminding us that only men of refinement recognize the nobility of hopeless love; the vulgar crowd jeers at them for wasting their time. Only the idle and free can afford the luxury (the anguish) of making an absence into the very rose-heart of their lives. Only they have the extravagance of time to languish, shed tears, exalt their pain into poetry. For others time is too regulated; every day repeats itself.

I wasn't rich, but I was free and idle enough to ornament my liberty with the melancholy pleasure of having lost a Bordeaux boy with a claret-red mouth. All the while I'd been with Jean-Loup I'd admitted how ill suited we were and I sought or dreamed of seeking someone else either tepidly or hotly, depending on the intensity of my dissatisfaction.

Now that Jean-Loup had left me for Régis, I could glorify their love and despise them and hate myself while sifting through my old memories to show myself that Jean-Loup had been slowly, if unconsciously, preparing this decampment for a long time.

When I am being wicked I tell people, "Our little Jean-Loup has landed in clover. He'll soon be installed in the château for the summer and he can fill the moat with his *bandes dessinées*. The only pity is that Jean-Loup is apparently at Régis's mercy and Régis is cunning. He holds all the cards. If he tires of Jean-Loup, the poor boy will be dismissed without a centime, for that wedding ring doesn't represent a claim, only a—"

But at this point bored, shocked friends laugh and hiss, "Jealous, jealous, this way lies madness." Jealousy may be new to me but not to them. My condition is as banal as it is baneful.

And then I realize that the opposite is probably true: that Jean-Loup had always dealt with me openly, even at the end, and had never resorted to subterfuge. As soon as he knew of his deep, innocent love for Régis he told me. I am the one who attributes scheming to him.

He always wanted me to describe his ass, so I'll conclude with an attempt not to sound too wet.

I should admit right off that by all ocular evidence there was nothing extraordinary about it. It wasn't a soccer player's muscled bum or a swimmer's sun-molded twin *charlottes*. It was a kid brother's ass, a perfunctory transition between spine and legs, a simple cushion for a small body. Its color was the low-wattage white of a winter half-moon. It served as the neutral support (as an anonymous glove supports a puppet's bobbing, expressive head) for his big, grown-up penis, always so ready to poke up through his flies and take center stage. But let's not hastily turn him around to reveal Régis's Daily Magic Baguette, as I now call it. No, let's keep his back to us, even though he's deliciously braced his knees to compensate for the sudden new weight he's cantilevered in his excitement, a heavy divining rod that makes his buttocks tense. Concave, each cheek looks glossy, like costly white satin that, having been stuffed in a drawer, has just been smoothed, though it is still crazed with fine, whiter, silkier lines. If he spreads his cheeks—which feel cool, firm, and plump—for the kneeling admirer, he reveals an anus that makes one think of a Leica lens, shut now but with many possible f-stops. An expensive aperture, but also a closed morning-glory bud. There's that *grain de beauté* on his hip, the single drop of espresso on the wedding gown. And there are the few silky hairs in the crack of his ass, wet now for some reason and plastered down at odd angles as though his fur had been greedily licked in all directions at once. If he spreads his legs and thinks about nothing—his fitting with the tailor, the castle drawbridge, the debs whose calls he can no longer return—his erection may melt and you might see it drooping lazily into view, just beyond his loosely bagged testicles. He told me that his mother would never let him sleep in his *slip* when he was growing up. She was afraid underpants might stunt his virile growth. These Bordeaux women know to let a young wine breathe.

Egypt, in One Sense

Clifford Chase

Vast old terrazzo floor of the terminal; not knowing where to go for currency, then for visas; the signs all in Arabic, guidebook warnings of graft, my fear of error; the brusque yet unhurried little clerk carefully making tiny marks on his forms, as if Arabic were a dream language invented solely for my bewilderment; released at last into the balmy night air again and the new perils of dishonest taxi drivers.

Soldiers with machine guns had surrounded the plane as we filed down the tarmac in the balmy floodlit night.

For some time I had been harboring panicky thoughts about John, such as, "We've been together four years and I still don't have a key to his apartment!"

We sped along the elevated highway wedged between plaster orange–lit buildings, and though the road was certainly no worse than any expressway in New York, it all felt utterly makeshift, about to collapse, yet not collapsing, maybe suspended mid-collapse, and every window and roof and dark alley appeared in some fundamental way *different* from anything I'd ever seen before, and my capacity for astonishment awakened.

The first time John ever spoke to me was in astonishment—we were standing next to a small pond in early spring listening to weird-sounding frogs—"Wow," he said, and I knew I wanted to know him—just as now we exchanged glances again and again in the cab.

Gigantic billboards around the traffic circle advertised Egyptian movies with gigantic hand-painted faces of Egyptian movie stars.

The hotel appeared not to have been renovated since the 1920s and thus exuded a shabby, postcolonial glamour.

The poker-faced handsome lobby clerk with a Coptic cross tattoo on forearm.

I strongly suspected John had slept around in New York while I was away for three weeks earlier that summer, but I had said nothing.

We smiled at one another as we ascended the worn, carpeted, creaky steps, and again as we entered our huge, dilapidated room with its tall shutters, worn red velvet drapes, tiled floor, and sagging maroon twin beds with massive dark-wood headboards.

I place these disparate memories side by side to remind myself that they all simply coexisted at the time and need not be resolved in retrospect either.

I had decided the only answer was to go back into couples therapy and, putting off telling John, hoped that our vacation in Egypt—far from ordinary distractions—would be a good time to talk about it.

"I feel strangely at home here," I said, lying on my back and looking up at the cracked ceiling. "Me, too," he said.

Indeed Cairo offered no ordinary distractions, only extraordinary ones. Abdul and Ali said they were "student artists" and they could help us find the American Express office. John and I had been puzzling over our map, near the museum. After John had cashed his traveler's checks, we offered to tip the two young men for their trouble, but they wouldn't hear of it. They wanted to help us get our international student IDs, which I had mentioned was our next task that day. With these John and I planned to save money on the already absurdly low entrance fees to museums and other sights. We were poorer then (this was ten years ago) but not that poor. We weren't students. I was thirty-nine and John was thirty. The process took several hours: Abdul and Ali took us to an old photography studio hung with decrepit portraits and a forty-year-old poster of Nasser; a dingy storefront full of desks, where we submitted our photos and small fee; and a less dingy travel agency, where we made our train reservations to Aswan. We were jetlagged and I had a bad cold. I actually believed the two young men's names were Abdul and Ali and that they were indeed art students. Neither of them was particularly handsome but I was certainly attracted to the idea of them. They were extremely nice to us and any doubts John and I might have had about their intentions were outpaced by our wanting to be liked and of course by the fact that they were taking such good care of us. Our IDs and tickets in hand, we offered to tip them again, and again they refused, instead asking us to accompany them to their cousin's papyrus-painting shop. John rolled his eyes but we went. At least now we knew what they had wanted all along.

The deserted shop located on a side street was hung floor to ceiling with the stock colorful images of pharaohs and barges and various gods on brown crinkly paper. Abdul expounded on the paintings' authenticity as to content, technique, and materials. "Did you paint any of them?" I asked naively, but they said no, they were still learning. We didn't like the paintings and bought only a single small one. Our miserly purchase was enough for Ali but not Abdul, who asked if we would go with him to the duty-free shop to get him some liquor, which Egyptians weren't allowed to buy. "We'd be happy to do that for you," I said. They had spent all afternoon with us, after all. But when Ali declined to come along, it began to dawn on us that something wasn't right. Until then we had walked everywhere with them, but now as we rode in a cab with Abdul around a huge, insanely busy traffic circle, I realized with a kind of internal lightning bolt of fear that John and I had no idea where we were or where we were going or what might happen when we got there.

Soon enough we arrived at the store, which was in a decent neighborhood, and the three of us went in. Several men sat at a counter, behind which the large warehouselike space was stacked to the ceiling with boxes. Abdul spoke in Arabic, and John and I were asked to sign some forms. Then the clerk took us down a long passage between boxes into a little room where a young woman in a headscarf greeted us modestly from behind a metal folding table. Abdul remained at the front of the store chatting with the clerks. The woman began stamping the forms and our passports. Something in the way she looked at me made me examine more closely what we had just signed. One charge for thirty-eight, two for forty-five. Dollars, not Egyptian pounds. I pointed to the forty-five dollars and glanced at her. "Radio cassette," she answered. "No!" I said. "No, no. No radio cassette." She tore the two forms in half. And the thirty-eight dollars? "Liquor," she replied. Surely more than the two bottles we'd promised him. "No," I said, and she tore up that form too. I don't think I thanked her. "Let's go!" I said, and John and I ran down the corridor of boxes and out to the street. Abdul must have been close behind us. To our relief a cab stopped right away, but we had to circle back around past the store, and there was Abdul flagging us down. We rolled up the windows. "Don't stop! Don't stop!" John yelled, but the driver did stop, and Abdul began calling to us as if in all innocence, "What has happened? Where are you going?" I shouted back something about the two "radio cassettes." My brain seemed to be burning down the middle. Abdul said, "You come tell me. You don't just go." For a split second this seemed only fair, but John said, "You weren't straight with us." Abdul tried to open the passenger door. "I come with you." "No, no!" John shouted. *Fuck* you!" he yelled back, "I waste all my time on you." The clash made John hyper-reasonable: "And we were happy to compensate you," he said. I shoved a ten-pound note through the driver's open window—about three dollars. Abdul grabbed it. "And you pay *him* ten, too," he ordered, meaning the cabby, who grinned toothlessly. "Whatever," I said, like a jerk. We drove off.

Back at the hotel I was afraid Abdul might yet come after us—I had told Ali where we were staying—so John pushed the dresser against the door. We lay there talking about the encounter late into the night. We had wanted to believe we were making two new friends, young men very much like ourselves, only Egyptian, but instead had discovered nothing but a giant divide. Abdul clearly meant to rob us, yet he had also genuinely helped us, and his outrage when we fled appeared genuine. We of course were gaming the system ourselves, with our fake IDs, and we ended up giving Abdul next to nothing for his help. It also appeared that he and Ali really did want to be friends, or at least they were as curious about us as we were about them, especially Ali, the gentler of the two. Or did we simply flatter ourselves? And why hadn't we seen the scam coming? Why hadn't we put a stop to the whole thing sooner? Finally John said, "I guess it was just bound to end in tears."

┼

Dusty crumbling buildings in hazy morning light.

Huge trays of fresh tan pita carried on bicycles through the streets.

I drank the fruit juice despite the ice, even though the guidebook had warned us not to; John frowned.

The old telephones in wooden stalls took only older Egyptian coins, difficult to obtain since they were no longer in general circulation, nor did my phone card work, so we failed at calling my friend Gabby in Israel.

In the brand-new subway station two heavily veiled women giggled in delight as they stepped onto the escalator—evidently their first escalator ride—and so John and I also giggled in delight.

I went back to the hotel to rest, but John didn't want to; I wrote in my journal that I wasn't feeling "in love" with him.

My throat was sore and my nose required constant attention.

Behind the shutters and velvet drapes—blinding dusty street, rubble sidewalks, and blaring call to prayer.

That night the tower restaurant revolved uneasily on its Soviet-engineered track, creaking and lurching like an old ride at Coney Island.

"Cairo is to New York as New York is to San Francisco!" I said.

Turning and turning with impossible smoothness, the dervish lifted his wide, multicolored skirt to form an inverted cone around his head.

154

My mother complained to me about my father nearly all my life.

Generally I avoid conflict, and I tend to see dilemmas everywhere.

The question of whether John and I were "just too different," for instance his rarely needing to go back to the hotel and rest, whereas
I—

In the street or a café or a mausoleum or a mosque, the place pouring into my senses, pouring into John's senses, pouring into our
senses together.

The lit-up streets full of men, the bright tacky shops stacked high
with goods: we went into a toy store and bought an Egyptian version
of Clue.

Of the dervishes I wrote, "Ecstasy is an action, not a state of
being."

Like a cartoon car the little taxi seemed to suck in its sides for the
tightest passages, then bounce back to normal, as we motored
through Cairo's slums. The driver slowed for a battered pickup piled
ten or twelve feet high with roughly hewn furniture. It stopped to
unload a table, and though the alley had scarcely widened, once
again our Fiat squeezed through and we accelerated into the next
crooked channel. The driver achieved all this antic motion through
no apparent effort, one palm resting lightly on the steering wheel,
the other resting just as lightly on the gearshift. The trip lasted perhaps fifteen minutes but like a roller coaster ride seemed to go on
and on. Powdery bright sunshine and blue black shade, motorbikes,
donkeys, beat-up vans, men and children and covered-up women in
dusty clothing pressing themselves against the flaking windowless
walls as we sped by. We burst into a small ruined square—if you
could call a gravel pen a square—and suddenly a thriving produce
market revealed itself—tomatoes, greens of all kinds, brown-flecked
yellow tamarinds, bananas in various sizes, all laid out on a plastic

tarp amid the rubble. We rumbled on into another darkened alley, where a slender woman draped in cloth floated ahead of us, a lettuce the size of a basketball atop her head. John and I looked at one another in astonishment. I comprehended the poverty, yet poverty hardly seemed to describe the profusion of images passing by our windshield.

Whether in rebuke or simply the next twist of the kaleidoscope, the Ibn Tulun Mosque—our destination—was as empty and stark as a de Chirico. Fortresslike walls surrounded a vast courtyard, a stairway circling the small minaret. Inside, we were greeted by a small boy with eyes as huge as those in a velvet painting, who asked to be our guide by saying, "Guide?" and pointing to himself. We were relieved to be dealing with a child instead of a possibly unmanageable adult. Besides the ticket taker we seemed to be the only people in the vast mosque. The boy's tour was as spare and minimal as the building itself. "Carrrving," he announced, pointing upward to the intricate stone archway of the colonnade in which we stood. He pointed out other features such as "courtyard" and more "carving." "View," he said, unhooking the chain and leading us up the winding staircase. There was an austere pleasure in learning absolutely nothing about the place beyond what we could see for ourselves. Like figures in a dream, John and I looked out over the courtyard, the walkways above the four colonnades, the domed structure in the middle, all dusty and sand-colored, as if made of sand. "Citadel," the boy said, pointing in that direction over the city. Indeed, John and I had just come from there, so it was the one sight besides the pyramids that we already knew. Down the winding steps, we each gave the boy twenty pounds for the tour. He looked disappointed, so John also handed him his lighter. We were perpetually confounded by how much to pay or tip in Egypt—what was "appropriate" for any given service remained a mystery, and what about a child?

That night my friend Gabby arrived from Israel, where she was living that year. In Cairo's huge labyrinthine marketplace, John went off to explore while Gabby and I sat down in a gaudily tiled tourist café. There I ordered the meal that would make me sick for the next year and a half. "I saw your eyes in a portrait in the Coptic museum today," I said to Gabby. "That's uncanny," she replied, "because people keep commenting about my eyes lately!" At that moment everything seemed uncanny to me. My Egyptian cold medicine contributed to the effect. It was called Flu-Calm, but actually it made my heart race. Gabby and I spoke of déjà vu, past lives, destiny . . . until the awful food arrived, breaking the spell. I had ordered Egyptian Pancake with Egyptian Hotdog. I had assumed this was tourist-speak for a crepe filled with merguez. It wasn't a crepe and it wasn't merguez. It was a flat dougy thing studded with orange chunks. I ate it anyway. I had never had stomach problems before, so I was cavalier about food, to John's dismay. Soon Gabby and I realized we had been talking a long time and he hadn't yet returned. I finished my tea and began to worry. Café noise, fluorescent lighting, the smell of flavored tobacco; outside, the crowded square was strung with bare lightbulbs. John was often late, and I was mad at him now for making us wait for him. I kept looking at my watch. At last he arrived, breathless and exhilarated from having been lost in the innumerable winding passageways of the Khan al-Khalili. He told us about it. At first he was simply following his wonder, past the dozens of tourist shops full of perfume bottles, silver, or inlaid wood, and on into the real market—piles of baby clothes, towels, surplus plumbing fixtures, tools—until he realized everything was closing and the narrow streets were becoming more and more dark and deserted. He didn't know the language and didn't know where he was. Then he felt a hand firmly grasp his arm. He looked to see a teenage boy, who silently led him back through the maze to the brightly lit square. "Do you want to meet my friends?" John asked him, but whether or not the boy understood, he shook his head and disappeared again down the curving alley.

In the middle of the night I sat in the stained marble hotel bathroom shitting my brains out.

I say brains because I had apparently entered an altered mental as well as physical state, a vortex of panic that had sucked into itself all my unvoiced doubt and confusion over John.

"Are you OK?" he called through the door. "No," I said.

The sagging mattress no longer seemed charming.

Tea and toast in the dark-paneled hotel dining room; John said, "From now on you have to be more careful about what you eat."

He and Gabby went to see the Blue Mosque and to find me some Pepto-Bismol.

I shit the tea and toast away.

I lay in my hammocklike bed staring at the cracked ceiling, muttering, "Fuck, fuck, fuck!" at each new twist of my gut.

I debated whether to break up with John, right there in Cairo.

It would have been a lot simpler to see a doctor, but in the mental maze I'd entered I must have thought a parasite was the least of my problems.

I was no better the next day and tried to decide whether I was too sick to travel to Aswan that night, as John and I had planned. I couldn't stay in Cairo alone; should I go to Israel with Gabby?

Lying there fervently wishing John would proclaim to me, "I'll come with you to Israel and make sure you get well!"

John said we had already bought our tickets to Aswan and moreover he didn't know when he would ever get back to Egypt, so he wanted to go to Aswan.

Panic: "My boyfriend is selfish and won't take care of me!"

Like my mother with my father, I wasn't willing to make open demands.

On the other hand I was sure I would be well soon, as I always had been whenever I caught a stomach bug.

I agreed to go with John up the Nile, but even at the train station I considered turning back.

I climbed up into the top bunk and began to shiver uncontrollably—a fresh symptom.

The carriage shuddered and began to roll.

John asked the steward for an extra blanket, but its warmth had no effect.

The guidebook had warned of fundamentalist rebels shooting at these trains; I imagined the black window strafed by bullets.

Click-clack, click-clack.

Weak and sweating through my clothes, almost beyond thought now—except for the conviction that getting on this train with John had been the biggest mistake of my life.

John said, "Look," and I sat up to behold in the window of our compartment the hazy gardens of the Nile, plots of the purest green and rows of spindly trees, filing slowly past in the ancient early morning light. "Wow," I said. My fever had broken. In the next field a slender figure in a white turban and light blue robe, his back to us, walked calmly between the calmly glowing furrows. Now and then a glimpse of the river and the sandy banks on the other side. It was as if the train had traveled backward in time while I slept, and even now was crawling still further into previous eras, slowed by the effort. The landscape before us had nothing to do with the train or anything else invented in the past five thousand years. John and I were invisible, gazing out like spirits on an untouched world.

—✠—

The hotel in Aswan: a rundown '60s high-rise of chipped pink stucco, with balconies overlooking the distant Nile.

We were on the far edge of town on the far edge of Egypt.

Hard to find anything I could eat.

Locating a decent doctor here seemed out of the question.

We had prepaid for the room and it felt too extravagant to move to a better hotel where, say, toast and tea were served.

Living under full sway of my illusions will forever be one sense of the word "Egypt" for me.

John went out to explore the city, returning at lunchtime to tell of dark-skinned men offering him "Nubian banana" on the corniche.

It's definitely more like Africa here," John said.

The afternoon alone in the hot room—sleeping, sweating, writing in my journal, going to the balcony now and then.

Distant palm trees, the silhouette of a felucca on the shimmering water—the very boat John was on?

Once, when I was four, during a period when my father was out of town a lot, I saw him in the kitchen and wondered, "Who is that nice man making popcorn?"

Here the desert went right up to the Nile's banks.

"I want to run away," I wrote, "not only from here but from all of my life."

"A warm knife in my belly, another in my head."

You had to take a taxi convoy to the temple of Edfu because a single taxi was subject to rebel attack, but in any case I doubted I would be well enough to go.

I stared longingly at the guidebook's photo of Edfu.

I began debating again whether to break up with John.

"I seem destined to see little more than this crappy hotel room."

"Oh, this happens. This is life."

If, say, during lunch I had stopped to observe even for one moment his wide face and green-brown eyes, I might have brought myself to my senses, at least a little.

I wondered if maybe I was feeling a little better.

I could muster walking for fifteen minutes before stopping to rest on a bench overlooking the Nile.

I had never seen a sunset like this: lacy rags in clumps, connected by ropes of cumulus, sometimes the ropes crossing at right angles, all of this in a plateau just above a golden sun, above the Nile, above sand hills; an orchestra of ragged clouds, rows of gray, dark gold, bright gold, arranged around the conductor of the sun—

A man in a long, blue gown stood in front of me—"Smoke, smoke. I take care of you"—I moved to another bench.

I'm not usually one to see pictures in the sky.

Four cassocks seemed to be dancing wildly off to one side, their hands linked, and soon they were spun apart by their own dancing.

As it turned out, I would be much better the following day, both in mind and body, and John and I would see amazing things together in Luxor—the gigantic pillars of Karnak; a cramped tomb painted above with grape vines; the vast temple of Queen Hatshepsut cut into the hillside, where fifty-eight tourists and four Egyptians would be gunned down and butchered only a month later . . .

For now I continued sitting by the Nile, gazing into the sunset, asking myself again all the riddles of the day.

And then there it was, a parting in the clouds in the exact shape of a question mark, gigantic and elongated, with a small chink below for the dot.

I stared at it in thwarted wonder, until new shapes appeared—a plus, a circle.

I stumbled back to the hotel to wait for my boyfriend.

Lamb of God

Ty Geltmaker

When I lived in Rome people used to ask how I could put up with so many machine guns on the streets. I would say I didn't much notice, just like now people don't believe it when you tell them Rome back then was dark and all the buildings were black with soot from all the time gone by and all the cars and buses. The churches were smoky, full of wax and little candlesticks hardly able to breathe. You took flashlights in to see the paintings, dropping coins into electric votive candles, and dim floodlights illuminated all the Immaculate Conceptions, Annunciations, Assumptions, and Resurrections. My favorites were the frescoes, high in the vaulted ceiling in Sant'Ignazio, of American Indians confronting their European conquerors; and Santa Teresa and the other mystics like Santa Caterina, frozen in ecstatic states above the marble altars of Rome's baroque churches. Caravaggio's muscular men and women, their feet and hands pushing out from the canvas, were a secret pleasure all dressed up in a game of shadow and light, just like wondering who you might run into walking around Rome's little alleys, bursting into a piazza. You could walk back and forth from the Pantheon to Piazza Navona, strolling between those two huge outdoor living rooms, without knowing you were hearing Vivaldi and Mahler in the background. The fountains were gushing and you could buy flowers from the long skirts of old Agnese, long since called la Nonna, who was said to steal her bouquets from the cemetery after each morning's burials. Church after church after church, and one glance to the next; it was like doing the Stations of the Cross.

In all this darkness life went on. And even though it rained a lot, Rome seemed so bright and full of sun around five o'clock each evening, with people splurging, now and then offering each other espresso and grappa and ice-cream cones in little bars while window shopping the boutiques and bookstores near the Spanish Steps and Parliament up and down either side of the Corso, going home to cheap apartments in Testaccio, and around the Colosseum, and out to Garbatella, coming out again as many nights as not, for dinner at someplace you could get good-enough food and wine, cheaper than you could cook for yourself at home, at places like La Quercia off Piazza Farnese, where bossy Italia told you what to eat.

No day ended without having wandered in and out of one church or another, never avoiding paintings like that of *The Calling of St. Matthew,* playing cards, in the Chiesa di San Luigi dei Francesi; and you would go to bed wondering what all the fuss in the world about sin was. In the unmarked church just next to Chiesa della Pace behind Piazza Navona for a hundred lire you could see that German nuns protected a treasure of castrated marble male genitalia, while up the way at the bottom of Via Veneto tourists paid even more to walk through a chapel of skulls and bones of dead holy brothers arrayed in decorative patterns. Still, in Rome in those days, you would read in the papers that homeless, sleeping immigrants from Africa were found torched to death in and around these sacred sites.

San Juste comes to mind, from Cameroon, watching over a band of gentle, desperate men from Africa encamped at the Isola Tiberina, begging with their tubercular coughs around the Ospedale Fratebenefratelli halfway across the river between the Jewish ghetto and Trastevere. No one could resist his muscular voice, playing guitar at the fountain of Santa Maria in Trastevere and before that on the steps of the cathedral of Perugia, where I had first met him the year before.

But there were always other people like *le gemelle,* the twins, who lived high up in Monte Mario with a concierge and an underground garage. Clelia and Gina were rich, attending the Rome Simultaneous Translation School on the edge of Villa Borghese, both blonde and bilingual and known around Rome, moving from one scene to another on their pastel green and pink Vespas. I knew them from my job as an announcer on the radio station of the *Rome Daily American.* They had an afternoon show and used to dedicate songs from Earth, Wind & Fire to me, whom they addressed with a coded nickname, Tiberio. Once I gave Clelia a poem I was writing and she noticed I was using "o" instead of "a" at the end of my adjectives and vowels and figured out that meant the object of my love was masculine, not feminine, or that I had confused my genders. *Dio, Tiberio. Hai sbagliato.*

Ever since then, Clelia and Gina would play Van Morrison's "Into the Mystic" and dedicate it to me. Once, at dinner in their apartment with their grandmother and their mother, both of whom had defied convention and gotten a divorce once it finally became legal to do so in the early '70s, all the while running a haute couture boutique, I was asked—"as an atheist"—to comment on Zeffirelli's latest television special on the life of Jesus Christ: *Tiberio, tu che non sei credente, che ne dici?* They didn't really care what I had to say as a "non-believer," or that my name was really Eric, not Tiberio, or that they all knew I was gay, and went on to talk about how sad it must be to be such a talented homosexual like Zeffirelli.

Le gemelle could catch you off guard saying the strangest things, like that as self-proclaimed Fascists they thought Rome's few public parks would have been better off left as the private property of the old nobility. Walking through Villa Celimontana, Clelia once said, *Mah, certo è bello, ma sarebbe più bello se fosse ancora mio.* More beautiful if only it were still hers? She explained that her ancestors had owned the place as *nobiltà nera,* the so-called black nobility allied with the Vatican against political forces advocating secular control of Rome. And to think a young Roman girl could be saying such things a hundred years after losing that fight, as if she herself had been on the barricades at the moment of the fall of Rome and the unification of the Italian state. Still, we were friends, sharing snacks of thinly layered white-bread *tramezzini* and one apricot or pear *succo di frutta* after another in the bars around the *Daily American* just off the Corso behind the Galleria just across from the parliament, in Via di Santa Maria in Via, which confused people but meant The Way of Saint Mary in Flight.

In the flow of any normal day then, most working men and women kept shop from eight in the morning until they went home at one in the afternoon to *mamma,* a wife, or a grandmotherly *nonna,* cooking stews and sauces and pastas, and then took naps with their clothes off in bed with their *moglie* or *marito* before returning to work from four to seven. You could walk around Rome in the so-called *ore di pasto* when all newspaper ads said it was safe to call by phone to rent a room or for whatever it was you were seeking, and hear a uniform clinking of forks and plates, against the background theme of dah dah dah dah dahdah dah dahdah dahdah dah dahdah! That was the theme of the Rai, the national radio and television network. There were no privately run television channels, and just a few pirate radio stations on the low end of the dial run mostly by political groups of the left.

Big company men and a few such professionally employed women, and state employees, ate in corporate cafeterias and neighborhood restaurants, idling their time as they saw fit, like the horde of foreign journalists working around the Trevi Fountain who ate at Tarcisio's *osteria* with a daily pasta and predictable meat and vegetable dish. *Cucina povera* and what Italians now call *slow food* were just how people ate. No one thought it wrong to have a little wine and when the weather was nice go off to a park for a nap or a tryst in a wayward spot and then go back to work, often enough with an espresso topped off with steamed milk at simple cafés around the Trevi Fountain like Crema and Panna. For special occasions people walked over to Tazza d'Oro and Sant'Eustachio near the Pantheon for the best coffee in Rome, or Giolitti across from Parliament for ice cream. People forget now that Rome had four rush hours every day, everyone trying to avoid coming in and going out in each direction twice. What a mess! *Che mascello!*

It took at least two years back then to get a telephone from the national service, known as Sip even though no one ever seemed to know beyond *Società italiana* what the "p" stood for; something like "for," as in *Società italiana per telecomunicazioni,* with the "t" dropped off. People find it hard to imagine that there were no cell phones, and no e-mail or calling cards of the magnetic or coded variety. Even from a phone in your home you had to call the operator for long distance, which was anything outside of your immediate town. Public phones required the deposit, or rather constant dropping, of a *gettone,* at fifty lire each worth about half a minute; an average call could require hundreds of these heavy copper tokens. The only way to make an international call was to go to a central Sip office like the one in Piazza San Silvestro just off the Corso and place an order, waiting in lines that could take an hour, finally getting a *cabina* with a private phone to which you would be summoned as your call was placed. Waiting, you would meet people from all over the world, often running into acquaintances from the United States you had no idea were in Europe. "Betsy, what a surprise; Richard, so good to see you. Getting married? So soon? How lovely; Oh, no, I'm stuck here in Rome; so sorry I can't attend." You'd go to San Silvestro to pick up a dirty sleeping bag an African refugee had told you to get, and wonder why everyone was calling places they had voluntarily left.

In Rome back then if your intention was to stay for more than a month or so, you were lucky to find an apartment any sooner than you would ever get a telephone. Rent control was strict and once moved in you could hardly ever be evicted. Landlords preferred short-term foreign renters who they knew would leave sooner than later, betting on the fact that conditions in Rome were too primitive for even the most desperate Romantic. Everybody still somehow seemed to find a place to live, usually around some past or future hoped-for, had-been, would-be lover; or they left Rome and went back home to their *paese* somewhere south and disappeared forever, occasionally showing back up sad and lonely; mostly male homosexuals riven with guilt, afraid to cut their hometown family ties, destined to be the *frocio del paese* or *scappolo della famiglia*, hometown fag or family bachelor.

Once in a while an American woman would make a dramatic return to Rome, shocking her past lovers, years after having given up her dreams of living in Rome forever, now with lots of money, her bad Italian rusty, accompanied by an irritable spouse reminding her—if she needed to be told—that she no longer fit in here anymore, if she ever did. Occasionally such women returned alone and with a vengeance. Patricia Breakstone comes to mind, buying an old castle in the *campagna* and an apartment in the *centro storico* on the bet that her trust fund would allow her to throw parties and live in impoverished luxury to the end of her miserable life, all the while complaining life was better back in New York.

Nobody in Rome could imagine living anywhere else, but it all depended on whom you knew. You could know no one and suddenly be told a famous director had seen you in a club like Superstar or Easygoing and you were in demand. That's how I met Brantomi and after a little sex he put me in a couple films and loaned me the deposit for my apartment. I paid him back a year later with a hundred thousand lire stashed into my signed original print of Isherwood's *Berlin Stories.* That's when I met Enea, too, at St. James Club. He was such a *mauvais garçon*. Wasn't that strange: the first guy I ever had sex with was a hustler who didn't want money from me.

I would wait around the Spanish steps and go upstairs to his apartment in Via Frattina once he had finished his trade, flipping through magazines while he took a shower. He was a whore, which didn't bother me in the slightest since I loved everything about him, his black head of hair, his smooth chest, his lanky body, his *Vado in Sardegna domani, vuoi venire con me?* Of course I didn't want to go to Sardinia tomorrow or ever with him or anyone else; I wanted to move to Rome and live with an Italian lover.

People did not think of sex in the way sex was commonly understood elsewhere. People had sex just having dinner or at a bar or at a table in a piazza, checking each other out, letting go at the sight of what might have been, not worrying that to eat and drink might be considered something more than innocent flirtation anywhere else. You really were a piece of meat, less desired for doing it than being thought to have been available, with other people knowing it. People really only cared about two things: sex and food, in reverse order. That's the mistake most Americans make. It's all about seduction. Sometimes it's about the illusion of seduction, and never doing it at all.

Sex in the get-it-on sense of really doing something and holding on was all about fantasy and furtive moments on Sunday afternoon in a borrowed car with newspapers stuffed around the windows in the Parco della Rimembranza if you were straight, or a rendezvous at the dunes after a train ride and bus trip south of Rome from the Pyramid to Ostia if you were gay. Very little sex ever happened on Saturday night when the dance clubs around Piazza Bernini at the bottom end of Via Veneto emptied out. Life was all about being seduced and being abandoned. Besides, most Italians lived with their parents well into their thirties whether they were married or not. Every now and then a young runaway boy like Renato from some out-of-the-way place like Crotone, on the east coast of the toe of the boot in Calabria, would show up and everyone would take him in, passing him around, having sex; and then an aunt or two would arrive and stay, moving into your apartment, cooking and looking for jobs. It took me from All Souls to the second Sunday of Advent to get Concetta and Pinotta to believe that I was not keeping Renato and had no idea where he was.

Rome when I lived there was a city full of expatriates and eccentrics. At one point Guido Mannheim was harboring Renato, begging me to take the waif in, playing his mournful saw in Piazza Navona, his music ever more haunting as his consumption of heroin increased. He was not alone in his drug habit, as Italy was plagued with an epidemic of delirious addiction such that on your way home late at night or on the way to work in the morning you had to dodge the syringes tossed aside by what I used to think of as the *fratellanza dell'ago,* the "brotherhood of the needle." Really hot guys like Christoph Schmidt would come up to you at Bernini's Fountain of Four Rivers and say, *Quando facciamo all'amore?* And all you could scream was, *Quando smetti di bucarti.* "I'll fuck with you when you stop shooting up." This was summer; in winter it was worse, addicts crouched against the cold on the gated steps of Borromini's Sant'Agnese church.

Second- and third-generation expatriates with mixed Italian parentage like Guido and Christoph did nothing much in particular and would invite groups out to a grandfather's *castello* on the outskirts of town where it was once the country but was now surrounded by public housing high-rise apartment buildings, *le borgate.* Everyone was supposed to find an appropriate sexual partner or two after a dinner of veal and polenta and then be given fresh linens and airy rooms, crawling with mice, to fall asleep in.

On other nights, young people like me were invited to simple dinners of tuna and mozzarella, garnished with sliced tomato, up among the rent-controlled apartments of established postwar film and dance critics like Kirkland James and Burnham Gibbons. They had lived their entire adult lives as semi-closeted homosexual exiles in Trastevere and in the cheaper blocks behind Piazza Navona, near the Oratorio di San Filippo Neri, and always seemed perplexed that someone like me would have come to Rome "at such a late date"—*così tardi*—lamenting their backwater status, wondering if they had not made a mistake in having "not gone to Paris."

The center of Rome each Sunday seemed empty until everyone came piling back in to be seen having a cappuccino at sunset. The crowded bars in Piazza Navona, the Pantheon, and Sant'Eustachio were the places to go. In summer men wore jeans and loose white cotton half-unbuttoned shirts, no socks, and colorful cotton-topped straw-soled *scarpe basche,* what the French call *espadrilles,* which turned into wood if it happened to rain and get too wet underfoot. These shoes were made on the Amalfi Coast in Positano; now they are made in China. It was cool for men to show their ankles and a little chesty cleavage. Women pulled their skirts up for a glimpse of the naked calf.

On weekdays it was Café Greco people went to after work in the evening, but never at the back tables and booths where elderly matrons still carried on about how Fascism had done so much good, paving the roads in Africa; and only until 8:00 p.m. at the front of the house, when just before closing, professionals who swarmed the place left their unfinished cocktails on the black marble counter, rushing home in time to run out to dinner at the hot places of the moment: restaurants with piano bars like Kozmo, Proletaria, and Rum.

The most handsome young men in Rome in the late 1970s were to be found across the Piazza di Spagna at Babington Tea Room every night around six. They would all fawn over a fat little rich girl known only as Rosetta. She draped herself in oversized white buttoned-down dress shirts and was famous mostly because her mother was a painter of celebrities and their cats and dogs. Before she eventually killed herself in one of those epidemics of suicide that occasionally swept through Rome, Rosetta led a lonely existence, feeding her many admirers dinner each night in an ensemble of apartments in the once fashionable Via Margutta, emerging after a nap around midnight into the local warren of gay bars where for fifteen thousand lire you could get a drink and be ushered down a flight of stairs to a tiny basement dance floor. Years later the local press revealed that Rosetta was in fact a boy who had been raised as a girl.

Everyone was too polite to call anyone much of anything, much less a fag hag or a transvestite, even if the roads leading out of the city were filled with men dressed as women selling themselves. It was only with the later suicide of the gay theoretician Mario Mieli in the early '80s that the issue of transexuality became a national issue of some limited importance. Mieli's best-selling *Elementi di una Critica*

Omosessuale, which I translated in a private edition as *Prolegomena to Any Homosexual Critique,* had on its publication in 1977 caused an outrage, even as the author was hailed a genius, an academic Pasolini.

Out in the Parioli suburb, where people lived in modern, what we might now call mid-century apartments, you had to be seen fashionably dressed, cashmere sweater swung around the neck, at the Café Ungaria in Piazza Ungheria, preferably with someone in a hot car waiting for you. And not a minute beyond *ferragosto,* the August 15 holiday after which leather boots and even a fur were required for women of a certain class, saying, *Cara, fa così freddo.* My dear, how cold it is. Young cool Fascist guys liked to hang out here. This is where I met Riccardo, whose family farm north of Rome made a decent *grappa,* and who turned out to be the brother-in-law of one of the Australian typists at the *Daily American,* where in the summer of 1976 I landed my first job in Rome. Riccardo was the very model of the dark Italian man in his early twenties everyone still fantasizes about, even as I wonder why we never had sex.

We would carry on as if engaged in sacramental discourse, especially our love of the Baroque, and always disagree about politics. I just could not stand his insistence that "things were not so bad under Mussolini" and that "the racial laws of 1938 were just an imposition to buy time from Hitler," or that "if only the partisans had not gone after the Germans, less lives would have been lost." How could I be so attracted to someone who said such things, even though he was so handsome? He was the only guy I knew back then who just wanted me to love him and move in together and lead a normal life. But what could a *vita normale* back then in Italy have been for him and me? It was tempting, but he was a Fascist and said so, and so I couldn't. I look back on that time and wonder how Riccardo could have said such things and still wanted to live together with another man and if people like Clelia and Gina really believed what they said about politics and homosexuals. As if they were all nostalgic for an imagined simple time they had never lived in.

Late on Sunday in any season no one in Rome's center was to be found anywhere except at Birreria Marconi and er Buco near the Trevi fountain or at da Ivo in Trastevere, along with the other *pizzerie* and *wurst* joints, especially er Baffo, not far from Piazza Navona, everyone drinking beer that night of the week, never wine, which would be the sure sign you were a tourist, as would the usual objections to the use of "er," which in Roman dialect is "il," for "the." It was amazing how people who knew so little invested so much in their drinking preferences and their limited grammar.

I was still learning that blue jeans, corduroys, and Hush Puppies, which Italians called "Clarks," were the required trousers and shoes in winter, for the kind of Italian guy I wanted to become like and sleep with. Guys with staccato names and ways of speaking Italian, like Roberto Manin, wearing V-neck sweaters, nothing underneath, at the weekly meetings of FUORI, the gay rights group I had started to attend. And the women I liked were feminists who wore knee-length skirts of silk with a floral print.

No matter where you went in Rome people always carried a newspaper or two, neatly tucked under the arm you didn't write with, as a kind of public badge of political identity, also serving as a purse in which to keep things rolled up, when not being read alone in bars and restaurants. *Lotta Continua, il Manifesto,* and *la Repubblica* were popular with people like me on the left. Around the San Lorenzo university quarter, on the edge of the Verano municipal cemetery where buses unloaded mourners coming in from the provinces each morning, just being seen with one of these daily papers was an automatic passport into conversation, mainly with students from southern Italy and the Middle East, with lots of refugees from Lebanon. Northern Italians tended to go to university in their own cities or they would find apartments they could afford in Rome outside of the crowded college district, showing up only for classes and exams. But everyone shook hands in what must now seem like such formal times, men and women also giving each other a double kiss, cheek to cheek, with none of the airy phoniness that has long since become so fashionable.

Still, you took pains to be discreet even if people were not afraid to criticize or mimic each other, as I would do a few years later, stepping onto a little barge in Venice going to the Zattere, when I looked at a man and his bare feet, a few years older than me, and said, "That is me; that is who I want to become."

2
Coming Back

On
Going Back

Brian Bouldrey

Then I returned, and I saw vanity under the sun.

Ecclesiastes 4:7

I.

Anthony, my partner of many years and now the butt of all my ex-boyfriend jokes, is the best traveler I know. He is miserable at home, but on the road—whoopee! I remember once looking out the window of a secluded Tuscan villa within minutes of our arrival and, hanging in the lintel like a younger, hairier Helena Bonham Carter in a tasteful, saucy Merchant Ivory film, I sighed, "I want to come back to this place already."

But Anthony shook his head. "The world is like a giant lawn, and it is my goal to mow every corner of it."

The first time my father let me mow the lawn, it was fun. Ever after, he never could pay me enough to do that kind of work. And you'd think a fairly bright guy could extrapolate from this life lesson and realize Anthony was right: he did not say, "The world is like a giant lawn, and it is my goal to mow every corner of it twice." But I did not extrapolate, and I did mow twice. Once.

The first time I walked to the pilgrim shrine of Santiago de Compostela in 1996, I met several lifelong friends, and among them was Petra, a German girl who has been my backpack mate for a decade now: together, we have mown Corsica, Hungary, Austria, and Canada. On first meeting, what had deeply impressed me, being a boy and therefore being competitive, is that Petra had made the pilgrimage to Santiago twice, two years in a row. It was her second time down the road when I was making my first journey. The first day I encountered her, we both, separately, chose to part from our companions to walk alone on a detour that added two miles to the day's walking, with only a remote Knights Templar church as a reward. We walked alone, together. We had the trail to ourselves, and we got to be fast friends, fast.

"Is it easier to walk this way a second time?" I asked her then, thinking I already knew the answer—knowing where you're going, you know what stones will trip you, what house will throw boiling water on the hobos.

"No, it is much more difficult!" she said. "In your mind, you know what the next town looks like, and in your imagination, you are already there." I imagined her imagination, the map of the world collapsing, time taken out of the equation, destination the only goal for each day. Think of the way you're a character in a play scripted to be slapped, and you telegraph a wince before the actual slapping.

So when Jean-Philippe, another, other fellow pilgrim, suggested that we make a second trip down the road to Santiago six years later, I decided that Petra's wise words did not apply, because six years had passed, during which time I had, as it were, forgotten my lines and when to wince; also I would be doubling the time, mileage, and misadventure by starting at one of the traditional starting places in central France: Vezelay. What had taken a little over a month to execute the first time would take two months this time, and half the road would be new.

A couple of weeks into our walk from Vezelay, we were directed by our makeshift guidebook (a folder full of photocopied maps and directions created by "Les Amis de Chemin de St. Jacques") to stay at the convent of Sainte-Marie de Frugie, in La Coquille, somewhere in the dewdropped Dordogne. Blackberry brambles were almost ready to fruit, choke cherries almost gone by. Cumulus clouds danced in orderly fleecy rows, dragging the occasional thunderhead, raining on its own parade. Rain is delicious as long as it doesn't touch you.

I was taken, all along this road, with the way religious and daily life are never separated in countries in which everybody is pretty much of the same faith (and by countries I mean France and Spain and Italy). (And by faith I mean Catholicism.) Because of this, there were odd juxtapositions, even contradictions, at least to somebody like me, the sacred and the profane not only next to each other, but informing each other: a big crucifix at the edge of a village overlooking a great pile of junked, rusty, abandoned cars; a restaurant's piped-in muzak featuring "Ave Maria"; a basketball hoop installed in one church door, and in another, the goals for soccer established at the door of a modestly sized cathedral. From my own small bed in our Sainte-Marie cell—for that's what it was—I noticed a little disposable air freshener beneath the crucifix. Jean-Philippe had tied one end of his laundry line to Jesus's hand, the other to a nail in the windowsill.

This convent was decidedly old-fashioned, full of ill-lit massive statuary of obscure saints, impassive as cigar-store Indians. Next to my head in bed, Saint Francis watched over me, his arms crossed with little white birds in his tonsure; beasts gamboled at his feet. This was just fine, until I woke up in the middle of the night and felt the profound disorientation I feel when spending the night in an entirely different place every single night, and saw the looming shadow of My Protector, and nearly hit my head on his wooden head.

The evening before the concussion, the nuns insisted we join them for dinner. Since the town had no restaurants, we decided to accept. We ended up eating in a large hall lit by stained glass windows of perhaps more secular subjects, meaning geometric shapes, so that Jean-Philippe was bathed in the light of a red square while he ate his blue omelet and I kept being startled. We were joining a well-watched group of two dozen wayward boys, troublemakers set on the straight and narrow with a cadre of tough-looking priests (hellion-to-priest ratio roughly 3 to 1) and led by nothing less than the bishop of this region! A bishop, I wondered at the introduction. This guy was young, younger than me by ten years at least, and I wondered what I had done with my life; somebody ought to knock some ambition into me. The bishop had to wear the simple black but gave vent to his vanity by fiddling with his tonsure. He'd taken great care with his mustachios and with sideburns that ended in complemented points; he had even experimented with a "fade." If I had had the Gall vocabulary, I might have complimented him on his "fade." What, I wondered as I dug into my own geometric cobalt-colored omelet, was the French word for "fade"?

"Where will you go next?" the bishop asked us, to make awkward dinner conversation.

Jean-Philippe and I gave each other a conspiratorial grin. "Thiviers," he answered for both of us. There is a reason that we knew the word was loaded, a reason I will give in a moment. We enjoyed an outburst of froggy braying from two or three of the bad boys, quickly silenced by one of the priests.

We knew the bishop would react somehow—inhale, exhale, bug out or narrow his eyes, smile, not smile. He squirmed a little and said what he knew he would say, "Well, but I advise you, do not go to the monastery called 'Partage.'"

We had heard of the Partage Monastery in Thiviers from our various evening hosts for more than a week. The name Thiviers was anathema. We were very excited. But we never heard the same explanation for the Thiviers Evil more than once, though the direness of the offense grew more colorful the closer we drew. In Limoges, the perceived problem was comical: the Thiviers monks were guilty of giving bad haircuts. Someone else told us they were rejecting the word of God. According to the Perigordians, the monastery of Thiviers was practicing medicine without a license ("Do not show them your horrible pilgrim feet, monsieur!"). The bishop of Sainte-Marie now said, "There is a Vietnamese abbot there, and he is performing exorcisms. It is a very strange business."

Vietnamese Exorcisms! That was a new one!

Jean-Philippe leaned in to me and took a chance that the bishop would not understand his English. "They take Visa and MasterCard."

The next morning, we were not allowed to leave le Frugie, to continue our walk among the brown cows and spools of hay of the Perigord, without first taking Mass. *Pas de* problem, of course, since they never charged us a single euro, and they had served us the omelet dinner and promised an omelet breakfast. As the priest entered (somebody we hadn't seen the day before), he opened the Mass. In Latin.

How odd, I thought, knowing from the catechism that Vatican II had commanded all Masses be performed in the local language. Isn't this Latin forbidden? Well, of course it was. We had stumbled upon a bunch of renegade Catholics who followed a fellow named LeFebre, who wants nothing to do with reform. Jean-Philippe was no help; he is an agnostic (when I lit a candle for my favorite saint, Saint Roque, he watched me drop two euros into a canister and said, "A beer also costs two euros. You feel better after a prayer, but I feel better after a beer."). I was able to follow the Mass without much problem because of all the requiems I had heard by Verdi, Mozart, Faure, what have you (and by "what have you," I am afraid I mean the original cast recording of *Evita,* in the opening funeral Mass). The real challenge was going down to my knees to take the communion, feeling the sacrifice in my sore feet and legs.

Renegades! When everybody is of the same faith, when there is no separation of church and state, people look for ways to differentiate themselves. This explained a lot of things at de Frugie: the youthfulness of the visiting bishop, the great dusty library, and the chapel there, glutted with too many candelabras and fading gladiolas, a reliquary or five, mismatched sconces, more wooden saints. Jean-Philippe leaned over, right during the Apostles' Creed, and pointed out a note on the door beside us: *Cost of a marriage: ninety-two euros. Cost of a funeral: ninety-two euros.* "Coincidence?" he asked, using the French pronunciation.

After good renegade coffee, we were happy to be on the road again. At the door of the convent, I admired another of the impassive statues, this time, of Sainte Matthilde. She had a plate in one hand, which may have been used for calling cards at some point, but now, as we could see with a few centimes of a euro scattered casually as "seed donation," we knew we were expected to give a little bit. I liked her, and so did Jean-Philippe, for she seemed to be lifting her skirt for us with her free hand.

"Who is Matthilde the patron for?" Jean-Philippe asked me, like I'm some kind of authority.

"Perhaps for you," I suggested, since she'd offered her political leaning, *sans coulotte*. "I will drink a beer for her," he affirmed, but he and I both dropped five euros onto the plate. We looked into our makeshift guide. The advice given about the Partage Monastery was to avoid it, because of "the legal proceedings." Nothing more. It was as if, every day, as they warned us off the monastery, the invitation were renewed for us. Perhaps I would get exorcised of all my inner demons!

3.

I had been warned, too, about the region of land beyond Thiviers called Les Landes. Friends had motorcycled through it. A flat, sandy, piney region that looked as if it might be peopled by beaver traders, it was planted at the command of Napoleon with forests and forests of regularly spaced pine trees. "You'll die of boredom," my cycle hog friends told me, since they had nearly done so, spacing out looking at spaced trees until the regularity of the road nearly brought them to crash. But Les Landes was a sweet respite for a walker used to getting disoriented when a road curves even slightly, and when a small hillock can create a great effort. Under the shade of the infinite pines, with the soft needles pillowing an even softer sandy ground, we drifted through that region as if in a dream—the one where the corridor stretches out forever and forever before you.

Travel by foot differs from travel by any vehicle. You move, but you seem to move in "real time." And yet you feel as if you are making great haste: There is a funny little footnote in the 1895 edition of *Uncle Remus: His Songs and Sayings,* written by Joel Chandler Harris himself: "It may be interesting to note here that in all probability the word 'skedaddle,' about which there was some controversy during the war, came from the Virginia negro's use of 'skaddle,' which is a corruption of 'scatter.' The matter, however, is hardly worth referring to." Things hardly worth referring to seem important when walking, and vice versa; footnotes become keynotes, and vice versa. Scattering and skedaddling, from the same source, pull away from each other, one sapping energy, the other, a source. All sorts of things seem contrary to the way you have always perceived them. It's like finding out a person you thought was straight is actually gay.

It may be that walking helps make other fine distinctions you could never perceive while moving so quickly through a noisy world. I have discovered that the difference between being alone and being lonely is big, and only comes to you when walking, which one must do alone, even if you are with a dozen other people. The fact is, I never learned how to be alone until I grew older. There's something in our culture (and by our culture, I mean gay culture) that equates "alone" to "failure." And while gay men seem lonely, that's not the same as alone. After I worked all this out while tromping down the long sandy corridor of Les Landes, I began to have a bad feeling about walking over the same trail twice, which I would soon do, once I crossed the Pyrenees into Spain. Going a second time meant I was not only not lonely, but not alone.

Anyway. Somewhere along the piney corridor of Les Landes (that sandy soil makes hydrangeas red, and cornflowers purple), a shiny Renault zipped past us on a stretch of asphalt we had to pass along. It slowed, then stopped. I had a moment's panic. Though I'd been buoyant believing I had thoroughly skedaddled, I couldn't really run quickly if this were foul play, not with a backpack pulling down on me. But as with any suspected instrument of foul play, the Renault turned out to be a beneficence, manned by a priest in a white cassock, a Père de Blancs, as Jean-Philippe explained to me as he approached us, his hazards flashing, his car door agog. He spoke to Jean-Philippe as if he knew I wouldn't speak a word of his French. "I see you are going to Saint Jacques," he said. You can always tell a pilgrim by the cockleshell pinned to his backpack.

We nodded—you caught us.

"Have you had the communion yet today?"

Hell, we hadn't had communion in weeks, not since the renegade convent of Sainte-Marie de Frugie. So we said no. And right there along the side of the road, with other Renaults whizzing by and people staring at us, on our knees, backpacks still over our shoulders, this priest gave a mini-Mass (not in Latin this time but in inscrutable French) and offered us communion.

It may seem funny, but this was one of my fondest, most incongruous memories of that second pilgrimage. I wish I could go back and find that stretch of unimportant freeway where I received communion by an anonymous priest. But that's a foolish wish, isn't it? The desire to go back is the desire to be an expert, a master, to go native—and that isn't even possible in the place where I live and work. I want to make all those incongruities and dichotomies smooth, or hold them together with some sort of mental glue.

4.

Once Jean-Philippe and I had crossed the Pyrenees into Spain, we were on familiar terrain, and this was, as I suspected, not a good thing. There was, first of all, the impulse to tell all those people (and by other people, I mean fellow pilgrims) to "get off my property," though we were the ones tramping through the backyards of villagers every day. Jean-Philippe and I were so much our own little unit that it was hard to meet us, if you were a fellow pilgrim. Somehow, we were intimidating, because most of the pilgrims who joined us on the other side of the Pyrenees were just starting out, and we had a kind of skedaddling inertia hurtling us forward. Our feet were in good working order: wounded, then toughened by a month of France, while these newbie pilgrims spent the first hour after stopping treating weeping blisters and wrapping ankles and knees in all sorts of bandages. There was some crying; there were some who were doing this international walking thing for the first time—retired people, overweight people, girls from the city, boys stunned to find nobody spoke French beyond the mountains we just crossed. The man running the *refugio* had mixed up a "sopa de peregrino," or pilgrim soup: a big bin full of water, vinegar, and salt. People took turns soaking their feet in it. It's only pilgrim soup after four or five walkers have used the same batch.

I struck up a conversation with four German students washing their clothes in the backyard of the *refugio,* and the T-shirts they hung on the lines had strong lefty sentiments silk-screened into them, most of them quite anti-American. I hadn't made anything like the friendships I made when Petra and Jean-Philippe and I walked last time, but I was not really heartbroken about that. I felt as if I were preserving and honoring that journey by remaining apart. They all seemed like kids, and I was too old to be playing with them.

Nevertheless, I tried to tell them about the heritage I knew from the pilgrim road. Earlier in the day I showed them the famous poisoned river that Basques led unwary travelers to during the rowdy middle ages, so that their horses would drink and die and they could skin the beasts and eat their meat. None of the students were impressed. Nobody likes a know-it-all.

And the jokes I retold from the first pilgrimage didn't work any more. For example, there is a way that nearly every town in Spain is laid out, with the municipal sports arena (pool, gym, soccer field) to be placed at the outskirts and called the *Polideportivo.* For those who have walked all day long, it's the first thing you see when coming into town, and imagining any sort of running, swimming, or jumping (and when you do imagine, it is always imagined done with a heavy backpack) casts the soul into a Cimmerian pit of despair. Petra, who had done the pilgrimage twice first, was the one who used to moan whenever she spied the latest *Polideportivo,* and we would have a rejuvenating laugh thinking of all that pole vaulting and gymnastics with a backpack still strapped to us.

But here, now, when I tried to crack a joke about the first *Polide-portivo* I passed with the lefty German students, they failed to see the humor of the situation. Nobody was impressed. Nobody likes the guy who tells the same jokes over and over.

Jean-Philippe was miserable too, but for his own reasons. "It's so dangerous to return to a place like this," I told him.

"This food is terrible," he muttered.

"At least I don't have to eat any more damn omelets," I hissed. And that was what kept me going the second time: I felt much more at home in Spain, not just because I knew the language but also because of a familiarity with fried food, the love of conversation, and a desire to be just a bit self-destructive with pleasure (Spain is about 20 percent more dangerous than anywhere else: 20 percent more alcohol served in every drink, 20 percent more exposed wiring hanging from every wall, 20 percent more black tobacco in every filterless cigarette, 20 percent fewer seat belts on thrill rides and cars [same thing], 20 percent more children clad in flammable costumes next to festival bonfires flaring out of control; Spain is walking on one side of a high fence and hearing somebody on the other side rev up a buzz saw or car or other big machine and somebody near them shouting, "Oye! Oye!"; God bless you, Spain). And an odd comfort with this specific stripe of macho wasn't foreign to me; it was something they exported successfully to the New World centuries before.

We passed into La Rioja from Navarra and the landscape changed from sticky mud to purple hills with matching clouds; thistle, mowed hay, dill, the sweet anis pacharan; brusque, obvious barmen; sandstone brown churches; smiling mild statues of the Virgin; the smell of frying potatoes; television in the dining room. I'd heard this joke before: I'd already dated this guy, this joke called the Camino; we had gone our separate ways six years before, and here I was, trying to have what is indelicately referred to as a "re-rack."

When one is working on something of any size, whether it is a book, a journey, or a child, one has the curse of time to fully realize that sometimes that thing will be a failure. A cheap imitation of the true thing, the original thing. And you have to go on, anyway. We call this feeling, of finishing something that will fail, "exhaustion."

You get to see it all when walking: the graffiti on walls, for instance. In pre-dawn León, I came across some that was meant to bait
skinheads: *Yo soy un Yanki Rojo Maricón Judeo Negro.* "I am an American Communist Gay Jewish Negro," with all the glib nasty words
used, so if I were a better translator, I would offer: "I am a Yankee
Commie Faggot Jew Nigger." In Europe, a "Yankee" is as marginal as
a faggot or a commie. Graffiti is a part of the whole exhaustion of
cities you witness when walking all the way—the exhaustions of
cities at their outskirts, the sputtering, the self-unraveling, the peter-
ing out. There are death rattles: a half-finished factory, a promissory
pile of cinderblocks, then freeway or dirt road, then trail again. Bruno
Schulz's "eponymous Street of Crocodiles" is described like that:
"The misfortune of that area is that nothing ever succeeds there,
nothing can ever reach a definite conclusion. We shall always regret
that, at a given moment, we had left the slightly dubious tailor's
shop. We shall never be able to find it again. We shall wander from
shop sign to shop sign and make a thousand mistakes."

We spotted more graffiti entering del Bierzo: *El rey es subnormal,
y todo el mundo lo conoce!:* "The king is retarded, and the whole
world knows it!" Well, I hadn't been informed, as yet.

I knew every place along the road, and it was not as I knew
it. One can be lost and found at the same time. There were ghosts
at every turn: *there,* I said to myself in Viana, I had lunch in front of
the church with an annoying Dutch man, Petra, and Matthias. And
there, the crazy old lady Felisa, who had passing pilgrims sign in her
book and offered "figs, water, and love." A foot journey, whether to
a pilgrim site or anywhere, is a love affair, I suppose; I'd had my
chance with this lover. I wish I could travel with Anthony again; he
is the best traveler I know.

I went to a bar far from the *refugio,* to be alone. There were six
hard-drinking Madrileños who asked me to pull up a chair with
them: they were impressed with my Spanish, and I'm easily flattered,
although I quickly volunteered that I didn't quite understand the
subjunctive. How is it going? they asked, and I told them what I was
doing and my dilemma. It had been hard to come through again, a
second pilgrimage. One of the men of the group took a moment

from his avuncular, alcoholic happiness to say with great seriousness, "*Segundas partes nunca fueron buenas,*" second times never went well. Or Einstein said it another way: the definition of insanity is doing the same thing over and over and expecting different results.

2.

We approached the Partage Monastery in Thiviers at the end of a long day of lupines, rich-red poppies, signs for approaching accordion festivals, shirts with horizontal stripes, butterfly trees in royal purple, the smell of pipe tobacco, force-fed ducks, lace in the windows.

As we entered through the gate in the stone wall of the monastery, it was clear that it had fallen on hard times. A grand edifice with stained glass in every window, it was protected by tall boxwood hedges that had not been tended in a long time. Jean-Philippe looked at me. "Are you ready for another crrrreh-zee experience?" I am always perhaps too ready for a crazy experience, as long as it is always a new crazy experience.

We walked in and presented ourselves as Saint Jacques pilgrims to a painfully skinny man not dressed in any habit I could recognize, and though he was pleased to have visitors, it was clear that the legal proceedings forbidding the Thiviers monks from haircutting, or exorcising, or practicing medicine may have been completed, but whatever energy it had had, renegade or religious, had been sucked from the group. In all, there seemed to be only four or five monks remaining, along with a little Algerian boy who looked to one of the men as his father. They seemed either silent or dispirited, and perhaps a little dicey. We were taken to the head of the order, a man who didn't look religious at all, who had a gut I'd call beer- before I'd call jolly-. He smoked down to a nubbin foul-smelling stogies (evidenced by five or six button-ends in his ashtray, from which he never strayed far) and had long smears of ash down a shirt he'd clearly worn for quite a few days. As a sweaty, dusty pilgrim, I felt cleaner. I certainly hoped he was washing his hands before performing any unlicensed medicine. Or exorcisms, for that matter. Or haircuts.

But he was also welcoming, hadn't seen a pilgrim in months, and explained that he had always wanted to go to Santiago but something always held him back and that his monastery was free of charge and he would have our pilgrim passports stamped and dinner was at nine o'clock and would the skinny monk please take us to our rooms?

Rooms! For the entire time before and after Partage, Jean-Philippe and I had to share a room, step over one another's wet laundry, shut our ears to our idiosyncratic brands of snoring. We followed the monk down the hall. He had so many pimples. On the walls of the long cloister, there were prints of famous works of art, Van Gogh's mad sunflowers, Rembrandt's self-portrait, *The Birth of Venus,* the *Wreck of the Hesperus.* I passed a room that was the infirmary—dozens of beds, impeccably made, crisp cotton sheets, real hospital quality. Is this where the medicine was practiced without a license? Where was the Vietnamese fellow? Where was the machine that would take my Visa imprint?

My room was gigantic, big enough for five pilgrims, and I had my own bathroom, and my own pointless armoire. I opened up the big cumbersome thing, as I would naturally open up any pointless armoire, and found, stacked neatly, dozens of well-framed religious prints—the Virgin Mary as seen in the vision at Guadalupe, the Sacred Heart of Jesus, a rather nice Ascension, and so on. I thought of Van Gogh's *Sunflowers* in the hallway, and looked around my room. Not even a crucifix over the bed. But there was a long, delicious shower waiting for me.

While I hung up my hiking clothes to dry in the little garden of the cloister, one of the monks, rather upright but smiling, came by with an Algerian boy at his side. They were reading about Robin Hood. "Ah, you are English," he said after hearing me jerk out two or three words of French.

I corrected him: American—Yankee—a correction I have come slower and slower to make in these recent years under the recent administration.

He was unfazed. "Then you know this story of Robin Hood," said the monk, in order for the boy to see that I was not too strange a thing. "Perhaps you can remind us, who it was, who ruled in Nottingham that forced Robin Hood to steal from the rich? And over whom Robin Hood prevails?"

"I think it was the sheriff," I said.

The priest smiled, for I had given the right answer. "Ah yes, the *sheriff.*" The boy recognized the word too, even in my pronunciation. He giggled. And the monk bade me come to dinner, and walked away, bathing in my answer.

Dinner was more than an hour away, so we went to a bar across the street. Jean-Philippe ordered us both a Pernod, though the name of the bar was "Bar Ricard," and Pernod is the competing anis. It was a locals bar, and everybody seemed to sport a mid-'80s brush cut; they rolled up their sleeves. I spied a couple of disturbing pro LePen posters, but chose to concentrate on translating the handwritten signs, "Pas de Credits" (No Credit) and "Reservee pour 3 viognos" (Reserved for the three winos). The best part of the place was a little stumpy-legged dog that played with billiard balls for toys and had been trained to take your payment in euro bills behind the counter— "but he won't bring you change," Jean-Philippe pointed out. A lady came in and put her wallet on the floor and the dog opened it up and pulled the correct denomination out, a fiver. Monsieur Ricard, behind the bar, told us all, "Now he just takes a five. When he goes out on the town, he usually takes a twenty."

We were going to have a conversation, until we made the mistake of telling Ricard that we were staying in Partage. He did not ask us if we wanted another round.

But we were suitably lubricated, so we returned to the monastery and sat down to a long table in the refectory. They served us generous portions from a potato pie, a delicious chicken and peas and cheese, and an untimely "Three Kings" cake, and in the slice I received I found buried in the crumbs a tiny ceramic Lisa Simpson figurine—and being the winner, I nearly chipped a tooth on the surprise.

The founder of our feast, still sloppy and smoky, started asking us all sorts of questions. They must have been so eager for company. "From Switzerland!" he said to Jean-Philippe. "Are you familiar with the work of your compatriot, Bakhunin?" Bakhunin . . . Bakhunin . . . this name rang a bell. I looked over at Jean-Philippe, who had suddenly understood just a moment before me: Bakhunin, the Swiss incendiary.

"Yes, he was from the town next to mine," said Jean-Philippe with a smile. I figured it all out about five seconds after him: we were being hosted by far-left communists. Communist monks!

Oh, the way we all live in uncomfortable contradiction to ourselves. Conservative renegades, good thieves, fascinating bores, communist monks, Catholic homosexuals. This is also what makes us feel alone: we are one-of-a-kind monsters, neither fish nor foul. I thought of how ridiculous the monks of Thiviers seemed. I thought how ridiculous I was—how we all kept heading toward the end of our project, one we all knew would be a failure, surrounded by comfortable people who never have to live in contradiction. The communist monks of Thiviers live to this day, as far as I know, in a monastery deep in the heart of ultraconservative, xenophobic, LePen-following southern France. They have been abandoned by their own Church, reduced to a handful of bedraggled monks, and a boy, probably still considered armed and dangerous. For God's sake, they took down the religious iconography and replaced them with Van Goghs! And here we were, trapped with them!

And five seconds after this, the monk watching over the boy with the Robin Hood book asked me, "Tell me, do you have radical syndicalists in your country?" We were Yankee Commie Faggot Jew Niggers, the lot of us. We were all outsiders at this table, and could it be that this was the closest thing to "home" I have ever had on any of my journeys outward? Being who I am, there are moments, just now and then, when I have felt at home like this. But it only lasts for a night or so. Then home, or I, or both of us, skedaddles.

For the rest of the evening, we talked warmly of Bakhunin and Woody Guthrie and the rise and fall of the Soviet Union, of causes not abandoned long after they were pointless or clearly a failure, and then of aporia, the losing of the way, and going on anyway. The monks of the Monastery Partage did not have a statue of Sainte Matthilde in the foyer, and they would not take our donation in the morning. "Just send us a postcard when you have reached your destination," said the stogie-smoking head of the order. I haven't sent them a card yet.

I wonder about myself sometimes: must everything be so flinty, so difficult? I am the one who reads the guidebooks only after I have made the journey, to discover that the sarcophagus I stood before was a great queen, or the ground I walked on was bloodied by Roland and his men. Only after. I read the guidebooks for nostalgia, but find instead that I have missed a thing I should have seen. "What is a divine mind?" asks Jorge Luis Borges in a mere footnote to his essay "The Mirror of Enigmas." "I prefer an example. The steps a man takes from the day of his birth until that of his death trace in time an inconceivable figure. The Divine Mind intuitively grasps that form immediately, as men do a triangle. This figure (perhaps) has its given function in the economy of the universe."

What is nostalgia but this picking through the ruins of living—not living, but *remembering* living? Walking among the renegades in France was the adventure, and after entering comfortable, stomped-over Spain, it was as if I had entered the gift shop and never left it for a month, selecting souvenirs, when I had plenty of them back home.

And do you know what the real trouble is? I haven't changed my song one bit: I would still hang my head out that window in Tuscany and tell Anthony, ex or not, that I want to come back to this place. I always want to go back, but I did go back once, and it wasn't a smart idea. I returned to the pilgrim's route to Santiago a second time in order to walk a new stretch of it, and because I wanted to meet new walkers on that way. "*Segundas partes nunca fueron buenas,*" Spaniards told me all the way to the end: "Second times never went well." And that's the truth. If there's something to walking off from the prison, of escape, of every theory I've ever imposed on myself, I should have seen that the Spanish *dicho* warned me from the first. Think of Orpheus going after Eurydice, or Lot's wife's botched rescue from Sodom and Gomorrah, or Stoker's Dracula climbing out of the coffin in order to find his love again—second times never go well, Count. Nostalgia scares me, for it seems to turn gladness into ghosts, grief into grievance; one alone becomes only lonely.

The Drive
to Fort Myers

Andrew Holleran

It's Sunday morning and I'm driving down from the town in north central Florida where I live to southwest Florida to see my sister, who has started renting a place in Fort Myers a few months every winter. She's following a pattern noticed by the *New York Times:* People gravitate to the towns in Florida where friends have already settled. That's how Naples started—retired General Motors executives—and that's what it remains, in part, today: a destination for people from Detroit. My sister lives in Pittsburgh, and a friend has a condo in Fort Myers for rent every winter, and this is the third year she has taken it, which surprises me, since my sister hates Florida and doesn't like to be around old people. But now my sister and I are beginning to be old people. Still, she tells me, she and my brother-in-law, who has just turned seventy, are not the norm in their gated community; the people there are mostly much younger.

"There is always a feeling of death going South," Scott Fitzgerald wrote about taking the train to Alabama to see Zelda when he was courting her. But in Florida there is a reversal of the energy flow. In Florida you leave the torpor by going south. North Florida belongs to that band of pines and live oaks and Spanish moss that runs from the barrier islands off the coast of Georgia to New Orleans. North Florida was part of the Confederacy, and trailers back in the woods here still fly Confederate flags. When you go to south Florida, you're leaving the culture of south Georgia; you're going to a place built by Northerners. The woman who founded Miami—Julia Tuttle—was from Cleveland. The man who founded Palm Beach—Henry Flagler—came down from New York. When you head to Fort Lauderdale and Miami, or even Tampa and Sarasota, or once sleepy Orlando, everything picks up: traffic, congestion, population, energy—which is why I always dread going down there.

This Sunday morning, however, Highway 441 south of Gainesville is virtually empty. There are only six or seven other cars on the road. Maybe that's because it's Sunday, or mid-April. The first empty expanse I cross is Paynes Prairie—a plain south of Gainesville that was once a lake the eighteenth-century naturalist William Bartram described in such exotic terms that Samuel Taylor Coleridge was reputedly inspired to write "Kubla Kahn." To the east is Cross Creek, where Marjorie Kinnan Rawlings chose to settle and wrote *The Year-ling.* This part of Florida is green and lush, with small towns composed of white clapboard houses: our version of New England or the Midwest. But not much further south, when Highway 441 joins 301, the traffic begins to thicken. On the radio I hear the Mass being said. "They have pierced my hands and feet with nails, they have numbered my bones," says the man reading the Scripture. This might just as well be said of Florida, it seems to me: *They have built highways through my woods, they have numbered my land into lots.* Once I join Interstate 75 the traffic is what I feared. Driving at high speed behind SUVs, enormous trucks, and a swarm of large motorcycles near Tampa, I am struck with the scale of the caravan. In my town they can no longer fit all the cars in the garage—which is full of junk anyway—so they park them on the lawn. Everyone is going about eighty. It feels like piloting a plane that never takes off. I am behind a Coca-Cola truck for a while, and then a horse's ass—a big white butt—in a horse trailer: The former mode of transportation, it occurs to me, is now being transported by the thing that replaced it.

Florida is such a long state—so flat and featureless when seen from a car window—that driving its length can be very tedious. There's also a lot of kitsch. A friend from Virginia came down in a car with his mother years ago but got only halfway, near Orlando, before turning back, because, they said, everything was so ugly. Another acquaintance, more recently, drove down to Naples to see his stepfather, and e-mailed that every restaurant he stopped in was next to a center for cataract surgery and contained only two types of customer: old people in neck braces, and teenaged girls dressed like prostitutes. That's Florida, the human zoo: the place Ratzo Rizzo goes with Joe Buck at the end of *Midnight Cowboy* because every kind of trash eventually rolls to the Sunshine State, which was a pit stop, too, for the killers in *In Cold Blood,* not to mention Andrew Cunanan. (O. J. Simpson now lives in a very nice neighborhood of Miami.) In fact, the highway on which I started out this morning was where Aileen Wournos used to pick up the men she killed; and I live not thirty minutes from the prison where Ted Bundy fried. Florida is too heterogeneous to describe, much less comprehend; a climate where not only exotic pets, and invasive plants, have run amok, but human beings too. It's a Southern state that isn't Southern. It's a new state that's very old. It's standing on the bridge over the St. Johns River in Palatka watching ospreys nest below while waiting for the space shuttle to take off from Cape Canaveral. It's Palm Beach (a movie set for plutocrats) and Belle Glade (a migrant workers' town that in the mid-eighties had the highest AIDS rate in the country). It's Cuban Americans obsessed with Castro, and Haitians, and Baptists and Jews, the London Symphony summering in Daytona Beach, and crackers who would not let the government designate the St. Johns River a national treasure because, they said, that would lead to control by the United Nations. It's the state that is trying to restore the Everglades and converting more and more of it to suburban developments and sugar cane plantations at the same time. But one thing it is almost everywhere—flat and monotonous, which makes for very dull driving. In fact, it's only when you stop driving and get out that you begin to see its strange, exotic beauty. Florida is many microclimates that succeed one another, it seems, every ten or twenty miles, if you are attuned to the subtle change in the kinds and sizes of oaks, palms, the ground cover. Driving down to Fort Myers on I75, however, just to get there, makes it about as interesting as the steppes of Russia: this drab, flat, featureless landscape whose beauties are invisible until you get out and walk, which more and more Americans refuse to do.

I make only one stop on the way, however, and that's to see my uncle, who lives in Bradenton. South of Tampa Bay I leave I75 and begin following the instructions he has given me on the phone. At eighty-five he has just moved into an adult assisted-living facility after renting a place in Sarasota on his own for many years. My uncle has never married and has always been extremely independent. I watch him for clues about aging. A single man in his sixties has to wonder where he will end up. Everyone has to wonder where he or she will end up. The facility my uncle wanted to get into in Sarasota had a waiting list, so one day some women taking a neighbor to this place in Bradenton told him, "Get in, you'd better come with us." He did, and signed up the same day. His new home is run by Presbyterians. It's in the old part of Bradenton, downtown on the river, in a quiet residential neighborhood where this Sunday they are having some sort of seafood festival. I park on one of the narrow tree-shaded streets and walk to the tall white building on a little green promontory jutting into the river.

The first time I tried to visit my uncle here I was with a friend, and my uncle discouraged me from coming by saying the traffic was so bad it was not worth the effort. I could not tell if he didn't want me to see him in his new place or really believed a visit was not worth the drive. So I'm relieved to be here now. The high-rise is not brand new, but there's something clean and reassuring about it. On my way to the dining hall, where the receptionist tells me my uncle has gone, I walk past a nice wood-paneled library, a chapel, an auditorium, a pool room, a mail room. In the dining room I pause at the threshold and ask one of the waitresses for my uncle, but when he is pointed out to me, I think there must be a mistake. The man the waitress indicates is seated with his back to me at a table with seven other people; he wears a blue blazer, but his head is no bigger than a coconut. This small gray head seems too small for my uncle, so I go back to the lobby and wait. Sure enough, ten minutes later, he comes out of the dining room in the blue blazer. It was my uncle sitting there. He's simply smaller. But he's his perennially cheerful self. He takes me around. He seems to know everyone, or have a word for everyone he passes. My uncle has always been good-humored. He has never once complained about anything but the American tax code, stockbrokers, and traffic. His mood never alters. Whenever I call he answers the telephone in the jaunty voice of a man who is ready for whatever is thrown at him; and it's not fake. He seems to be contented even here. "I've just finished assembling everything for my tax return and sent it off to the accountant," he tells me when he takes me upstairs in the elevator. The view from the eighth floor is lovely: a line of narrow windows runs the length of the building, overlooking the river. The stucco walls are white, the carpet blue, the flowers artificial, and the long corridor of doors makes you feel you're on a ship—leading me to think: I could live here.

Why not? People used to enter monasteries to get away from the world. Maybe this is the way out, I think as we enter my uncle's room—if he can do it, so can I. In Japan men go to prison for the peace and quiet; they commit crimes to get put in jail. In California a friend of mine in his fifties has already entered an adult assisted-living facility in Napa Valley. My uncle's studio apartment has a small kitchenette, a big bed, a sofa, another chair, and a long, fairly narrow window looking out over an inlet of the river. He has reduced all his possessions to two suitcases in the closet. I can't even clean up my bedroom. I can't throw away letters, old magazines, books, papers, clothes, or swimming goggles. But here is my uncle, unencumbered as a monk. There's something Buddhist about what he's done. He has detached himself from material possessions. He serves me cheese and crackers, we chat, and then we go back down to the first floor. At the elevator we meet the librarian of the place, a calm, intelligent woman with whom I discuss the way she acquires books. Then, when the elevator comes, the doors open and a woman walks out and walks right past us in a daze. My uncle and the librarian call to her to ask if she's on the right floor. "She has a bad cancer," my uncle informs me as we go down to the lobby. There he gives me a tour of the public rooms, including the chapel, where, he says, he recently fainted. He is on several committees; they want him to be on more. As he shows me the dining room he confesses, "I could sit with the same people at every meal, but I don't want to get trapped that way, so I make a point to move around at dinner. But now a guy who just lost his wife insists on eating with me every day, and when I suggest we split up and meet new people, he starts crying. So I guess I'm stuck with him," he says with a laugh. We go outside and he shows me the swimming pool. Then we return to the entrance, where two people are seated on a bench by the doors, dozing in the spring sunlight. There seems to be no reason to stay longer; Fort Myers waits. I shake my uncle's hand, thank him, and walk down the street to my car.

I drive off with mixed emotions. Because on previous attempts to visit my uncle, his warnings about the traffic seemed so exaggerated that I suspected he didn't really want me to visit, I didn't drive down. He was right—the traffic was bad—but this time I made the effort and am happy to have seen him. My uncle is fine, I think; he has chosen a nice place; I am glad I saw him. At the same time I feel as I drive away that I have left him in a death camp. I feel, as I retrace my route to I75, that I have left my uncle in Hades, in some strange twilight land of the almost dead, in the anteroom of the life to come.

Maybe that's why the rest of the drive to Fort Myers feels rather subdued. *So that's how our family has ended up,* I think as I rejoin the unceasing stream of migrating vehicles. My uncle, who never married, who came to visit my mother and me every Thanksgiving, who served in the Army during World War II, who spent his life with AT&T, who lived in Washington and worked with top secret communications installations, then retired to Sarasota, played golf for years, and finally developed the arthritis of Time—the metaphorical arthritis, since he seems to be quite limber—has now shrunk to the little old man in a blue blazer whose small gray head seemed too small to be his when I stood in the dining room looking for him, a man who now is simply waiting for what Henry James called the "distinguished thing," though it seems deeply vile to me. My uncle, my sister, and I are all that remains of my mother's family of seven kids, my father's of five, and at this moment all three of us have ended up in Florida. But since Florida is such a big state, many hours of driving separate the three of us. I am in a small town an hour from the Georgia border; my uncle is in Bradenton, halfway down the state; and my sister is in a town not far from the Everglades, at the next stop on I75.

If you look at the map you see that Fort Myers, on the west coast, lies on about the same longitude as that gay Mecca, Fort Lauderdale, on the east, but the difference between the two places could not be greater. I have always regarded the west coast of Florida as less glamorous—for no good reason. But if the east coast draws people from the Northeast, the west coast is home to people from the Midwest. It has, both geographically and demographically, an entirely different feel. The Atlantic is bright and sparkling, and has a surf, nor'easters and autumn storms, and, along its length, a single strand of white sand runs up and down the coast almost continuously from Key Biscayne to Jacksonville, so that when I am on the gay beach near St. Augustine I can look south and imagine walking all the way to Miami Beach. The west coast is different: Florida's most beautiful beaches, it's said, are not around Miami but near

Panama City, on the Redneck Riviera (where gay men gather on Labor Day); but once you hit the Big Bend (that curve of land between the Panhandle and the peninsula of Florida), marshes predominate all the way to Tampa/St. Petersburg, and broad rivers empty into the Gulf of Mexico. This mix of marsh and river mouth and bay, this beachless mélange, is the opposite of the east coast—as if the Atlantic has pushed onshore a single barrier of dunes, but on the west coast, the Gulf provides a murkier meeting of water and land. All of this is of course a gross generalization.

I never even bother to see the beach in Fort Myers—I cross the Caloosahatchee River on I75 several miles inland, turn east, and drive down a big divided four lane highway till I see the signs for a veterinarian and a Baptist church my sister has told me to look for. The fact that the landmarks are signs for a vet and for a Baptist church is telling. Both typify the car culture, the man-made landscape that makes so much of Florida look the same. (If you were to show someone pictures of ten different stretches of highway in Florida, chosen at random, I doubt anyone would be able to identify the locations.) This is the grid that men have laid upon the infinitely subtle, delicate ecosystem of this unique state: a grid of highways, strip malls, and housing developments that has taken something that used to be as exotic as Africa and turned it into another corporate, standardized replica of what Henry Miller called years ago, after his own trip across America, the Air-Conditioned Nightmare. In other words, to quote Joni Mitchell, in a sentence that should probably be stenciled onto the Florida license place: "They paved paradise and put up a parking lot."

It never was, of course, paradise—there are still bugs and humidity and heat in summer, and hurricanes and boredom—but having lived here for more than forty years one becomes attached to the landscape. The problem now is that most of the people I have lived with here are gone. Florida, like life, is supremely transient. Florida, the joke goes, is where people go to die and then don't. People come here toward the end of their lives, as if by escaping snow and ice they can escape death; instead their relatives descend and take them back to their points of origin just before dying—which brings me to the question: How does a gay man exit? My only gay friend in town is thinking at eighty-one that he will have to move to some adult assisted-living community, and once he goes I can't imagine life without him. With whom could I watch old movies—or talk about the bag boys at Food Lion? Who will drive me to the airport? The idea of retiring to Key West is an option no longer; Key West is now too expensive to even be someplace I go more than once a year. (There's no more spectacular drive than the last half of the trip from Miami to Key West.) Fort Lauderdale is where gay life has apparently regrouped after Key West was de-gayed; and life there is a round of book clubs, mahjong groups, restaurants, bars, baths, and gay beaches; but Fort Lauderdale is nearly as expensive as Key West now. So where does one go for the last decade and a half? Where are the Golden Girls?

Not in Fort Myers, I'm sure, as I stop at a guard house and give the man my sister's name—though the Golden Girls are what we're all looking for: some house in which we can live with our friends, making wisecracks like Bea Arthur (whose name was on the marquee of a theater in downtown West Palm Beach the last time I drove south; that's where the Golden Girls end up in real life—touring). Even married people are stranded by death. People get hitched at the same moment, but they don't unhitch simultaneously. So everyone ends up in adult assisted-living communities, rest homes, trailer parks, places we never dreamed of being. Even my sister wants me to share a house with her now. But I demur. So she and her husband have rented an apartment in this gated community west of Fort Myers for three months every winter.

Somewhere south of Bradenton I have found a radio station that plays lush arrangements of '50s music; and, after leaving the guard house, the cascades of tinkling piano keys that express "Autumn Leaves" begin to fall as I drive along a golf course lined with flowering oleanders that resemble azaleas. The gated community, you could argue, is, like the SUV, a variant of white flight—affluent European Americans barricading themselves against an increasingly colored and chaotic country—and I am finding it a bit surreal. In fact, my sister's condo is on a street that looks like a painting by Magritte: every unit is exactly the same (pale yellow stucco with white trim, tile roofs, little balconies; a vaguely Mediterranean look) on a curved sidewalk lined with lampposts. At the end of the street is a small swimming pool everyone can use, with the mailboxes in an adjacent covered loggia. Only the parked cars provide evidence of human beings. Most people have gone north already. Yet someone toils here: every blade of the St. Augustine grass between my sister's unit and its twin is perfectly clipped. (This means: Invisible Mexicans.) I knock on a door flanked by two perfectly groomed hibiscus bushes; a voice calls, "It's open!" and I enter the condo and turn the corner. There, at the far end, on a big, overstuffed sofa, my sister and brother-in-law are watching a golf match on TV—like Daisy and Jordan reading the *Saturday Evening Post* in *The Great Gatsby* when Nick Carraway finds them on his first visit, anchored, like balloons that have just returned to earth after a flight around the room. The light comes from a screened porch beyond them overlooking the fairway. A line of pampas grass separates the golf course from their small backyard, a patch of lawn, and a young tree. We catch up, have dinner, watch "American Idol," and then I take the dog out for a walk.

Finally I feel at home—I always do when I take the dog out for a walk. At least, I seem to belong: I'm a man walking a dog—a dog that lives there, even if I don't. This feeling, of being both at home and not-at-home, comes, I've always thought, from being gay. It may be more universal than that. But I tell myself it's the reason I'm wondering where to live, and why I don't travel anymore. This year I told myself I should go to California, the San Juan Islands, Vancouver, British Columbia, Colombia, Quito, then overland by bus or train to Buenos Aires. I did none of it. I feel too rootless at the moment to go wandering. My sister, utterly rooted, is traveling a lot. That is the paradox: the person who is single, has ties to no one, and is free to go feels trapped in his loneliness. The person who is married, has family ties, and could come up with a dozen reasons she can't leave home travels. Or maybe it's just temperamental. I feel anxious for some reason; and, after the long and hateful drive, being out at night with just the dog is the first time I have really relaxed all day.

It's dark out but the silver clouds floating overhead are illumined by a crescent moon, so that the sky belonging to this gated community to the east of Fort Myers, Florida, looks most like the sky in El Greco's night view of Toledo. It is neither warm nor cool. It is utterly still. Of the houses I pass, only one in thirty is lighted, though some of the man-made ponds they are built around sport geysers shooting uselessly into the air, while the golf course is being watered by gigantic sprinklers. The staggering wealth, the luxury, of a country in which so many people not only have one home, but two (or more), is all I can think of as I walk along, passing house after house in various styles. All of them face either a fairway or a body of water. On the screened lanai of each dwelling I can hear as I pass the sound of a fountain plashing into a small swimming pool. Given the water shortage that Florida—the entire country—faces, there is something awfully sybaritic about these fountains, spilling into the swimming pools of empty houses. How long can any country afford this waste, I wonder. The network of streets, of vacant houses with splashing fountains, goes on and on, till I reach the golf clubhouse and turn back. There is no one out. The dog occasionally lunges toward the shrubbery—an armadillo, a rabbit? But otherwise nothing stirs. A single, lighted house looks forlorn among the mass of dark ones. I imagine someone inside reading, all alone, in this community whose owners have all gone north, like a house guest in Palm Beach who remains during the off-season, living in a back room of some mansion, working his way through his host's library, like a termite, in the Florida summer. The Florida summer, of course, is what's coming on—what everyone has fled. That's why no one is out—not even an insect—as I walk from the clubhouse to a dog park, then a nature trail, then turn back toward my sister's.

It's like Versailles—Versailles for the middle class, or rather the upper middle class, considering the money required for a piece of this. The landscape is as anal-retentive as Le Notre's. The sidewalks are immaculate. When the dog poops, I inadvertently leave a smear of shit, after picking it up with my cellophane bag. I have ruined, with my clumsiness, the efforts of the Invisible Mexicans, who, presumably, keep this place looking the way it does. I cannot leave shit on their sidewalk. With a leaf I try to scrape the smear away. Then I return to my sister's block, say good night to the moon, slip into the condo, and take the leash off the dog.

My bedroom is a biopsy of American affluence, small but cozy, with framed watercolor prints of tropical scenes on the wall, ruffled pillowcases, flowered bedspreads, a digital clock, and a lamp. My little heap of things sits in the corner: the face mask and snorkel I always hope to use in south Florida, my sandals, my knapsack, my magazines, my newspaper—the accoutrements of a brother who has never quite grown up. The room is slightly suffocating—like my life, as it narrows with age, or the room in the gay guesthouses I used to visit in Key West where a chintz-bomb seemed to have gone off— but though I could lie awake wondering where on earth I am supposed to go next, I sleep, knowing that for the moment I am with my sister, and therefore home, in a sense.

The room is full of stillness and softness when I awaken the next morning: it's the same feeling I have waking up in my bedroom in north Florida. It's an amalgam of the air, the silence. It's another day in paradise, it's what drove my father to drink after retiring here. It's what Goethe meant when he said, "Nothing is so difficult to endure as a succession of fair days." Florida is almost all fair days. That's why twelve million more people will be living in this state by the year 2025, why five hundred immigrants arrive every day. A stupid reason on which to base one's life, one would think—the weather— but now only one of the reasons they come; others include the absence of an income tax, the presence of new jobs. Still it's a shock when I leave my bedroom and see, at the far end of the condo, my brother-in-law reading the newspaper on the porch. It hasn't hit me till this moment that he is retired. But now, as I stare at him in his wicker chair and bathrobe, he looks like someone in *Village of the Damned*. It's the beginning of old age, the last act. My father stopped working at fifty-nine, taking an early retirement package his company offered; he ended up sitting in his bathrobe at a table on his porch, his back to the lake he lived on, playing a game of Solitaire over and over again; the sound of the cards hitting the table, of his fingers drumming as he decided what play to make, the sound that clods of dirt make falling on a coffin. But I have never seen my brother-in-law in this mode. In fact, I have only seen my brother-in-law at this hour in a suit and tie, bound for his office. To glimpse him now, in a white wicker chair, reading the Fort Myers newspaper with the dog at his feet, is a shock.

The Drive to Fort Myers

My brother-in-law says that on occasion he can hear a woman who fights with her husband across the golf course but mostly the only sound here is just the breeze. The golfers go by in their golf carts, then a golf cart with beverages for sale goes around to the golfers. An hour later, my brother-in-law puts the paper down and takes the dog out onto the apron of grass between the porch and the pampas grass lining the fairway. Minutes later a muscular young man comes out of the unit next door in sweat suit and baseball cap with a miniature dachshund. He and my brother-in-law converse—as I wonder, looking at the dog, the baseball cap, the huge chest and arms: Would a young gay man live in a gated community? Of course, everyone goes to a gym now. Everyone has a chest and big arms. Everyone wears a baseball cap. But still, there is something about the affability of this neighbor, the way he stands holding the leash, a certain angle of the hips that makes me think: maybe for A-list gays, affluent, ambitious gays, in the Fort Myers area, this is a premium address.

An hour later I take my sister's dog for a walk and wander past the end of the golf course to the fence surrounding the community—which reminds me that it is, after all, like Disneyworld, a carefully maintained illusion. Over the fence I can see the four-lane highway lined with businesses like the veterinarian and the Baptist church. A palm tree has fallen over in one of the flowerbeds. I wonder if I should call someone. How long can a palm tree lie on its side before it dies? The man-made landscape stretches in every direction. Two Latinos in a golf cart come by. In Washington, where I live half the year, to escape the ennui of Florida, I often see, on my way back from the grocery store, Central American men washing windows, refacing brick, planting flowerbeds, and I think: I am going upstairs to work on a book review. The sun is getting hotter. The dog rolls in the grass. I walk all the way to a maintenance shed. Over the fence I see a Publix supermarket. The developer has built a parallel connector road so that you can drive from the gated community to the mall containing the Publix without having to get onto the highway. This means you need never enter the thing that has laid waste to Fort Myers and so much of Florida: the car culture. The gated community is the eye of a hurricane, the cause of, and escape from, the very same thing: sprawl. It's a sort of monastery, a cloister. You could hole up in this place for months—write a book!—and go back and forth to the Publix without ever having to enter traffic.

On my way back I see a man in a bathing suit with a chiseled chest and a Naugahyde tan, working on his car a few doors down from my sister's. I imagine he's one of those men I'd find on www.silverdaddies.com, living in an improbable place. Maybe the A list of gay Fort Myers has decided this is the place to live. It's obviously not for retirees. It's young, not old, people here, which my sister likes. My sister dyes her hair blonde and looks younger than I do. She has infinite amounts of energy. The most poignant moment of the visit comes when she confesses—regarding the other people at the golf club the past few months—that it's harder to make friends when you age. Even she!

This morning, however, she takes me house hunting. My brother-in-law tells me she makes every visitor do this; it's her favorite thing, besides playing golf. The first house we visit is on the market for 1.7 million dollars. Inside a well-dressed African American woman who is paid to babysit the house is in the living area reading a book on making money; the author, she says when I inquire, is a financial guru on television. That's how books get sold. Americans don't live in the United States. They live in television: an alternate universe composed of electricity and marketing pitches. After making small talk, the woman returns to her book and lets us wander around by ourselves. The house is very well done. My sister likes the way the indoors/outdoors issue is handled; outside there is a second kitchen on the lanai and a pool. The pool is rectangular and elegant. A fountain at one end sends a sheet of water cascading into the main body of water; like a fountain in a villa in Pompeii before the eruption, in one of those historical novels I read in eighth grade. The master bedroom is really too plush, the thick carpet, the big duvet, inconceivable without air conditioning. The bathroom is green marble, the kitchen countertops gray granite. The study is chocolate brown. Grays and blacks dominate the house. Dark wood, maple floors give it a northern look. The theme, we're told, is Old Florida. (What Old Florida, I wonder—some pine-paneled hunting lodge near the Georgia border?) It's for people from cities like Pittsburgh, where wealth is expressed in a more baronial style; but it doesn't sell, the woman in the next house we view tells us, because in Florida people prefer lighter colors.

When you buy, we're informed, you have the option of purchasing the furniture too. It's fun to dish the way the decorators have furnished each model we see; the variations in mood, and design, and taste. Everything's theatrical; everything's a page in a magazine or catalogue. We're part of a floating crowd of critics. Each house we enter has people already there, talking to the house sitter or real estate agent. The minute we leave one house my sister insists we see another; and so we work our way across the entire community, empty under the April sky. "The poor thing," she says of an old woman bent over as she walks from her van to a model house. "That's why I'm going everywhere I can—before that happens to me." In one house we meet a real estate agent who reminds me of an actress on "Designing Women." (There is something very Atlanta, very L.A., very Orlando—L.A.'s surrogate—about all this.) She drives us to another part of the community. People from the same place tend to end up on the same street, she says. One block is all people from St. Louis—"people who like to party." Though uniform in style, the place draws people from all over the country. A neurosurgeon from Pittsburgh has bought the house my sister likes most. Another house is owned by a wealthy man who owns a huge fern nursery in Iowa. The real estate agent herself has moved here from Orlando with her husband, an unemployed chef. Her older daughter is living with her ex-husband in Kissimmee; she is not pleased with her younger daughter's school here, so she may move again. We go from one model to the next, driving around the vacant streets that remind me of childhood, when every thing you see, an empty lot, a pile of dirt, is simply a place to play. We go from house to house the way the houses' owners go from state to state—everyone afloat on a tide of money, in constant motion. One house we see is owned by a decorator who furnished the last one we were looking at. (Developers merely assemble the land; lots are sold to different firms who build the houses on them, then decorators stuff them with furniture.) The decorator from Orlando comes here only twice a month. Her house feels very different: There is no pool on her lanai because she does not want to have to maintain it, and one realizes how crucial babbling water is to the sense of luxury. Her view of the golf course, however, resembles a plain in Africa: broad open spaces edged with high tawny-colored grass on which one feels a zebra should be standing instead of a man with a four iron.

Indeed, the theme of the next house is Around the World: the child's bedroom is French; the master bedroom, with wrought iron grilles on the windows, seems to have been inspired by the Spanish Inquisition. In every house the formal living room tends to be much smaller than the den, or the bedrooms, dining room, or lanai. The biggest space of all is inevitably the kitchen; as if at this point in our history there is nothing left for Americans to do but eat. There are also game rooms, and pool rooms, and media rooms, and studies, and wet and dry bars, which remind me again of *The Great Gatsby*— of Gatsby's shirts, to be exact: the sadness in American abundance. Everything is swollen and fat: the master bedrooms, the duvets, the chairs, the carpets, the bookcases, the chandeliers. And in every house but one (the decorator's) the maddening water splashes from a hot tub/fountain into the pool—which bothers me so much I finally protest to the sales agent, who assures me that the water is recycled. Still, the main image I carry away with me of this place is walking past the screened porches at night with the dog, hearing the sound of fountains in the houses of people who are not even there.

Our hegira ends in the smallest and simplest model— $400,000—with the agent who reminds me of "Designing Women" sitting on the sofa, talking with my sister as if they have known each other forever. "Won't you go halfway with me?" my sister says when we leave. "You could live here the whole year; we'd come down only in the winter."

"I can't live here," I say.

"Why not?"

Because I'm gay, I want to say. But what comes out is: "Because I don't play golf!" (In my family it amounts to the same thing.) "You're here because you play golf," I tell her as we drive off. "Anyway, you can't buy a house."

"Why not?"

"Because then you won't be able to shop for one."

She laughs and drives home to pick up her husband. Then we head for Fort Myers, which means entering the stream of cars, the ever-flowing river one sees everywhere in Florida now, necessary for almost every human need. Looking at the endless traffic I wonder why Americans have been so willing to base their lives on these machines. People pass us in their little metal boxes, pressing the accelerators and brakes with their feet, like women in New England mills in the 1800s operating looms for hours every day; except those women were trapped in factories, whereas in a car one can go wherever one wants. That is the problem: the car is now equated with freedom, appetite, escape—though my brother-in-law sits quietly in the front seat while my sister drives like a child being taken to soccer practice. Our mission today, however, is much simpler: buy fresh fish. We cross the broad blue river. The town on the other side looks slightly run-down, and therefore older; in Florida, a decade's difference can inspire nostalgia. On the far side of the river are cement ranch houses, sleepy streets, an atmosphere of desuetude that reminds me that people move to Florida—have always moved to Florida—to drop out. "Gentle" is the word Henry James used to characterize the state when he came down in 1905. Gentle it remains in certain places. We go back across the river with our fresh fish preserved in an ice chest and stop for lunch in a restaurant set on the edge of a vast parking lot beside a mall. It is two in the afternoon when we finish. There is a strange disembodied feeling when you emerge from a dark, air-conditioned cave into a blazing parking lot in the middle of the afternoon. It raises the question: Do you exist? We drive to another mall. While they go into a wine store I stand under a tree. A flock of crows is flying around the parking lot, landing on the handles of discarded shopping carts, like something out of *The Birds*. A young man in khaki pants and a polo shirt, morose and overweight, comes out of the wine store to collect the shopping carts. Time seems to have stopped. When my sister emerges she says the money they saved here will probably be cancelled out by the cost of shipping the wine home.

There are not that many historic sites in Florida, though the few we have are much older than you'd think, because Florida's European history goes back farther than even New England's—St. Augustine is the oldest town in the United States. Yet most places it feels as if the state started in the twenties; which includes the Thomas Edison–Henry Ford compound that my sister points out on our way back: several white frame buildings in a park on the river that evoke the space and graciousness of an earlier, less-populated era. She says I should take the tour. But I don't. Florida is dotted with the homes of tycoons—Thomas Edison, Henry Ford, John Ringling, John Deering, Henry Flagler: industrialists and inventors who have influenced its history to various degrees. (Flagler is virtually responsible for its development; Deering and Ringling merely built Venetian mansions, one of which, Vizcaya, is the site of the White Party in Miami every winter.) I want to get back to the gated community. The minute we drive in I feel the way a monk must when he returns to the monastery; within these walls, everything is orderly, quiet, and calm. On the way home they drop me off at the clubhouse, where I take one of the kayaks available to residents and their guests onto the Orange River and paddle upstream.

It's five o'clock—rush hour. But I'm the only one out. The banks of the river are a thick, dense tangle of trees that look like the jungle in a Tarzan movie, though those films were actually made farther north at Silver Springs. There are palm trees one never sees in north Florida, moss-hung oaks, and trees I cannot identify; the water is as dark as coffee. This is what the Amazon should look like—but doesn't, when you finally get there—even if the river, as far as I go, is lined with houses on both sides, houses engulfed in shrubbery for the most part, but still there. On the left side are the luxurious structures of the gated community; on the right, dwellings that are more real and ramshackle. A boy is fishing from a dock. A woman is returning from the grocery store in her car. Tendrils of moss and curlicues of pollen swirl on the dark water; overhanging vines and rotting docks accompany me all the way up to a concrete overpass, where I turn to go back downstream to the clubhouse, past people getting home from work.

All Florida is eaten up now—the only portion left is the Big Bend, and much of that is owned by the St. Joe Paper Company, which has recently decided the land on which they grow their trees is worth more as a development; so that is going, too, and finally Florida will be what is called "filled in," i.e., every inch of it will be built upon. It's extraordinary but nothing can stop it. The history of Florida is four centuries of forlorn emptiness, when governors, and colonists, begged people to move here—gave land away—and no one did. Now the problem is the opposite. But there's no solution. Nothing can stop growth, not even the traditional means of cooling development off: hurricanes and freezes. All the things that used to make Florida uninhabitable—insects, heat, obliterating storms—have all been controlled with pesticides and air-conditioning; there is no reason people cannot live here all year round. So they do. The real streams—the beautiful rivers that originate in springs of pellucid beauty and empty into the Atlantic or the Gulf—are now dwarfed by the metaphoric versions (I75, I95). The metallic rivers are now more powerful than the liquid. The rivers one can canoe while remaining in the forest are all in state parks. Only a float down portions of streams like the Ichetucknee, Suwanee, Santa Fe, or Ocklawaha still give you a sense of pre–World War II Florida. Eventually the only places you will be able to see Florida untrammeled by man is in county, state, and national parks. The rest is gone or going. Bye-bye, Florida: one of the subtlest, most beautiful marriages of land and water on earth, once so full of wildlife that birds blocked out the sun, and, the saying goes, a squirrel could go from Tallahassee to Miami without ever touching ground. In place of that unbroken canopy are now the habitations of one species only: its gated communities, golf courses, towns, cities, and developments.

In time I suppose some of the latter will look better than they do now—softened by the maturing of their instant landscapes. Nor are all of them ugly now: developers aim to please; there are constraints. But in the larger sense these don't matter. The state's bones have indeed been numbered, in the offices of developers, law firms, banks, and county courthouses all across Florida.

There are two gay campgrounds I consider visiting when I say good-bye to my sister: one near Dade City, the other south of Sebring. But I don't feel like doing that, so I point the car east and head to Fort Lauderdale. I have never seen the county south of Lake Okeechobee so I might as well take a look before it vanishes, too.

Driving east the land has been newly cleared for yet more developments; but in truth there isn't much for the eye to enjoy anyway in this part of Florida. It's very flat and agricultural. At one point I find myself in a town devoted entirely to tomatoes. The signs are all in Spanish. (The history of Florida has always been a tug of war between the Spanish and the English; what's happened to Miami, with its influx of South Americans, is really nothing new.) All my life I have seen Lake Okeechobee only as a big blue space on the map, and it feels frustrating to be driving just south of it, but not being able to see it; so finally I take one of the roads that promises to take me to a scenic view, but when I do, I find only a parking lot beneath an enormous levee, and when I walk up on top of that, the lake is still too far away to see. This girdle of concrete and asphalt, built after a killing flood, stands for man's relationship to not the Everglades but the whole state. Lake Okeechobee is not only shrinking but also loaded with the toxic by-products of agriculture and industry; a recent hurricane stirred up so many of the chemicals that had sunk to the bottom that an enormous algae bloom resulted. The lake has been controlled to death.

In Clewiston I stop at a Wal-Mart to buy a TracFone. Inside its cavernous depths a handsome Mexican adolescent trying not to cry comes up to the cashier who has just waited on me and says he is lost; the person who brought him to the store has disappeared. The clerk makes an announcement on the PA system: "Will Susan Koch please come to Electronics?" A British couple (what on earth brings *them* here?) wait with me to see if this person shows up. We all feel sorry for the boy—could one be more lost: abandoned in a Wal-Mart in Clewiston, Florida? For a moment I think: Why don't you take this young man home, adopt him, and send him to college—it's Good Friday, isn't that what being a Christian means? But I don't. I go out into the parking lot with my TracFone and head for Fort Lauderdale through fields of sugar cane and other crops tended by people from Central America and the Caribbean. Then I see Fort Lauderdale in the distance, and the ribbons of concrete begin to weave together in a pattern of extraordinary design, funneling me toward the center of town, and I re-enter a culture of enormous wealth.

Fugitive
Emissions

Mack Friedman

Like a cat burglar, I steal Mom out of storage. Only some. Dad won't notice she's gone. She rides shotgun in a plastic bag on the passenger seat, like a drug.

Mom and I go through the border gate at Brownsville. Before the shantytowns in hazy twilight, three fluorescent hours are spent negotiating Mexican car insurance. Mom's Spanish is better than mine, and she's a good flirt, but it still takes two hundred dollars and the whole afternoon. The air is different almost immediately, the exotic incense of trash bonfires. We drive on empty tanks through dusty clapboard towns, splurge on a motel with a hot tub the first night. The morning sun through the wood lattice Jacuzzi roof is as strong and complicated as love. We come from the sun and I want to go back. That afternoon we set a tent by the Gulf, a dune on the beach in the nonexistent town of Tepeguajes. It's right on the Tropic of Cancer. No one lives there but seagulls, gray hawks, and butterflies in a forsaken cemetery on a bluff. Daggerwings and sprites skip over dangling crosses and crumbling headstones, flutter into a pink thatch of peonies. The waves are wide and slow, relentlessly silk-screening the sand, imprinting the land with their flow. I braid my hair with a bundle of small rubber bands and pad to the edge of the Gulf, to piss.

At dusk the sand has grown cold underfoot.

I'm the only person for miles. There hasn't been any other traffic all day. Unless you count the seagulls.

The next day, along the score of suspension bridges to Tampico, my gas station shrimp disagree with me violently. I unroll the window and vomit into the black, blinkered gulf until I'm completely empty inside. My Pontiac smells like I remember it. She helps me make ramen noodles in a pension we take for the night. I want to find that place in my mind, the jungle's edge where we can live, just Mom and me and our navy dome tent under the snaking vines of wild hibiscus. I learn Spanish from being lost. In San Luis Obispo I buy a bottle of brandy (El sabor de la noche! The flavor of the night!), nursing it in empty marble halls while she sleeps. Our grand hotel is a void, dispossessed. Housekeepers sleepily sweep halls for themselves, their broom strokes echoing, eerily, like fingernails against stone, the frenetic scratching of someone who's been buried alive.

We decide to go west, toward our destination, dust and road.

In Pátzcuaro, in the western central highlands, the elevation makes for cold nights. We buy three soft wool ponchos to wrap ourselves. The townspeople dress in four or five layers. As it gets progressively warmer during midday, up to 80 degrees, they strip down to T-shirts, and then bundle up again at sunset. They are always taking something off or putting something on. The streets are steep, leading up a hill to Our Lady of Good Health. From the old colonial church, you can look out at the descent of rust-red shingles, a testament to invention that is almost an optical illusion, a real-life Escher.

I buy Mom some Mexican chocolate, thin crispy medallions tightly stacked in a pink paper sack. She shares with me. They are as thin and airy as the breeze off the nearby lake, where the Purepecha kings would frolic and fish. She tells me the old myths that claim Janitzio, a tiny lake island, is the door of the sky where the natives descended. These days Janitzio is ringed by black sludge from the oil of motorized boats that take tourists around, but indigenous folk on the small island hillock still use cowhide canoes and butterfly netting when they dredge for whitefish. On the hard-pebbled shoals, men hack flesh into pieces, fling them onto makeshift stone braziers.

I carry Mom up the cobblestoned hill from our campground to the square, the Plaza Vasco de Quiroga. We learn from our campground owner that the celebrations for the Day of the Dead are incomparable, and in early November the town is besotted with orange marigolds, the Aztec flower for remembering the dead. Every year the fishing boats on Janitzio carry a procession of relatives who honor the entombed with offerings of flowers and pan de muerte, the bread of death. He gives us the recipe: it calls for orange peel and anise. Unfortunately, we're two months late. Today is market day, and the blackberries are plump and wet. We buy two paper bags worth and share them with three small children. I take color pictures of the red juice dripping from their happy mouths.

And once again, after this calm break, we cross the lonely mountains and into the atmosphere. Away from the lakes, the air becomes arid and crepuscular. The mountains are dry and brown and so remote that not even helicopters fly overhead, spraying their poison over papaverous hillsides. Every ten miles we stop to pour water into the radiator. After three days of desolate endless ridge I know no one can find me anymore.

"I feel safe," I tell Mom. Nothing can live here but scrub brush, and even that looks sick and parched.

I don't, Mom answers, staring out the double plastic of her bag and her window. *We need to keep going west. You could die here in the Sierra Madre and no one would ever know.*

"Isn't that the point?"

What's wrong with you? I can see her make a face as she regards me, then looks back to the sky, puts on her shades. I am driving us into the sun. *How are we on gas?*

"Quarter of a tank." I imagine touching her thigh, cool and plump. "We'll be okay, remember? We've got each other."

Shit, she says, *I feel like dirt.*

I'm glad we can talk to each other like adults. I feel closer to her than I have in years.

And gradually, in the lavender twilight, we begin to descend. The long plateau gives way to switchbacks and horseshoe curves, and my tires squeal pathetically. The needle's on empty but we can take it in neutral. Dirt becomes soil and bare hills are now verdant, emerald vines with long, fat leaves. The air is thick and wet.

Can you smell it? she asks me, excited now. *I think I can smell the ocean.*

I know that's where she wants to go. I'm not ready yet. "Look!" I respond. "Can you see it? The green and white?"

I see her craning her neck to my side: *The Pacific?*

"Not quite. But I think there's a Pemex station two or three miles down." And there was, and past that, ten miles of hilly rain forest kissed by the coast, and just beyond, the deep black dusk of the sea.

We splurge for a cheap hostel bungalow in Playa Azul. We are so tired we don't bother to move our twin beds closer. The next morning, Mom asks for flour and oranges and anise seed and I walk around town to find the ingredients. I also buy tiny cookies, galletitas, as a treat.

Thanks, she says on my triumphal return. *If you want to go to the beach, just go. Have fun. I am just going to relax in here. Later we can bake some bread.*

I cruise up and down the shore, partly for the exercise and for the cool feel of the sand, the grit that turns to sludge beneath wet feet. The coast is an endless, sunbaked quagmire, which keeps me moving, north and south alongside, all day long.

I talk to strangers:

An older kid, maybe twenty-five, at the hostel. He's bald—shaved clean—but a blond goatee slides off his shin like angel hair. He sprained his ankle walking down the beach all day; or it was the tai chi, he doesn't know for sure. He's trying to get a job here, and get crutches. He's from somewhere in Brooklyn and commands the communal TV, which makes me suspect he's just faking his injury to watch his favorite shows.

A younger kid, maybe seventeen, who's from Seattle and here with his extended family—his cousins, grandparents, his maniacal mom, who's good-looking in that deep dark tan, bottle-blonde, aerobicized way. He asks me about bodysurfing. He's seen me get dragged into the sand. I teach him my technique; you have to tread and wait for cresting waves to come, then kick so you're horizontal and duck your head and stroke as if you're part of them. If you imitate the ocean's thrust, a good wave can take you all the way to shore. Then I look up from his two-tone Pumas. Two taut thighs. There is only darkness where they meet. His grin's punctuated by rubber bands that circumnavigate his gum line. He's sturdy, like a soccer player. The first time he sees me, water jetting from my nostrils as I struggle up the beach toward him, he smiles so big his rubber bands almost pop loose.

Two kids: a shy, brown-haired boy, fourteen; and his friend, a fifteen-year old girl, smiley and chunky, a Playa Azul native. The boy is originally from Chicago. He is short, maybe 5′3′′, pale and skinny. His pale eyes are the blue dawn of his swim trunks, almost transparent in equatorial sunlight. They lead me into a quarry where tiny silver fish flock. Their quick darting defies laws that my father knows. The girl is interested in me, but I throw her off by acting like a big brother. When she tells me about her twenty-year-old boyfriend, I say, "If you were my sister, I'd be worried about you, because guys are always out for sex." The girl says, "I'm a virgin. I'm not even attracted to him. He's ugly. He gives me stuff." I want her to leave so I can consume her friend. If I concentrate hard enough I know I can make his suit disappear, but she is distracting me. We talk about surfing. The boy does not surf. The outline of his cock makes a thin shadow in his shorts. When the girl realizes she's not my quarry, they leave me; he trails after her, apologetically. He does not come back. I stick my hand in the warm shallow water and the glossy fish disperse.

On the beach of an Americanized resort, a boy, maybe twelve, is with a much younger brother and two older sisters. "Can someone bury me in the sand?" he shouts loudly. "Anyone? Please you guys," he implores his wading siblings. "Please?" I take him up on the offer, ask them if it's okay. His sisters couldn't care less. Like a seal pup, he is hairless and wriggles. He throws sand over his crotch so I don't have to touch him. As I consolidate small stones over his stomach, a woman comes over.

"What are you doing?" she asks, shadowing me from the sun.

"I'm burying this kid in sand. He asked to be."

"Do his parents know what you're doing?"

"No, they're not even here. I asked his sisters. It's fine with them."

"You better stop. I don't want you to get in *any kind of serious trouble*," she says menacingly, and pads back to her perch, glaring back over her shoulder. She has two small girls with her.

"The fun police," the boy cracks. I'm trembling again and sit down, deflated, a kite torn by a power line.

"What is she even talking about?" I ask him.

"Stranger danger," he shrugs. "It's OK, I'll just bury myself."

Nearer the street, a sixty-year-old curly-haired New Bohemian from Nebraska gives me a Salem 100. She seems anxious to talk as the sun hides behind stray clouds. We talk about her son, who lives here and has married an Azulia, and her own incredulity upon arriving in Acapulco. "It took me two weeks to believe I was here! I've wanted to come here since I was a little girl! I just wish I could swim at the resort in Acapulco. Their beach is contaminated this week." She drove her RV for three weeks to make it. We discuss her suggestions for a drink: "Duke's, though I'm not sure who's singing tonight." Duke's is a beach bar, where Toltec sacrifice reenactments are staged for American tourists on the hour, where the bartender simply pockets the leftover change from my Pacifica. I like the frizzy, grizzled woman. She seems lonely, and happy.

A thirteen-year-old plays chess on the tables above the public beach. I buy a cactus salad across the street and return, bid for the next game. Homeless, toothless old men and women cohabit with the chess players and the bike cops. Under the picnic grove–style roof, the salty wind is tempered by wafts of urine. I ask the boy where he's from—Philly, it turns out. We share the joke: "Don't talk to anyone—" I say, "—Unless you want to get shot," adds the boy. He moved here three weeks ago with his parents; his dad's on assignment, whatever that means. He has smooth legs, short curly hair, glasses, a Math Champion T-shirt, and boy-scout-length tan shorts. A pimple is forming along one of the wings of his freckled nose. He asks where I'm staying, says, "I stayed in a hostel in Sacramento once. I didn't like it." What did he think of Sacramento? "It kind of sucked," he says, and checkmates me in sixteen moves. I'm distracted and outclassed and play too aggressively. He collects his chess pieces, seals them in a plastic bag, and rides off on his bike.

A nuclear American family occupies a square in the sand near what seems like the gay beach: a mom, a dad, a boy, a girl, the first half graying, the second half in full bloom. I ask them for the time. The dad says it's ten to six. I say thanks and almost walk off, but the son, who'd been supine on his stomach, gets up. His hard-on plows up his red trunks, and he half-lackadaisically, half-frantically tries to cover up with an unbuttoned button-down. Self-consciously needing a reason to stare, I fish for a smoke and ask if they have a light. Tracking the son's awkward movements, I pirouette like a Rittenhouse pigeon. "No," says the father, firmly. Some nearby German men in bikinis grin at me while I stand and chart the boy's fumbling: his dick up against his stomach, then straight out, tenting his suit, and finally, uncomfortably stretched down as he walks, bowlegged, to the sidewalk. He's about my age.

An old Japanese tourist walking down the pier with his wife offers me his lighter. I sit on a bench and smoke and watch the boy lace his shoes and button his shirt. As the family walks to the intersection of Morelia and Guerrero, I tag along. They wait for two lights to change. A white stretch limousine rolls past us, and the father explodes.

"Is there a reason why you're following us?" he demands in a voice that has nothing to do with the sun or the sky or the morning glories that stretch across stucco.

"Wha—?" I squint, caught slightly off guard, like the boys I like to look at, I'm supposing. "No . . . I'm just lost. I walked up and down the beach today and I'm just trying to find my way back home."

"Well, you won't find it from us," slams the dad. The light changes from a red wand to a pale silhouette, legs akimbo. And the family runs off to their fancy hotel, or wherever. I feel like I just got kicked in the balls.

A Mexican girl bums a smoke from me in exchange for another light. I stumble down the boardwalk and watch the boys boogie-board until the sun's flames fizzle into the water.

Back at the hostel, the owner's wife greets me. "Where you from?" she asks. "How long you staying?"

I tell her Wisconsin, and I really don't know. Maybe a week, maybe more.

"Wisconsin?" she says. "Up north, right? We haven't had a guest from Wisconsin in quite a while. Quite a while."

How long, I wonder. She seems to read my mind.

"Almost twenty years," she says. "Wonderful people. I still remember their names. We have a picture of them," she says. "Have you looked at our photos? Come look."

I follow her over clay tiles glazed with white birds with blue eyes and terracotta beaks. She turns on the lights in the common room (the TV-watchers groan) and points to the bulletin board. In the middle is a woman with freckles and wavy red hair, her arm around a man with a Jewish afro and thick red beard and soaked button-down, holding a screaming wet toddler.

"Nadia, Shlomo, and Ivan," she says proudly.

"Nadia, Shlomo, and Ivan," I whisper after her. We've all been here all along.

"Those are my parents," I tell her in Spanish. I don't want anyone else to know. "My name is Ivan but they call me Eye."

"No," she says, disbelieving. "No! But you do look like him," she smiles. "Welcome back," she says, also in Spanish. "I'm Estrella. You know, you're the reason we drained the pool. It is still empty today. Too much worry, and the sea is so close. Three times you jumped in! Three times! And each time your poor father jumped in to save you with all his clothes on." She laughs, shaking her head at the memory. "The last time you turned blue and he had to give you breath. And now look at you. Almost a man! Tell me, how are your parents?"

"My dad is okay. He's in Germany. I brought her with me. Nadia. She's in my room. I'll go get her."

Estrella is horrified when I show her Mom, but Mom's really happy to see her, I can tell.

"My God," she says, crossing herself. "What happened?"

"She was studying ruins in Chiapas. She got really sick and had to leave. No one knows exactly what happened." My Spanish isn't good enough to explain any further. The docs seemed to think she'd consumed corn laden with DDT and warfarin, but I still think she was cursed by an angry Toltec mummy. "She was hospitalized. She was allergic to the medicine. This is part of what's left of her. She wanted to come back here." The tears come hot and salty, like the water in the quarry. I turn away and whisper. "She wants her ashes to fly over the Pacific like your white butterflies. It's what she's telling me."

"I am so sorry," she says, wiping her eyes. "She was so alive, you know." She pulls a pin out of the corkboard and hands me the fading Kodachrome. I try to politely decline. "Take it," she orders. "You must take it, you must. Stay as long as you need. Do what you must. Do what your mother wants."

Back in our room, I unclip the metal screen door, duck past whistling hinges into luminous cool, the locust buzz. Sounds like wolves are making love, or mourning the migrating monarchs, gone north to Carlsbad, or the Sonora. Soon I may follow them. The latch clicks shut behind me.

It is too easy to escape, and then again too hard. I cannot leave them behind. I cannot leave her fully, yet I have to leave her here, this part of her I have to jettison. Overhead, the waning moon reminds me: soon. When it disappears again, before it renews. All those light-years off and all that time long gone now. All those towns that drifted slowly by.

A corner of the building peels away, the straw and mud. I walk around the kitchen windows to the broken kiva, sit where flatbread used to bake, and smell propane. Carlos is the owners' son, so it's good shit, homegrown. Deep breathing, eight good hits, then hyperventilate. Thoughts are dandelion dendrites, panic spores. Words slur into axions. Still, there are certain things to know for sure:

I'll be twenty-one soon.

My name is Ivan but they call me Eye.

Eye is the same backwards and forwards.

Mom's in a bag on the bed.

My brain is a ball of well-wound rubber bands, bouncing around the following: it's four thousand miles from Jersey, give or take. Also, you can see a storm miles away here, when it's perfectly sunny. Walking showers, they're called. Everyone's favorite song is "Soy la Basurita," meaning *I am the little piece of trash.*

As the broom of the gods, the wind of the night, sweeps the dust from the sky, I can sense what I miss: her smile, showing small even teeth, an inner lip's wet sunset. Her angular cheeks, denting a lumpy pillow, as she jawbones her way through uneasy dreams.

Now the door clicks shut, the cherry's gone. It flickers out in the dark red dust. I flick off the lights, set the roach on a thick wooden windowsill, kick off new moccasins. The stone floor is cold on my soles. I sit on the ancient swivel chair to a muffled screech of iron, inflame a votive candle on the blue Formica table. I run a hand along its ridged chrome siding, stare at Mary, supplicant.

She looks like Mom, when I was little, playing Sorry!

I'm sick of missing being little.

Light a match, burn a fingertip a bit, to flinch.

Over tostadas tonight at the Rancho de la Playa, I fell in love with a busboy, redheaded Leandro, from the mountains.

She wants to be scattered in the ocean. She wants to set sail. She's possessed. Inside the bag, her spirit, pregnant, pressing. On the counter, the anise, the orange, the flour. Tomorrow I will become a man.

And so tonight, when I'm still little Eye, it is only safe to remember boyhood, to imagine Leandro's freckled shoulders upholding denim straps, naked arms milking the afternoon's long shadows.

I look to the other bed, the bulging baggie twisted into knots. She used to tell those stories of me as a toddler, tinkering too close to the water's edge, tumbling into pools before I could swim. *Your father saved you three times,* she would say, *corduroys, fountain pens, wallet, and all.* I feel protectiveness welling inside me, like I'd do just that. I'm still here, after all, and can hardly recall what the surface looked like from the bottom, bubbling with Dad's resolve.

Instead what I remember is the song he would sing on long road trips to the Badlands, to pick her up from a dig. Absent-minded, almost silent, he'd breathe his lullaby's life into the dry, quiet nights.

Go to sleep, my weary hobo. Let the towns drift slowly by. Can't you hear the steel rims humming? That's the hobo's lullaby.

Soon, I'll blow Mary out, close my lids to the flame's inlaid turquoise, stumble through the other room. Lift her nightshirt. Fasten lips around her navel, the tie in the plastic, like it's a third nipple. My nose will skim skin, the nape of her neck, thin fuzz of her mustache, and allow me a last glimpse of my first kiss: a maple leaf's spiral, a football, a nine-year-old boy, how it all began.

In packs, in some unconscious phalanx, the boys converge for waves. They float, supine, faces angled toward Samoa. Their asses gleam, half in canvas, beaded with saltwater, sleek with dusk. I watch them from the pier. The younger set, eight to twelve, stay near the shore. They fling their boards against the skim and race to leap on them. Waves fling them into somersaults, into the sea. The older set, sixteen to fifty-five, stay fifty yards offshore, bobbing steady until they feel whatever tidal pull precedes a big kahuna. They'll ride it in if it holds up. A spackling of guys play both these roles. They are the most interesting.

I borrow a shortboard that washed up, long ago, onshore. (The hostel has a collection of decaying sea devices.) I walk to the edge of the promontory, gulp, and vault into blackness as night falls. I am new at this, and other young men sense it. I lose my board on the back of a foaming crest. A boy saves it for me wordlessly. Like the adolescents, I bob between the shallows and the deep.

The ocean swells. Forty boys and forty boards float forward in silent unison. I am one of them.

Return to
San Francisco

Bruce Benderson

In 1994 I left judgmental, high-stress New York with a tense neck and aching temples, hoping that the gusty vagueness of northern California would ease my deadline-oriented mind. A French magazine was sending me to take a deep look at the counterculture of sunny San Francisco, a city that stood as a strange hyphen in my life and in my writing career. Twenty years earlier, from 1969 to 1974, I'd lived a bohemian existence there, stranded on public assistance and virtually without contact with the conventional workaday world.

From today's perspective, my life had been one of strange contradictions, a way of getting by that seems completely marginal now. It was a total rebellion against not only the work ethic but also current conventions regarding success, fulfillment, and security. My goals were personal and pleasure-oriented and had nothing to do with accumulating money, obtaining material objects, or winning respect and attention from the society around me. At the time, I was part of an entire, extensive subculture—still largely undocumented—that felt exactly the way I did. We thought the outside world was a rapidly dimming nightmare, fueled by concerns about money, security, and power, ready to be overturned by a coming libidinal revolution. As we awaited this event, we firmly believed that we already had the right to construct our own private paradises. We cultivated the art of living as an endless span of free time, full of infinite choices for leisure, promising any kind of fulfillment and requiring not the slightest effort.

Filling the cheap, sprawling Victorian homes of San Francisco with throngs of friends, we called our living spaces "communes" and forsook privacy and luxury for a festive, privileged poverty, open to both adults and children. Forsaking marriage, we chose promiscuity and celebrative group sexuality. All that remained was to find a means to pay for all of this; so we devised ways to trick the government—which financed widespread social service programs at the time—into providing us with a subsistence living. Every day, we purified our blood with macrobiotics and ginseng root but poisoned it with hallucinogens and cheap California wine. Our wardrobes came from both genders (it was not at all unusual to see a bearded young man in a woman's blouse or housedress), and our hair went uncut for years or was styled in the bathroom by a scissors-wielding friend.

With all the free time of my unemployed life, I spent hours a day in San Francisco pursuing intellectual pleasures, learning French from bilingual editions of Rimbaud and Baudelaire, without any connection to a university or school, or writing stories and prose poems to entertain myself and my friends, without the slightest thought of publishing them. It turned out to be a marvelous accidental education. While other young writers were developing within the strictures of competition and the pressure to succeed, I rambled through the terrain of literature, language, and the arts, pausing unpressured when anything enticed me, acquiring knowledge without the slightest goals in mind. I still remember this time as my golden period of creativity, in which I regarded poetry, film, music, and the plastic arts as no different than the pleasures of the body. If I at all merit the title of an original writer today, it's because of this unfettered, festive education, free of any worries about the future or any need for recognition.

All of this transpired twenty years before my second visit to San Francisco, in 1994. In 1974, I'd left San Francisco for New York, begun salaried work for a public arts program, and started to devote myself quite seriously to a freelance writing career. I left San Francisco because I'd become distressed by the static nature of so much freedom. I'd begun to think that life was boring and meaningless and wanted a taste of a world in which survival was a more pressing issue. But because of the leisure time of the previous five years, I arrived in New York with my writing talents finely honed. A mere few months later, the atmosphere of competition and ambition in New York had infected me. I was writing just as much, but, suddenly, being published had taken on an urgent importance.

When the offer came from the magazine to revisit my old stomping grounds, I jumped at it because I hadn't set foot in San Francisco in twenty years. The friends who'd remained still spoke of it as sustaining a unique, perhaps non-exportable alternative lifestyle, whose closest European counterpart might have been Amsterdam (but is currently, in 2007, Berlin). According to my friends, self-invented styles—from experiments with sex and gender to New

Age spiritualities—were still more visible in San Francisco than any place in America. I had to take their word for it, because little information about these phenomena had reached the mainstream press. Did the City of Love still hold any part of my lost past?

Like Europeans, but to a lesser degree, American East-Coasters are inexorably subjected to the pressures of history. The Ivy League universities, banking empires, and government centers of the East Coast tie that region to the foundations of America, most of which were imported from Europe. Power networks established several generations ago still hold sway over East Coast cities, and many can be traced back to America's illustrious first settlers; speech and manners are established and exigent.

The West Coast, on the other hand, has come to represent the ideals of old America. It's a place where new immigrants can develop without judgment and assimilate with relative freedom. To create an atmosphere where this can take place, the West Coast has managed to erase all the sharp particularities of its cultural types. The Catholics of southern European stock seem to have lost most of the gutsy emotionality prevalent in the countries of their origins. Among their Jews, there seems a lack of the irony and sarcasm that distinguishes them in the major cities of the East Coast. The only minority ethnicity that seems salient is composed of members of the Latino population, who have had a foothold in the region since its earliest days.

The first people I wanted to see in San Francisco were my friends Cara and Sal, who had somehow managed to survive the fade-out of sixties counterculture and were shining even brighter in 1994. At fifty, they still lived in an immense, semi-converted garage, bursting with mystical and hallucinogenic images and blessed by constantly changing pagan altars to celebrate the solstices and equinoxes. Whole fields of demon faces, Buddhas, and Mexican death heads—most of which were made of plastic or cheap, painted wood—grimaced from the shadows. Sal, with his long, ash-white dreadlocks, wore a sarong and a happi coat. Cara wore striped silk pants and a turquoise tunic.

The air in this dense atmosphere was infused with multiple incense sticks and marijuana. In the past few years, both Cara and Sal had dedicated even their bodies to the overflow of psychedelic imagery that filled their home and minds by commissioning huge, complicated tattoos. Cara's partly shaven skull was decorated with a large blue spider. An immense tattoo of a red and blue bird fanned over one shoulder. Sal's thigh was a dense tapestry of Indian gods. And on his shin was a portrait of his deceased Mexican and Filipino parents as Mexican death heads in a kind of macabre wedding portrait.

After several hookah bowls of marijuana, Sal led me to their ramshackle '62 Volkswagen so that we could drive up Haight Street, the center of 1960s hippie culture. Cara's dark eyes shot strange sparks of jubilation as she talked about the tattoo she planned to get on her ribcage in a couple of days. She described the pain of tattooing as building slowly, a worsening burn, especially if the work was over a protruding bone. Yet both she and Sal claimed the pain was a focusing meditation, a kind of exorcism that left permanent holy stigmata on their bodies.

Both Cara and Sal were interested in death imagery. They attended San Francisco festivities for the Day of the Dead every year on November 1 and 2. Though the threat of AIDS may permeate the current alternative cultures of the city, the San Francisco counterculture has always sought a cheerful, spiritual relationship with the Grim Reaper. When my friend of thirty years would die shortly after from AIDS in San Francisco, his room would be full of cartoon skulls, skeletons, and other, mostly lighthearted but still occult images of death. Death has always appeared in this city as a fellow celebrant, sometimes glorified by the established Church of Satan in San Francisco, whose High Priest had been the occultist Anton LaVey. I was to meet disciples of LaVey near the end of my visit and learn about their theories of sensuality, power, evil, and race.

Fifty years ago, San Francisco was a city with a strong working-class flavor and powerful left-wing trade unions. It was a magnet for famous rebels, dropouts, and cultists of the American postwar period. Marginal artists, poets attracted by the cultures of China and Japan, fugitives from the law, renegade psychologists and Satanists came to the area. None of them had much money. Aside from New York, this was the city where the Beat movement established its strongest roots. The writers Lawrence Ferlinghetti, Jack Kerouac, Michael McClure, Gary Snyder, Kenneth Rexroth, and Diane di Prima all made their reputations and found their inspiration here.

In 1994, however, the city's counterculture was already significantly changed. It was, as well, different from when I had lived there, for many underground types had full-time jobs. Counterculture had become a lifestyle deeply rooted in the American white leisure class and was playing a part in the gentrification of San Francisco real estate. A neighborhood known as the Fillmore, which was poor and black when I lived in San Francisco, had been mostly repopulated by the overflow of a new generation of white Haight-Ashbury hedonists, who paid high rents with professional jobs but still hunted for drugs, wallowed in the new cafés, or danced themselves into oblivion in raves that lasted all weekend. According to my friends, some of them still showed up at clubs looking like Indian gods, grasping mosaic canes, caressing their own hair, holding out drugs, laughing mockingly, or jangling cheap bracelets on their blue, red, or bone-colored arms. These days, a significant part of the culture of San Francisco served as a safety net for the middle-class rebel, who could enjoy a counterculture lifestyle in relative tranquility without really threatening the mainstream and while perhaps helping real-estate values rise.

Cara, Sal, and I got out of the car feeling very stoned and walked through a head shop cluttered with hookahs and hash pipes, "Free Marijuana" car stickers, and posters of Jimi Hendrix, Jefferson Airplane, and Bobby Seale. Imagery of the sixties, from civil disobedience to eastern transcendence, glared from every corner, yet the salesgirl, with her short, bleached hair and black T-shirt, had a Courtney Love, post-punk look. This store hadn't survived from the past; it was merely a nostalgic reconstruction of it, for only in the last three or four years had the "Love generation" returned to the Haight. Haight Street had become an emporium selling the old Haight. Bill Belmont, producer of Fantasy Records and manager of the Grateful Dead, had reissued all the old band recordings; and the Fillmore—the legendary concert hall that once hosted The Doors, Janis Joplin, and Boy Dylan—had reopened. It functioned as a strange placebo for certain people, for, in the face of a growing emphasis on cultural identity, the white, liberal majority had found itself identity-less. And pagan rites, trance music, distinguishing tattoos, and small eccentric communities were just what some of them had been looking for.

As the hookah bowls carried out their climax, Cara and Sal's life-long surrender to sensuality began to overwhelm me. I'd thought that I'd completely outgrown the indulgent, provincial playfulness of the Haight-Ashbury ghetto. But suddenly I felt my defenses dropping and I lost my objectivity. Endorphins were flowing, and my stiff neck relaxed to the torrent of psychedelic images, trance music, and vivid chatter pouring through me. Eager for new sensations and new pleasures, I left Cara and Sal to plunge into the world of the Radical Fairies, a neo-pagan group of mostly male, mostly white homosexuals who'd inaugurated their vision around 1978 with a mystical gathering in the Arizona desert.

The Radical Fairies were in part the brainchild of eighty-two-year-old activist Harry Hay, who'd founded the Mattachine Society—the first homosexual American organization—in 1950. Hay's vision had been of the sissy as shaman, in touch with a transcendent androgyny that gave such a person special access to the worlds of Nature and the supernatural, with a potential to heal the divisions of the social body and point toward a universal community of mankind. In other words, Hay saw the homosexual as a kind of "Magickal Faerie," who'd had a special spiritual leadership role in many previous cultures. The striving for acceptance and membership among the larger social body that he saw among the new politicized homosexuals distressed him greatly, and, in protest, he'd helped found the Radical Fairies, whose politics and mysticism are indistinguishable from each other and who live lives of deeply felt androgyny, revolutionary consciousness, and free sexuality.

A precursor of radical farieism had developed in the early seventies when I lived in San Francisco. Two communes, the Cockettes and the Angels of Light, had spontaneously developed out of members of the Kalifower Commune into a performance group that exhibited proto-Radical Fairy attitudes and ideas along with pop-culture parody. They raided the thrift shops of poor neighborhoods to find dresses, veiled hats, high heels, and jewelry from the 1930s and 1940s and created comic hermaphroditic personae that shocked and delighted a wide audience of supporters. Half terrorist-transvestites and half performance-group artists, they held Holly-wood extravaganzas in a Chinese movie theater after midnight and in parks. They wore slinky, transparent Jean Harlow dresses and glued glitter or sequins to their beards as well as their penises, which poked through holes they had cut in the dresses. They mimed polymorphous sex or staged primitive Busby Berkeley musical num-bers in front of baroque scenery, wearing coconut-shell bras and grass skirts, while a stoned audience that included me howled and screamed. They eventually became so well known that the New York media began to promote them. Truman Capote, Gore Vidal, and other notables finally flew to San Francisco to attend their perform-ances. But when they were brought to New York to appear on Broad-way, Manhattan's professional theater community reacted with con-tempt, and they flopped.

I wondered what the Radical Fairies would be like in 1994, with high rents, the politicization of homosexuality, and increased gay bashing added to their environment. How, especially, would their emphasis on free sexuality be affected by the AIDS epidemic that was ravaging San Francisco?

Twenty-two-year-old Billie Jack was small-boned and petite—elfin—a graceful boy-man with a dyed fluorescent orange beard and orange hair. Although he met me at the door wearing a woman's emerald green pullover and an Indian-print skirt, there was nothing ludicrous or even particularly feminine about him, perhaps partly because he also wore large, lace-up Doc Marten boots. He exuded a sweet, meditative calm that was both palpable and profound—the monklike manner of someone who has made a major, irrevocable life-time commitment. These qualities, coupled with his gentle speech and hallucinatory orange beard and hair, literally made me higher, as if I were in the presence of some mystical, fairytale vision. But what interested me even more about the luminous presence of Billie Jack was his intimate portrayal of his life as an HIV-positive person—he had discovered he was positive at the age of nineteen.

Billie was born in Iowa, one of eleven children in a strict Presbyterian family. He described his childhood and early adolescence as one of repression and sexual guilt, with the burning desire to escape his Midwestern environment. He had fled to Los Angeles at eighteen to become an actor and had begun a life characterized by a vengeful, rebellious emphasis on sexual pleasure. He had made several gay porno films but didn't blame them for his HIV status. Instead, he said it was compromising choices in general in his avid search for an erotic identity that made him take the chances that led to infection.

We were sitting in Billie Jack's room, on the mattress on the floor covered with a boy's quilt from the sixties, a pattern of smiley faces and peace signs. Billie lived in fairly cramped quarters with his family, a serene twenty-three-year-old woman of black and white parentage named Allegra and her two children, eight years and seventeen months, the older of whom was born when she was fifteen. Billie's room was a pastel landscape of tinsel, crayon drawings, and an altar that wouldn't have been out of place in a corner of Cara and Sal's converted garage. The altar took up the entire larger closet of the room, and in it he had hung bundles of white sage from the San Gabriel Mountains, which he used as smudge sticks to purify the atmosphere, just as Cara did before her parties. On his altar were things he had collected from the land when he felt the closest to his spirituality, such as a gourd and a phallic-looking rock from the beach.

Billie had just come back from Wolf Creek, Oregon, from one of the established communes of the Radical Fairies. There he did mushrooms with the Radical Fairies and "connected with the earth." They had celebrated the Celtic Beltane rite for May Day, which included a maypole dance and group safer-sex orgies. During this ritual, he had come to the conclusion that the HIV virus caused a heightened sense of life because it created a stronger sense of mortality. His HIV-positive condition had led him to a profound new spirituality because he had learned to "channel demons and release anger."

Perhaps I should have realized how the Radical Fairies would process the AIDS crisis. They would incorporate pain, illness, and mortality into their naturalist, cosmic view of the world. As we lay on Billie's bed, he stuck out his tongue to show me the long, steel barbell that ran through it. Shortly before New Year's, his tongue had been pierced at a ritual. The next few days there was swelling and an increase in pain. But Billie saw the pain as a positive focal point. He'd had a lot of trouble focusing his thoughts before, and now he was able to. He said he had used the entire healing process as a meditation.

I've always been amused by Californians' tendency toward hokeyness and the over-dramatic statement. When I had seen a filmed sequence of a rite at Anton LaVey's San Francisco Church of Satan, the Hollywood hamminess of the details prevented me from appreciating its spiritual aspects. The robes worn by the mostly big-breasted female initiates seemed to be made of polyester, and their hairstyles seemed more appropriate for the movie *Barbarella* than they did for any church, no matter how diabolical. But on the seventh day of this return visit, I was more open to the idea of authentic ritual, real paganism, and black magic. I knew that California was a haven for fanatical, mostly white cults, as if the West Coast were some last-ditch attempt on the part of Caucasians to drum up some salient, hard-edged group identity. After a week back in the San Francisco counterculture, I was still searching for strong medicine, and I realized that people whose lifestyle couldn't be justified by easy political theorizing or even a general laid-back attitude might be hard to find. As it turns out, I found what I was looking for in the persons of Danielle Willis and Violet, a couple, who, for better or worse, led what seemed an irrevocable lifestyle.

I first got Danielle Willis's name from the writer Dennis Cooper, when I asked him to list some women in San Francisco who were pro-sex and sexually empowered. For years Danielle had been working as a dancer at a porno theater, and the world of the night was the one with which she identified the most. She'd also written a book called *Dogs in Lingerie,* which contained some of the best writing about "abject sexuality" I'd come across. One story, especially, in which she took the role of a vampire in a freak show whorehouse who gave dangerous head, but who fell in love with a dying mermaid, had aroused my admiration. We fixed a date late in the afternoon of the next day, and she promised to show up with her boyfriend Violet, whom some people had already described to me as a "half man/half woman," but about whom I knew little else.

From the moment Danielle and Violet smiled at me over our table at a Vietnamese restaurant, I knew I was dealing with people who believed in the radical gesture. From the parted lips in Danielle's white pancake-makeup face and Violet's velvety white one poked vampiric canines. They were permanent, steel-reinforced porcelain caps, which a Harley-Davidson-loving dentist had installed in their mouths, and they were 100 percent functional. The physiognomies, clothing, and tastes of both Danielle and Violet were in perfect harmony with their fangs: both were tall, attractive, sinuous, and waxen, with long, raven-colored hair. They shared a penchant for velvet coats and cuffs with ruffles as well as Death Rock music. What is more, they were vampires.

Both Danielle and Violet, who sometimes dressed as a transvestite, were fascinated by the erotic and mystical connotations of human blood. Violet claimed to have a license as a phlebotomist, and when friends needed to go to the doctor's for a blood test, they sometimes took him along, because of his adeptness with needles. He had a large collection of syringes, tubing, and needles, which he used regularly to draw out his own blood and the blood of Danielle. Together with one other woman, the two participated in blood feasts. All three of them were HIV negative, although Danielle didn't set much stock in the absolute truth of medical tests.

For Danielle and Violet, blood drinking was a sexual and spiritual rite that symbolized their dedication to sensuality, the intimacy of their relationship, and their identification with the animal world, especially that of wolves. Although both claimed to be Satanists, they didn't worship Satan as their god but only saw Satanism as the precept of being for oneself and learning how to exert one's will over the outside world to get what one wanted—a kind of enlightened self-interest.

Danielle said she liked the way blood tasted and claimed that it gave her "a psychological high." Violet agreed with her: "When you're fucking it's great to seize your lover by the neck and ram a needle into her vein. I love the idea of reaching the very inside of one's love."

Both Danielle and Violet claimed a friendship with Anton LaVey, the Satanist, who, then in his sixties, was something of a mentor for them. Like LaVey, they were moved by archetypes of power and will, and both expressed great interest in what they referred to as the "archetypical Satanic images of the Nazis." Although these images were attractive to them for their mystical, and not political, significance, there was a certain amount of racial theorizing in the Church of Satan, at least as Zeena LaVey, Anton's daughter, practiced it.

At the time I learned about her, Zeena LaVey claimed to have dedicated her life to fighting "Judeo-Christian hysteria." Since then, I've been told that she currently lives in Germany and devotes part of her time to debunking the many lies her Satanist father perpetrated about his own biography. Zeena LaVey is an articulate writer. At times her sharp, literate utterances seem sadistically trenchant. However, they also smack of race fantasy, a base desire for a cleansed racial identity. As codirector of the Werewolf Order, Zeena LaVey was engaged in a thirteen-year ritual to revive atavism for the coming millennium. According to her, the North American land mass was a "cursed area" because it had killed off the descendants of the land's original tribe, who were currently seeking vengeance by hexing alien races and creeds. She saw her spiritual soil as existing in Europe, where the German myths spoke of a vanished but altogether epic, atavistic life.

Since LaVey is of western European descent, she claimed that her chemistry was most sensitive to the western European tradition. She subscribed to ancient Germanic magic traditions and predicted the end of the world and the beginning of a new Satanic era. She viewed the Germanic magic tradition as a broad spectrum that stretched from Faustian black magic to Paracelsus and included the runes and the Rosicrucians. She saw the German National Socialist leadership, which claimed inspiration from the Germanic myths, as having been motivated by diverse currents and unified only in its search for a European mythos that was not "an imported Eastern slave cult."

LaVey's ideas about blood and Satanism were much more formulated than Danielle's and Violet's seemed to be, and her references to race myths probably would not have aroused their interest to a high degree. Nevertheless, the meeting of Danielle and Violet was a culmination of a growing conflict for me. On the one hand, San Francisco had seemed to be the very opposite of categorizing, pigeonholing New York, where race, profession, class, and income are prime markers. But on the other hand, as the days passed, I had the increasing sense of being locked in a ghetto of uniform race and class that would have been impossible in crowded New York, where dramatic though brief encounters on the street immediately brought home the verbal, gestural, and dress style of the ghetto. In the New York art world and counterculture, the "blood" origins of thought and lifestyle were hopelessly "contaminated" (multicultural). For although the bohemian East Village style of New York was white-dominated, it was geographically permeated by the neighborhood's other cultural styles, especially Puerto Rican.

San Francisco seemed different, less cosmopolitan. The European orientation of the Radical Fairies mythology, the consumerist hedonism of the neo-hippies, and the race mythology of Zeena LaVey spoke to me of an identity that was potentially alienating to other races and classes. Now I was beginning to wonder: Were the experimental personae, mystical adaptations, and alternative medical practices of the people I had met made possible only because they had been grouped together according to common background, race, and education? What would happen, I wondered, if the urban ghetto floodgates were opened, and Americans who cared only about the next fifty cents or the next rock of crack were added to the mix?

The next afternoon, I trudged up the stairs of Danielle and Violet's home with my magazine's photographer. Although Danielle and Violet had offered to draw out my blood as a gesture of camaraderie before we photographed them, I had demurred. But to be honest, I had a certain thirst for theirs, as if it held the answer to all my perplexing questions. Was San Francisco, with its counterculture of shifting identities, kaleidoscopic mysticism, and sensual delights a place of freedom or the preparation for a new cult of white tribalism, yet another co-option of nature by the Caucasian horde? Would hedonism lead us to a pansexual world of peaceful tribes or to a blood feast?

Violet had wrapped a belt around Danielle's waxen biceps and was drawing blood into a huge syringe. She was naked from the waist up and serenely watched her blood flow through the tubing. When Violet was finished, Danielle sat in a chair under some meat hooks that hung from the ceiling and arched backward. The blood from the syringe raised above her by Violet began to trickle onto her face. She licked at it hungrily. When her lips and breasts were covered with blood rivulets, she stood and Violet stripped off his velvet jacket and ruffled shirt. His lean, hairless body looked like pulled tallow. His fang-parted lips dove to her chest and hungrily lapped the spilt blood—rivers of liberty and appetite in the bold San Francisco sun.

I flew back to New York with my copious notes the next morning. My San Francisco experiences had been intriguing but confusing, mostly because the culture I had once been a part of had taken directions I never would have predicted. The atmosphere of paradisiacal hedonism I had so supported now seemed clotted and a bit tortured, undercut by darker, more desperate quests for pleasure and meaning. I understood more profoundly why I had left this city: in the end, my project of ultimate personal freedom had been a failure. It wasn't just the fact that one had to face economic realities down the line. It had something to do with the limits of individual imagination and desire. It seemed quite obvious to me now that if I had continued to pursue a life free of any defining context, I might have lapsed into banality and repetition.

Then, suddenly, I thought of all the confining strictures to which I'd subjected myself in New York: breadwinning and the opinions of publishers, sarcastic friends and the judgments of the media, goals, deadlines, and competitive colleagues. Well, maybe San Francisco wouldn't be a bad place to visit now and then, after all.

No matter, because from what I have read, and from the reports of my few friends still living in San Francisco, the city is no longer very "pagan." Six-bedroom Victorian homes, which we rented for about $230 a month, now go for several thousand, making the casual formation of unemployed groups of friends nearly impossible. Those without money form burgeoning ghettoes of poverty and danger that the middle-class residents of the city assiduously avoid.

Counterculture types from my era have moved away, died, or "reformed." Liberal as the city is, San Francisco is now completely infused with a work ethic, making it little different than the rest of America. This, I think, makes my tales of a largely undocumented experimental period even more important. Let's pack these notes away now, hoping that some faraway generation will once again appreciate their value.

Saint Andy

Trebor Healey

Note: This chapter is excerpted from Trebor Healey's novel in prog-
ress, *A Horse Named Sorrow*, about a young man, Seamus, who,
having lost his lover, Jimmy, to AIDS—and in the process having
refused to help him end his life early—is left to fulfill a promise, and
through it, he hopes, gain a kind of redemption in taking Jimmy's
ashes back the same way he came to San Francisco a year prior.
Thus, Seamus sets out cross-country on the very same bicycle, re-
tracing Jimmy's route in reverse from Buffalo, New York, to Eu-
gene, Oregon, climbing over the Cascade Mountains from the coast
and heading east across the high desert of Eastern Oregon, carrying
with him a purple velvet bag containing the ashes of his friend.

Dayville was a swell ruin of a town in every way, in a little glen of cottonwoods where the road jogged up and over a small hillock before twisting down into the one-street burg, past a defunct and oversized Oddfellows Hall and a couple of four-story brick former banks or hotels, much too grand considering the town's size. But more importantly, there were those giant bough-heavy cottonwoods, splattering shade all over the road, and promising the little river that flowed somewhere beyond. I knew Jimmy'd been here because he'd circled it in red on the map and written a poem about it too called "Places Named for Time":

Not a where, but a when.

The sweat cooled on my face as I hit the shady spots under the trees because Eastern Oregon was all sun in September—three days running of cool mornings and blasted hot afternoons.

I ate at Ellen's Diner coming in and going out. In passing. Through. Where I tripped the bell that hung from the top of the door as I entered that hot afternoon of my arrival, jonesing for pancakes, which I was now eating for dinner as well—albeit with Coke instead of coffee on account of the heat. There was a counter and stools and four or five tables lined up on the opposite wall. The only other customer, a husky man in his mid-forties, was drinking coffee on one of the stools. He put his cup down as he said, "Howdy there," while a woman I presumed was Ellen said good afternoon, expertly produced a full smile like she'd been used to coming up with them in these circumstances, and thrust a menu across the counter where I'd decided to seat myself, two stools down from the man, who then barked, "Where you from?"

I had that sinking feeling that he was going to be one of those small-town characters intent on getting the skinny on me as if that were his and everybody's business. I didn't mind so much, but being gay and on a kind of goalless journey didn't seem like a promising reality to present to this local. And I hated lying, knowing full well my safest bet was to just be a harmless tourist. He was going to be some work while she was easy. I could tell right away that she was into minding her own business and seemed happy to oblige me in minding mine.

I answered that I was from California, which was almost as shameful as being queer to some of the Oregon rednecks I'd overheard in the past few days.

"I was in Sacramento once and Frisco too, back when I was in the service." I looked at him to gauge his age, so as to place him in whatever particular war before responding. He looked to be my father's age.

"Were you in Vietnam?"

"Yup. You ride that bike all the way from California?"

"Yup."

"What are you doing a fool thing like that for?"

What could I say? "It's the best way to travel—not too fast, not too slow," I said with a sigh.

"Not too slow?" he raised his brows incredulously. Then he craned his neck to look out at my bike parked at the plate glass window under Ellen's arcing red name. It arced the opposite way that her smile did when she looked at you, and I wondered suddenly if she were a sad woman. "How fast can that thing go?" he persisted, again incredulously.

"Fifteen miles per hour max, I'd say. I move along at about 10 or 12 most of the time, so in a ten-hour day I can cover just about one hundred miles."

"That's a fair distance, but no competition for trains and trucks and airplanes, and. . . . you know—what not," he guffawed, before taking a sip of his coffee. He turned to Ellen then. "Ellen, would you agree this boy is crazy?" *Ha, ha, ha,* he laughed heartily, in a friendly way. If he only knew.

"Yes, Carl, I'd agree," she said with a clipped, uninterested smile, as she wiped the countertop and asked me, with just a hint of sarcasm at Carl's expense, "So what will our crazy California man have for supper?"

I smiled and ordered pancakes. She raised her brows and I just smiled.

Carl turned toward me again and asked, "Why are you having

pancakes for dinner, and why are you doing this?" But before I could answer he said that Ellen made great burgers and that he saw no reason to leave home. He'd left Dayville once. "Just once," he lifted his finger, "to go to war. That's when I was in Frisco and all that. After my tour, I came right back here and haven't left since. I don't understand why people don't just stay home."

I felt it would have been presumptuous to answer him really, and it was all rhetorical besides. But he looked at me then. I formulated an answer, which I didn't give him: I'm more or less crazy, San Leandro sucks, I'm a homo, and Jimmy's dead. Instead, I nonchalantly answered that I guess I just liked to travel.

"You ever been to Vietnam? That'll kill the travel bug. Hot and humid, bugs, damn fungus and disease everywhere, cold in the mountains—lot of people don't know that—and all around, just plain unpleasant. And ugly as hell," he guffawed again. "Maybe I'm just lucky to be born in the most beautiful place on earth. Wouldn't you agree, Ellen?" he raised his voice as she'd disappeared into the kitchen.

"What's that Carl?"

"Dayville's the most beautiful place on earth!" He smiled at me as he said it loud enough for her to hear.

She came out with my Coke. "It's beautiful here, yes." She seemed tired. And I wondered what she really thought, what her dreams were, where she would rather be. I felt for her that she had to tolerate his banter. Not that he was a bad or rude guy. I was even sort of enjoying his chatter—once I'd gauged it was really more about him than me. He wasn't that different from Uncle Sean. But Ellen, like my mother, had probably gotten tired of his manly bullshit months, years—even decades—ago. What was pleasant for a morning cup of coffee at Ellen's, knowing you were moving on, was just not the same thing over time. Then again, this was a small town. People had to put up with each other somehow.

She raised her eyebrow. "Refill?" I'd just quaffed the giant plastic bucket of crushed ice and Coke in two or three gulps. And after I nodded, she added, "pancakes'll be up in just a sec."

"Thanks," I muttered, my cheeks filling with air as I subdued what would have been a resounding, even echoing, belch.

There was a lag in the conversation, which naturally caused Carl to look again outside at my bicycle.

"You rode that thing all the way from California?"

I nodded, sighing, "Yup, and I'm going all the way to Buffalo, New York."

He whistled. "Just for the heck of it? What's in that bag?" He looked at me quizzically.

I sipped my Coke and sat back. He really wanted to know. I wasn't hitchhiking, and he hadn't given me a ride or anything so I didn't feel I owed him conversation as I had Ralph. But this was his diner on some level—his town—and I was gonna have to pay in chitchat to sit in it. I'm not much of a liar, but I didn't want to bring up Jimmy, so I stuck to death instead.

"My dad died in 'Nam," I said, with some reticence, dumping the conversation back in his lap. It was always risky to bring this up, especially with vets, as they either felt very protective of me or else they'd go off on fucking gooks and tell endless tales of macho prowess. Either that or they were traumatized, in which case they'd not say another word. I could have told him I was a lost soul and that I was transporting the dead; I could have told him I had no idea what else to do and my heart was broken; instead I dodged him with my dead daddy. And I immediately felt guilty for it.

"I'm sorry to hear that, son," he said quietly, respectfully, sitting up straighter. It was going to be the protective shtick. "It was hell over there." Now, he got thoughtful. "I got lucky, spent most of my tour in supply. Where'd they get your daddy?"

"Some place in Quang Tri Province," I answered.

"Jesus Christ. That place was hell. I'm real sorry, son—Ellen, I'm gonna pick this up." And with that he yanked out his wallet. Say what you will about Oregon, I was getting a lot of free food there. I thanked him. And he quickly changed the subject.

"Well, what did you do before you got on this bike?" And he indicated it with a gesture of his head.

Who are you, and what were you before?

I wasn't about to tell him I took lousy photographs, painted lesbian Marie Antoinettes, fucked a lot of boys, met and took care of Jimmy until he died, and tutored small children—between visits to my shrink and the SSI office. "You know, the usual stuff."

"What line of work you in?"

"Uh . . . teaching."

"Well, I'm a handyman myself. I can fix just about anything, and I'm still as strong as a young man. My back's in good shape. I'm lucky. That's my Chevy half-ton out there. Just got it a few months ago. A beautiful vehicle."

"It's nice," I muttered, peering out into the street at it (big and beige and typical).

"So you're gonna ride that bike all the way to the east coast? That's amazing. I don't get it. Ain't you got a girl or something back there in California?"

"Or something." Would my mother count? Jimmy-in-the-bag?

"Ah, so that's it, you're trying to mend your broken heart out here."

I just smiled. *You don't know the half of it Carl, and I can't tell you for fear you'd run me down with that half-ton of yours, dead daddy or no.*

Either that, or he'd be one of those small-town queers, or *not-*queers as the case may be, as he took me home and plowed me with expletives through the night in his doublewide trailer. My next question would answer that.

"Is there a campground around here?"

Carl started describing some place by the river (relief)—a jumble of "left at the mailbox, then right past the old barn . . . ."

But Ellen interrupted him and said, "You can stay at the church— they always put the bikers up there. We're on the route, ya know."

"Well . . . ," he said and looked away, surrendering his effort to answer my question, and looking husbandly put-upon as she proceeded to go into detail about how to find it, and who to talk to once there.

I had an urge to ask her if she remembered seeing Jimmy last year on his way through here. I was wearing his clothes after all, the same Red Hot Chili Peppers T-shirt. And I wondered if he'd stayed at the church. There was the red circle on the map and that poem: *Dayville, Weekville, Monthville, Year / Gravity, Einstein, I'm a queer* (Or was that just my doctoring and Seussing of it?).

Ellen roused me from my Jimmy-reverie. "Dayville is on the Bike-centennial route. You ever heard of that? We get bikers every summer. It all started in '76 as a bicentennial celebration, and it's kept up since. 'Course the season's pretty much over." And she smiled, adding, "You're a straggler." Sure am, I thought, grinning at her.

I wanted her to hug me then.

I thanked Carl again for picking up the check as he said, "See you in the morning." Was that an invitation? Then I picked up Jimmy like a purse and went down the road to where they told me to, and saw the small steepled chapel on a little hillock above the road, surrounded in trees—oaks and alders, and those ubiquitous cottonwoods. As I walked my bike up the gravel drive, a short, thick little lady came out, with a *what-do-you-want?* scowl on her face. I told her Ellen had mentioned that bikers sometimes stayed nights at the church and asked whether that was true. She nodded her head suspiciously, sizing me up, and turned around to lead me toward the church, without a word. Christian charity, I thought. Thank God for it or a person like her would never help me out.

She started pointing things out along the way. "That's a mulberry tree; that's the cesspool valve; that . . ." And then she turned and looked at me sternly. "What's that on your shirt?"

"Uh . . . it's a cross. Of sorts." But she wasn't gonna buy that. "A rock and roll band," I admitted. She shook her head, clearly disgusted. I thought about how bad it smelled too and hoped she hadn't caught a whiff and that the church had a sink of some kind to wash it out in.

St. Andrew's Presbyterian Church was a small white A-frame with a blue slate roof. Next to the church, connected to the side of it, was a meeting room, where we now headed. When she got to the door, she pulled out her keys, and putting the key in the lock, turned to look at me again, kind of suspiciously I thought, as if I had transgressed somehow. I just smiled.

"You seen this shirt before?"

She just glared, but didn't answer me.

Inside the meeting room were tables and a countertop with a coffeemaker, foam cups, creamer, a stapler, some scotch tape, and assorted coffee mugs. The room was decorated like a classroom, with the usual Christian art: 1970s-era macramé, children's drawings, paper construction, lots of nature calendars with innocent scenes of butterflies and rabbits, and sometimes children with butterflies and rabbits—and of course crucifixes.

The lady looked at me and said, "You can lean your bike on the counter there and sleep here."

I rolled my bike across the linoleum-tiled floor and leaned it up against the counter before asking her, "May I see the chapel?" She looked at me as if to say *what for?* without asking, then led me through a darkened doorway into the shadowy little church with its tall, columnlike stained glass windows on either side. Like I say, I always liked churches. Three wishes coming right up. But would they count in a Presbyterian church?

Same difference.

"You got the Lord?"

It sounded like another disease, in which case it should be rendered in all caps, with periods in between. L.O.R.D.: the acronym. I wanted to say I got Jesus-Jimmy-in-the-bag.

"I was raised Catholic," I answered. Trying to pass. But Catholicism isn't much better than Satanism to some Christians, and I suspected too late that that might be the case with her. She just stared and led me back out of the chapel.

"You been born again?"

"Once was enough, thanks." I regretted it the minute I said it, but I've never liked being bullied by Christians and don't have much patience with the strident ones. I could sleep outside. Down by the river where Satan was blind and snapping like the rattlesnakes that lady'd warned me about back in Redmond.

I took a deep breath.

"You oughtta read the Bible," she said, pulling one out of the drawer and placing it next to the coffee machine. "Gotta get right with God."

I inhaled again and held my tongue. All her "got Jesus, gotta get right, got milk," ad infinitum was working my nerves, but she was putting me up (or rather the church was). I'd cork it until she left. Christianity like the acronym. It's not so much the thing itself, but the side effects that kill you: the opportunistic infections of mis-interpretation and politics, and the parasites that come with it.

"I'm glad you found something that helps you," I feebly answered.

"Helps me?—I'm saved," she exclaimed, self-assuredly gloating.

Like a hundred bucks in the bank, I thought. The delayed gratifica-tion of heaven; a condo in the clouds when you retire; spiritual insur-ance. "Well, I'm doing my forty days and forty nights," I added cur-sorily, not mentioning the forty-ouncers that often went with them.

"You read the Good Book, there. It'll help you." On a whim, I pulled out *Bury My Heart at Wounded Knee.*

"You ever read this book?"

"I only read the Good Book."

"This is a good book," I insisted. She looked at it perfunctorily. "This is a book about faith too. Faith in the U.S. government."

"Well, we all suffer for our faith," she said dismissively. At least she got my meaning.

"Well, we suffer with or without it," I added.

"And no point in suffering for nothing," she replied. "For the faithful, there's a reward."

"Didn't work that way for the Indians."

"They had faith in the wrong thing." And she pointed to the Bible again. "That's the word of God, not your silly Indian book."

"Well, I like history."

"The Bible's got history in it."

"I'll say. But it ain't mine."

"It's everyone's history."

"Not the Indian's." I wanted to add "not the queer's, either."

"Sure it is. God's story is everyone's story."

"Well, now, that we can agree on." I smiled and thanked her and turned toward my bike, hoping she'd get the hint that the formalities were over. I knew better than to get "into it" with Bible-bangers—what was I thinking? Christers: barnacles on a single metaphor.

"You have a good rest," she concluded, looking severe. She then headed back over to her little house nearby, sheltered by a clump of trees, looking back frequently as if expecting me to sprout horns. I felt lucky I didn't look like Jimmy, his tattoos and piercings, the dark eyes and dyed hair. I wasn't clean-shaven and I smelled carnal; the shirt was a bit disturbing on a symbolic level, sure, but other than that I was hardly scary.

I had to sleep in the church; just had to. I pulled my sleeping bag off my bike rack and took it into the chapel where I laid it out on the altar, before I spied the minister's vestments hung up in a closet half-opened in the far corner. I noticed a single gold thread hanging off the bottom. Which got me to thinking because Jimmy had tied strings all over the bike—he said each one was a poem.

I went back out into the meeting room and searched the bike frantically, and after a few minutes, sure enough, there it was! On the center column, under the seat. He was here! He'd grabbed a thread off that very vestment. Goddamn, I'm sure she remembers the shirt. I'm the second coming. Full circle. A closed loop. Jesus Jimmy.

I heard a knock at the door then. Quickly, I gathered up my sleeping bag and hauled it out of the chapel, threw it down near my bike, and ran to see who was there. But it wasn't the little lady as I'd feared. An old man stood there at the door, with a long beard, sun-glasses, and a baseball cap with stones sewn into it, forming a sort of shining garland that framed his face.

"Hello," I said.

"You on a bicycle?" he asked.

"Uh, yeah. The, uh, lady said I could stay here." He pushed past me into the rectory.

"Let me show you something," he said earnestly.

"OK," I answered, at a loss.

"My name is Woody." And he quickly sat down at a table, opened his backpack, and pulled out a box of gemstones and Indian arrowheads.

"I'm Seamus." But he didn't seem to care about introductions. He was a man on a mission.

"Sit down here," he ordered me. He explained that he was a prospector by trade as he dug through the box. He proceeded to tell me story after story involving old mines he'd unearthed, crystals he'd come upon, Indian burial grounds he'd discovered, etc.—secret places no one knew about except him. And now me. And, I was beginning to suspect, all the other thousands of bikers who came through this town.

He gave me three buffalo bone arrowheads, and then he stood up. "Don't lose these," he said, holding my hand in both of his. "They will protect you. Why, if it weren't for these arrowheads," he referred now to the whole box, "I'd be a dead man. There's kids around here who shoot at me. They always miss, of course, thanks to the arrowheads."

The bones of saints.

I didn't know how much of what he said I should believe, but I had a sense it was all at least *based* on fact. He was eccentric enough to be one of those old-time prospectors, and kids did run around with guns out here (my count of gun racks had surpassed my trip-long pancake count in one afternoon). Having been a kid, I could immediately see the reasons why kids would harass a man like Woody. He had that outsider-freak-homeless look that kids, in their own insecure way, liked to make fun of as if to test the powers of their success at human mediocrity. Likely, they used BB guns, but who knows? I wanted to tell him that I was crazy too—that it's OK, I understand. But what was it that Tolstoy could have said, but didn't? *All sane people are the same; all crazy people are crazy in their own unique way.*

He got up, wished me luck, and left as quickly as he'd arrived.

I looked at the arrowheads, and they made me think of pills and promises and the books and candles that were all Jimmy had left at the end.

I put them in my pocket—good luck charms. Good luck, Jimmy.

I took my sleeping bag—and Jimmy-in-the-bag—back into the church and spread it out on the altar and crawled in. And I wished I could hold him; I wished he had a body still. My hands grasped longingly at the velvet bag.

I wished I could hold somebody.

As full of people as it is, the road's an awfully lonely place.

I dozed off, but when I woke up in the middle of the night, that church was solid black, not a smidgen of light anywhere. So dark, I wondered if I'd gone blind. I thought how that church was white on

the outside, black on the inside. That's not an Oreo, that's a Good &
Plenty. Christianity isn't even a cookie then; it's candy. No food
value. Spiritual starvation.

I fell back to sleep and dreamed I was in a confessional. "Bless me
father . . ." And then I recognized the silhouette through the screen.
"Jimmy?—I'm sorry Jimmy; I'm sorry for letting you down." He
pulled back the screen—looked hot in that collar—and blessed me
in Latin. And for penance? "Better luck next time."

I heard the church lady in the morning and jumped up, racing to
get my things out of the chapel as I heard the door lock click open.
She'll think it a sacrilege for sure that I slept on the altar.

We met as I entered from the chapel and she from the door.

"Where'd you sleep?" she eyed me suspiciously.

I cannot tell a lie. "Uh, in the church," I fished for words—"it
was warmer in there. I mean cooler." She stared at me suspiciously,
and then past me toward the darker recesses of the chapel. I wanted
to, but I couldn't relate how I'd seen a beautiful boy named Jimmy
hanging from the cross. It was so ironically difficult to share a Christian moment with a Christian, that I just sighed.

"Hope that Woody didn't keep ya up." She kept looking past me
toward the chapel—expecting what? The refuse of my satanic rituals? The burnt offering was right there in the bag.

"I should have warned you," she went on, "he always comes
around when there's people staying here."

"It's OK, he's a nice man; I enjoyed talking to him. He gave me
some arrowheads."

"Poor soul," she shook her head.

He'll be inheriting the earth, I wanted to tell her, but I was not
going to get back into all that. She was already glaring at the un-
opened Bible. My cue to say adieu. So I thanked her and wished her
all the best and got out of there. And she stood with her hands on
her hips as I pulled out of the gravel drive on my bike, calling after
me, "The town of John Day's just over that next hill there," she
pointed, adding, "God bless."

So Jimmy'd been wrong about Dayville. It must have been
named after this John Day character. But perhaps he too was named

after time. Romantic bullshit. Like most places, as it turned out, Dayville was named for just another john. The earth's a whore and the conquerors are all johns—sounds like something someone once said, but I don't know who. Me perhaps.

I wondered then if there was a town named Jimmy or Seamus somewhere.

I went for pancakes at Ellen's and made small talk about the church.

"You meet Woody?"

I nodded.

"Poor soul."

Everyone called him a poor soul; it was getting old.

She looked off into the middle distance. "He lost his wife, and his mind went with her. Used to be a regular guy."

Death will do that, I wanted to say. Instead, I just reached for the arrowheads in my pocket, to make sure they were there. Gifts from a crazy brother. Three bones, three wishes—I'd never need the services of a church again.

I ate in silence, the only one in the diner, wondering if the Christian lady ever ate there, and did they like her? Was she having a secret affair with Woody, the wild man, John-the-Baptist prospector? Where'd he get that name Woody anyway? I know what a woody is. I thought about their cleaned-up Jesus with butterflies and rabbits and suburban school kids at his feet. I thought of how I got turned on to a crucified Jesus once in a church and had asked my mother why he was so scantily clad up there.

"Well honey, it's hot in Israel. And it was a different time; they wore different clothes. And they'd been beating him, so even if he had a robe or something, it would have fallen off."

"Don't you think that his loincloth probably fell off too and that he was probably really naked when they crucified him?" I persisted.

"Well, I don't think so, honey. You shouldn't think about such things. God does not walk around nude."

I thought then of Jimmy hung up on a cross, winced at how it turned me on. I contemplated how he'd look and I enjoyed seeing his body in my mind: the yellow-green paleness of him, the dark hair in his open armpits and at his waist, the vulnerability of his nipples, his torso stretched. He had one rib that stuck out—all of them did really, but this one was bent and protruded. I laughed, remembering one time he'd told me we couldn't have sex for a while. When I asked him why, he said that we were both so skinny that our bones banged together and he was bruised. "Like two skeletons having sex," he'd said.

Maybe so.

Now, I ain't even got his bones to make love to, I thought. Just the dust of him.

Dust to dust.

Poor Jesus. What did he ever do to deserve these followers? That was the last church for me. After that I saw plenty of them, but their crosses looked like Kalashnikovs held aloft by Muslim hotheads I'd seen in the news. Fathers of countries. Fuck 'em. What I needed was a brother.

Carl was already out on a job, but he'd left a ten-spot behind to cover my meal.

Well, maybe not a father or a brother, but an uncle.

A priest.

But some other kind.

A friend.

A stranger.

"Thank him for me."

Ellen said she would and that she'd give him my best.

I mounted and rolled out of town, spied the church up on the hill in its trees. Good-bye, St. Andrew. And I imagined him Andy, a boy saint—to cut the patriarchy with a bit of heart.

A dog followed me out of Dayville. I shooed her, but she wouldn't let up, and after I'd left the town a half mile behind me and nearly reached the river, I stopped and tried to send her back home. Not that I knew where that was but I figured she must live in town. Who knows how big a dog's territory or wanderings get out here. She just wagged her tail, having made up her mind she was going with me. So be it, I thought, and told her I thought she was acting like a dumb dog, disgrace to her species, etc. When I reached the river, she stopped and stared at me as I crossed the little bridge, and then I felt bad for scolding her. She'd known where her stopping point was all along. I left her there, and she watched me for a long time. And I wondered if she recognized the bike, the shirt; I wondered if she'd remembered the scent of Jimmy.

A Table for a King

Martin Sherman

(*Darkness.* DAVID*'s voice is heard.*)

DAVID. (*Voice only.*) A star fell on Albania. I saw it. Just a few minutes ago. And across the dark Ionian Sea, riding a cool breeze from the Levant, the heavens dance. The moon, burnt orange, shines like an illuminated teardrop. (*Pause.*) Oh, shit! What's an illuminated teardrop? What a dreadful sentence. Why do I sit here writing about the Levant? I don't know what the Levant is. Or where. It sounds so romantic, though. If only I wasn't alone. Why do I keep this idiot journal? I have to get out of here. Away from this island. Why did I come to Corfu? Will 1966 go down in history as the summer I chased my melancholy across Europe? Oh! Pretentious! Cross it out! Why can't I write a decent sentence? Do people look at me and laugh? What am I doing here?

(*The lights rise on the veranda of the Kistos Inn.*

A tiny village in Corfu. Summer. 1966.

The inn—small, very white and comfortable, stretches out behind the veranda. The veranda itself is occupied by a number of tables, some of them set for breakfast. A door on one side leads to the kitchen. There are steps on the other side that lead to rocks, which descend, in turn, to the sea that stretches out before the veranda. A group of beach chairs is piled on top of each other near the steps.

It is a blazing hot morning.

MRS. HONEY *sits at the center table—the largest table and one with a commanding view. She is in her early sixties, American.*

DAVID, *also American, sits at a nearby table. He is in his early twenties. He wears slacks and a long-sleeved shirt, buttoned to the top. His movements are awkward and insecure.*)

MRS. HONEY. Waiting! I'm waiting. Hello. I'm waiting! (COSTOS *walks in from the kitchen, carrying a tray. He is Greek, eighteen, handsome, wearing shorts and a T-shirt. He is humming "Yesterday" by the Beatles.*) Where is Yannis Kistos? Yannis Kistos or his brother Nikos Kistos? The proprietors of the Kistos Inn? I demand to see the Kistos Brothers! Tell them I'm waiting. For my tea. (COSTOS *puts the contents of his tray—breakfast—on* DAVID*'s table. He is still humming.*) And my toast. For my breakfast. (COSTOS *walks off with the tray.*) (*To* DAVID.) Glory Hallelujah! I declare . . . this is not a well-run establishment. I'm sure you've noticed. I saw you arrive yesterday morning. Time enough for you to observe how poorly run this establishment is. Sweet Jesus! And yet the Kistos Brothers own a popular inn. Oh, yes. Difficult to believe, isn't it? It does supply the most luxurious accommodations on this part of Corfu, but what does this part of Corfu have to offer, I ask you? A few goats, a dirty taverna, a puny village, and that dreadful view of the Albanian coast. Have you seen anything *move* on the Albanian coast? I have never even been to Albania. Yes, it is a popular inn, Chez Kistos Frères. Do you know who ate here Friday night? Lawrence Durrell! They wanted me to give up my table for him. This table. Quite the best table. I always insist upon it when I make my reservations. I have been here three times. I suppose it is a very special place, the Casa Kistos, don't you think? Serene. Well—what has he done, I ask you? Lawrence Durrell? Write a quartet. I'm not impressed. You're supposed to compose quartets, I believe, not write them. Have you read it? There's a wonderful hotel in Alexandria and I don't believe he mentions it at all. Of course, by wonderful I mean quite inexpensive. I suppose nobody in his quartet does anything inexpensive. Or clean. Well, well, well, I don't know. I don't know. I did give up my table. Yes, I did. So I do think I deserve breakfast. Lordy—I do. (*She takes a bell out of her pocket and rings it.*) Waiting! Call Nikos. Call Yannis. Waiting! I'm waiting! I carry my own bell. It's indispensable. Service is appalling everywhere, don't you think? (*Pause.*) We have a great deal in common—you and I—a great deal, well perhaps not a great deal, but one thing. We are both traveling alone. Now I will say this for the Kistos Inn. They have single rooms. Solitary travelers are the most despised race on earth, of course you realize that. It is usually impossible to obtain a single room. I always advised my children to marry at an early age so they would qualify for double rooms. Unfortunately, they listened to me. Unlike this waiter. (*She rings the bell again.*) He understands English perfectly. He's just insolent. So— you're a photographer? I saw your camera. It must be very heavy. I suppose that's why you stoop. I noticed your posture at once. What's your name?

(*Pause.*)

DAVID. David.

MRS. HONEY. Now *that* is a fine hotel. The King David. In Jerusalem. Are you Jewish?

DAVID. Yes.

MRS. HONEY. Lordy. An artist *and* a Jew. I do hope you're homosexual as well, they all three seem to complement each other, don't they? I, of course, didn't grow up with any Jews, not in Mississippi. I met them later, a few, on my travels. Where are those siblings? Nikos? Yannis! Will you take my photograph? I long to have my photograph taken. At *my* dinner table. Perhaps L. Durrell has left his spirit at the table. Perhaps it will materialize on film. Oh—please—will you?

DAVID. Well . . . I'm not very . . .

MRS. HONEY. It will be an adventure, won't it? I did have my photograph taken in Calcutta once. I had just purchased a camera. I thought my children should have a record of my travels. I asked a sweet little beggar to take my picture. I paid him, of course—he must have been terribly hungry and he had a stoop, just like yours, and only two fingers, one on each hand, which made it difficult to hold the camera, but marvel of marvels, he focused the thing and clicked it too, and then smiled the most wonderful smile and ran off with the camera. I tried chasing him but I think his two fingers gave him extra speed. It always helps to travel light. That, of course, was before I realized my children were not interested in seeing photographs. I wonder if he still has the camera? I have wondered, in the clear light of retrospect, you understand, if he was a leper. I've always had a morbid fear of lepers. Now where would a leper get a roll of film developed? I won't say that question has haunted me, but I *have* wondered . . . I think it's fair to say his stoop was a permanent stance. So you will—won't you—take my photograph? Please say yes.

DAVID. Well . . . (*Smiles.*) Yes.

MRS. HONEY. Thank you. Now, if only I can get breakfast. You seem to have yours. (*She rings the bell again.*) I must confess, the bell is hopeless. Never gets me anything. Still . . . (*She rings it again, vigorously.*) Waiting! I'm waiting. Sweet Jesus, I'm waiting!

(*The lights fade.*

DAVID*'s voice is heard.*)

DAVID. (*Voice only.*) I met an amazing woman this morning. On the veranda, waiting for breakfast. Her name is Mrs. Honey and she is from Mississippi and she travels all over the world and she never stops talking and I promised to take her photograph. Now why did I do that? I'm so stupid. I *am* stupid. And lonely. And sad. And confused and ugly and desperate. Why am I here?

(*His voice fades off.*

The lights rise on the veranda. Afternoon. It is very hot.

DAVID *is fidgeting with his camera. The camera is very old and a classic of its kind, resting on a tripod and using plates to record its images. It has a hood to cover the photographer when he wants to check the light.* DAVID *also has a small portable light meter in his hand.*

MRS. HONEY *is sitting at her table, wearing a very light cotton dress, her eyes closed, absorbing the sun.*)

MRS. HONEY. I feel like I'm under water. Floating. Not real. In a different time. (*She opens her eyes.*) That camera—my husband, the dentist, had one just like it. Many years ago. Is it an antique?

DAVID. I don't know. It takes the best . . .

MRS. HONEY. I can't hear you.

(*She closes her eyes again.*

COSTOS *enters, carrying a tray. He grins at* DAVID. DAVID, *embarrassed, ducks underneath the hood.* COSTOS *walks through the veranda, humming "Homeward Bound" by Paul Simon. He walks off.* DAVID *comes out of the hood.*)

DAVID. It takes the best . . .

(NIKOS *enters. He is Greek, in his thirties, and wears shorts and a T-shirt. His English is only lightly accented. He carries a deck of cards. He sits at a table near* MRS. HONEY *and starts to play solitaire.*)

NIKOS. A photographic session?

(MRS. HONEY *opens her eyes.*)

MRS. HONEY. Nikos! Yes—indeed. You have a distinguished guest. A famous photographer.

DAVID. (*Embarrassed.*) No, I'm just . . .

NIKOS. We have many distinguished guests here. This *is* the finest inn on this part of the island. It was very kind of you to give up your table for Mr. Durrell.

MRS. HONEY. Well—he is an artist. Artists make things grow.

NIKOS. (*Losing at solitaire.*) Son-of-a-bitch!

(DAVID *is circling them with the light meter.*)

MRS. HONEY. Nikos, you're in the light. Surely he's in the light.

DAVID. No. It's fine.

NIKOS. I am in the way?

DAVID. No.

MRS. HONEY. Of course you're in the way. Nikos went to Oxford.

DAVID. Really?

MRS. HONEY. I find, in general, that if you've been to Oxford, you're in the way. Of course, I can't imagine why he and his invisible brother run a hotel in such an insignificant village. Can you? Speak up, child.

DAVID. Well, I don't . . .

NIKOS. Now, my dear Mrs. Honey—I must ask you for another favor. (*He hits his cards.*) Bloody hell.

MRS. HONEY. You play solitaire with such passion.

NIKOS. It is not a sad game, not a lonely game, Mrs. Honey. Not for a Greek.

(DAVID *stands next to the camera, holding a small switch connected by wire to the camera.*)

DAVID. Now!

MRS. HONEY. What?

(DAVID *presses the button.*)

DAVID. There.

MRS. HONEY. Oh. I had my picture took.

DAVID. (*Removing the frame.*) I liked the look on your . . .

MRS. HONEY. Imperious?

DAVID. Yes.

NIKOS. Another favor. (*To his cards.*) There. That's better.

MRS. HONEY. What did you study at Oxford?

NIKOS. Political science.

MRS. HONEY. But that's meaningless. Especially in Greece.

NIKOS. That's why I run a hotel. (*To his cards.*) Beautiful.

MRS. HONEY. (*To* DAVID.) Take another photograph. With Nikos.
DAVID. Yes?
MRS. HONEY. The two of us.
NIKOS. No.
MRS. HONEY. Yes. Please. You would like that?
DAVID. I would.
MRS. HONEY. Speak up, child.
DAVID. I mumble. I'm sorry.
MRS. HONEY. You what?
DAVID. Mumble.

(*He circles them again with his light meter.*)

MRS. HONEY. Well, yes, you swallow your words. So did the dentist. Too much saliva, he said. I'd say a miserable childhood. Which would explain your clothing. You're so overdressed. It's blazing hot, isn't it? My, my, you're buttoned. What is the temperature, Nikos?
NIKOS. I must ask you . . .
MRS. HONEY. Oh, Nikos, ask not, ask not. Come—have your picture took too. Leave those silly cards. It is a lonely game, no matter what you say. I used to play it endlessly. While the dentist was dying. It's a game for *that.* Stand here. Put your arm around me. Host and guest. Milk and honey.
NIKOS. If it pleases you. (*Rises.*) Where?
MRS. HONEY. Right here. (*Motions her side.*) Do you like this, dear?
DAVID. Closer.
MRS. HONEY. Pardon?
DAVID. *Closer.*
MRS. HONEY. Swallow all the saliva and then speak. Closer, Nikos. Just stand still. He has to run around with that silly little thing and focus. You're a handsome man, Nikos. Nice legs. The dentist's legs were appalling.
NIKOS. Tomorrow evening, my dear Mrs. Honey . . .
MRS. HONEY. Oh, Nikos, you're so single-minded. Don't you ever ramble?
NIKOS. There is a special guest coming for dinner.
MRS. HONEY. When?
NIKOS. Tomorrow evening.

MRS. HONEY. Oh. You said that.

NIKOS. Yes.

MRS. HONEY. Well, that's nice. I hope he enjoys it. Will you be serving something with lamb?

NIKOS. I must ask you . . .

MRS. HONEY. You mustn't, you mustn't. Don't talk. He doesn't want your mouth to move.

DAVID. It's alright. I'm not ready.

(*He ducks under the hood.*)

MRS. HONEY. I think he said he's not ready.

NIKOS. I must ask you to give up your table once again.

MRS. HONEY. You ask too much.

NIKOS. For one evening only.

MRS. HONEY. One evening too many.

NIKOS. It is a special favor.

MRS. HONEY. It is *my* table. It has the best view. One of the olive trees. Of the beach. Of the sea. Of that empty little rowboat in the water. Of Albania. I come to this hotel because of the view of Albania.

NIKOS. I am serious.

MRS. HONEY. I am too. About the table. I do reserve this table, as well as my room, four months in advance. Do any of your other clients do that? I seriously doubt it.

NIKOS. This guest is very special.

MRS. HONEY. More special than Mr. Durrell?

NIKOS. Yes.

MRS. HONEY. He has written a quintet, then? Lordy, this insignificant village is crawling with great artists.

DAVID. *Almost ready.*

MRS. HONEY. You needn't shout. The dentist was the same way, if he wasn't mumbling, he was shouting. Smile, Nikos. Tell me, who is this very special guest? Is it Mr. Auden or Mr. Stravinsky or, gracious me, Mr. Picasso? Are they all rushing to Corfu? Do they think the view of Albania might inspire them?

NIKOS. I could choke you, Mrs. Honey.

(MRS. HONEY *laughs.* DAVID *stands next to the camera, holding the switch.*)

DAVID. Now.

MRS. HONEY. Oh. Now, Nikos. Smile. Just imagine your hands around my neck, and smile.

    (NIKOS *breaks into a broad smile.*)

NIKOS. He is not an artist.

MRS. HONEY. Then he doesn't deserve a table.

NIKOS. He is a king.

DAVID. (*Presses the switch.*) Got it.

MRS. HONEY. A king!

    (DAVID *quickly turns the plate over and replaces it in the camera.*)

DAVID. One more.

MRS. HONEY. Goodness—dime a dozen.

DAVID. This one will be faster.

MRS. HONEY. You meet kings and princes and dukes everywhere these days. Running around without their countries, looking for a free meal. Where is this one from?

DAVID. Can you smile again?

NIKOS. From here.

MRS. HONEY. Here?

DAVID. Please?

NIKOS. Yes. Here.

MRS. HONEY. Greece?

NIKOS. Greece.

MRS. HONEY. Oh, Nikos. Well, well, well. So it's *that* king. Your king. This king. *The* king. Dining at the Kistos Inn?

NIKOS. He has a home nearby.

MRS. HONEY. With Mr. Durrell? Are they lovers? Oh, you Greeks are so sly. Does the king come here for your legs?

NIKOS. Choke.

MRS. HONEY. (*To* DAVID.) Take one of Nikos—by himself.

NIKOS. No—no—no.

    (NIKOS *moves away, sits at his table again, and resumes his game of solitaire.*)

MRS. HONEY. Nikos is obviously more important than he seems. Oh, Nikos, Nikos. (*Pause.*) No. I won't give up the table.

NIKOS. You can sit at my table.

MRS. HONEY. It's too far away. It's near the kitchen. It attracts Greek mosquitoes.

NIKOS. You can sit with the honeymoon couple.

MRS. HONEY. *With* them?

NIKOS. I'll put them with the Germans.

MRS. HONEY. That would destroy their marriage. So would I. I have a wicked tongue. No, no.

NIKOS. You can sit with the French scientist.

MRS. HONEY. He'll talk to me. In *French.* No, no.

NIKOS. You can sit with your friend here.

(*He points to* DAVID, *who is dismantling the camera.*)

MRS. HONEY. He wants to be alone with his thoughts. He's happy that way. Alone. No, no, no. The king will have to sit with the Germans or the French scientist or even with you, although, if you did study political science, I don't think you would have anything to say to him. No, Nikos, I won't give up my table. If he were an artist, like Mr. Durrell . . . then I'd grumble and I'd protest, but in the end, I'd graciously give in. But a king! A politician! He has blood on his hands, Nikos. Quite simply that. On some level—even if he's a nice young man—he's a killer. You must know that. You studied that. A murderer. Oh, let him go to the local taverna. Let him dine with his deeply distressed subjects. But this table—is mine.

(*Pause.*)

NIKOS. I must have it.

MRS. HONEY. Mine.

NIKOS. I *will* have it.

(*He throws the cards off the table and stands up.*)

MRS. HONEY. I've paid for it.

NIKOS. (*Smiles.*) We've just killed each other not too long ago, Mrs. Honey. My people. Brother against brother. As they say. We watched each other die. (*Pause.*) A Greek isn't a Greek if he tells the truth. Pardon my lapse. For this is the truth. I will have the table. (*He kisses* MRS. HONEY *on her forehead.*) Dear lady. I always enjoy your visits here.

(NIKOS *leaves.*
Silence.*)

MRS. HONEY. Smooth. Don't you think?

DAVID. I don't know.

MRS. HONEY. Too smooth. There's a story there. How does a Greek boy from Corfu get to Oxford? Where did he learn perfect English? Why does he run a hotel? And where on earth is the other one, his brother? Oh, there is a story there. And we will never know it, you and I, we will never know it. When we travel, we pick up impressions, that's all. Never the truth. We're never invited inside. (*Pause.*) You and I. (*Pause.*) Will they be pretty photographs?

DAVID. I hope.

MRS. HONEY. Are you pleased?

DAVID. I think so.

MRS. HONEY. Aren't you hot? All those buttons.

DAVID. No.

MRS. HONEY. I have very little in life, you see. The dentist is dead. The children don't need or want me. I see deceit everywhere. I have very little. Occasionally, in some insignificant village, in some country I barely know, I have a table. Do you understand? Why are you so quiet? Look at your hair. It just sits there. You must give it some *style.* (*She runs her fingers through his hair, messing it up, trying to give it some body.*) Someday, you will understand.

> (*The lights fade.*
> DAVID*'s voice is heard.*)

DAVID. (*Voice only.*) Why did I bring this awful camera? No one travels with a camera like this. It's so heavy. The plates weigh a ton. Why do you think I can take photographs? When I try to carry the camera *and* the suitcase together, it's a living hell. I keep throwing clothes away, to make the suitcase lighter. It never gets lighter. It's a nightmare. The suitcase keeps brushing against my leg. And now the skin is falling off my leg. I have a rash on my arm as well. And my stomach hurts all the time. Maybe I'm dying. I think that I'm dying. What am I doing here?

> (*His voice trails away.*
> *The lights rise.*
> *The veranda. Evening.*
> DAVID *is sitting at the table, writing in his journal.* MRS.

HONEY *enters, wearing a nightgown. She is carrying a bottle of wine and two small glasses.*)

MRS. HONEY. Sweet Jesus! What an evening. Do you hear a cow out there? I have some wine. And glasses. I couldn't sleep. I saw you on the veranda. I had waking dreams, do you know them? Amazing landscapes, but one eye is open. Cows are much too noisy. Nikos Kistos has invaded my dreams. Manically chopping my table up with an axe. Here. (*She sits at her table.*) Move over here, to the table in question. (DAVID *joins her at her table.*) They've waxed it. See? Have some retsina. It tastes like nail polish. I don't drink too often. But this evening . . . well . . . it just isn't right, some evenings aren't, out there . . . there—in the world—not right . . .

(*She pours him a glass of wine.*)

DAVID. (*Takes the glass.*) Thank you.

MRS. HONEY. Drink it down very fast. Nikos Kistos is an evil man, mind my words, he's planning something. I smell enemies. I do, I do. Mind my words.

DAVID. (*Drinks his wine.*) Oh, my God.

MRS. HONEY. A bit like lava, isn't it? Have another. (*She pours him another glass.*) Glory be, child, don't you want to unbutton something?

DAVID. (*Drinks the wine.*) Ohh!

MRS. HONEY. It's good for you. Go on. Another.

DAVID. I can't.

MRS. HONEY. I insist.

DAVID. Well . . . (*She pours him another glass.*) OK. (*Giggles.*) It tastes awful. (*Drinks the wine.*) Do you, do you, do you . . . ?

MRS. HONEY. What?

DAVID. Do you . . . ?

(*He pauses for breath.*)

MRS. HONEY. Speak up, child.

DAVID. Do you know where the Levant is?

MRS. HONEY. Oh. Somewhere, dear. Definitely somewhere. Somewhere out there. (*Drinks her wine.*) We're not savoring this, are we? (*She pours* DAVID *another glass.*) Something to do with the Mediterranean. Places like Cyprus . . . Syria . . . Lebanon . . .

DAVID. (*Drinks his wine.*) Jesus!

MRS. HONEY. Do you know Beirut? That's probably part of the Levant. You must go there someday. It's an absolute jewel. I travel, you know—place to place to place . . . (*She pours herself another glass.*) My, this stuff grows on you. I'm never anywhere for too long. They know my name at every American Express office in Europe and Asia. Not Australia. Doesn't interest me. (*Drinks the wine.*) A tiny bit more? (*She pours another glass.*) Well. Beirut. Now, I'm not partial to nightclubs but in Beirut nightclubs are as natural as the sea. There's one that is, in fact, by the sea; it has a spectacular if rather grotesque stage show and, for a finale, a long, giant, life-size train winds its way across the nightclub floor, weaving around the tables, with chorus girls standing on top of the railway cars, and cages coming down from the ceiling, those too with chorus girls, and flowers raining down on the tables, and gold coins as well, falling past the chorus girls in the cages onto the chorus girls on the train. (DAVID *looks at her, dumbfounded.*) Lordy! What a silly thing to remember. Well. Beirut.

    (*She holds her glass in a toast.*)

DAVID. (*Holds his glass up.*) Beirut.

MRS. HONEY. The glass is empty. I do get fond of certain places. Usually much later. After I've left. I'll give you the address of a lovely hotel there. And that nightclub. You will go there some day. On your travels. Nikos Kistos worries me, boy.

DAVID. I'm sick of my travels.

MRS. HONEY. He wants this table, he does. It's only a piece of wood. Such a fuss.

DAVID. I'm sick of my travels.

MRS. HONEY. And he's devious. And it's a king. Spells trouble.

DAVID. I'm sick of my travels.

MRS. HONEY. What? Oh. Which travels?

DAVID. These. Here. There. This summer. My summer in Europe.

    (*Pause.*)

MRS. HONEY. Where have you been?

DAVID. Everywhere.

MRS. HONEY. For instance?

DAVID. Paris.

MRS. HONEY. (*Smiles.*) Ah!

DAVID. It was horrible.

MRS. HONEY. Oh.

DAVID. London.

MRS. HONEY. Ummm.

DAVID. A nightmare.

MRS. HONEY. I see.

DAVID. Rome.

MRS. HONEY. Roma!

DAVID. I hated it.

MRS. HONEY. Hated it?

DAVID. Venice.

MRS. HONEY. Miserable?

DAVID. Miserable.

MRS. HONEY. (*Laughs.*) I think you need these last few drops . . .
(*She empties the dregs of the wine bottle into his glass.*)

DAVID. Why is it so funny?

MRS. HONEY. Did you not find Venice a little, a bit, a tiny bit—
itsy-bitsy bit—beautiful?
(*She laughs again.*)

DAVID. Yes.

MRS. HONEY. Then why was it miserable?

DAVID. I don't know. Yes, I do. You see, it was me. I was . . .

MRS. HONEY. What?

DAVID. Nothing.

MRS. HONEY. Go on.

DAVID. No.

MRS. HONEY. Spit it out. (*Laughs.*) I used to say that to the dentist,
spit it out. Of course, he said the same thing to his patients. I
wonder who picked it up from whom.
(*Pause.*)

DAVID. I was lonely.

MRS. HONEY. (*Laughs.*) Oh. I'm sorry. I have a laughing fit. I don't
mean it. Glory be! Dear, dear.

DAVID. No one has talked to me. You're the first person on this entire
trip who has talked to me.

MRS. HONEY. It's all those buttons. You're so covered up. You do not invite conversation. I'm amazed you're not wearing a necktie. Are your parents the very religious type? Do they abhor the human body? I have heard that Orthodox Jews make love through a hole in the sheet—is that true of your parents?—and if so, do they tear a hole or is it meticulously cut? Well, well, well—you are not a happy specimen, are you? Still in school?

DAVID. Just out. Out. Into the darkness . . .

(*He stands up—can't handle it—sits down again.*)

MRS. HONEY. And child, your hair. It's so homeless. Did you notice, in London, during your nightmare stay there, that some of the young men are now wearing their hair long and wild and quite beautiful? Let your hair grow, boy. And slash away your trousers. Yes—show us your legs. Do you have a shape to you? Let's see it, child.

DAVID. I'm drowning.

MRS. HONEY. Oh, dear . . .

DAVID. I'm tottering . . .

MRS. HONEY. You're drunk.

DAVID. On the edge . . .

MRS. HONEY. Very drunk.

DAVID. Of an abyss!

(MRS. HONEY *stares at him and starts to laugh again.*)

MRS. HONEY. I'm sorry.

DAVID. I don't have nice legs. (*He starts to cry.*) I'm drunk. Michael! Do you have more wine? My legs are scrawny. My kneecaps stick out. He doesn't love me at all. He lied to me.

MRS. HONEY. Shh! You will wake the hotel up. Nikos Kistos will have us arrested for drinking. He's planning something, Nikos Kistos.

DAVID. I'm burning!

MRS. HONEY. It's the sun. It was extremely strong this afternoon.

DAVID. I'm on fire. I'm lost in an inferno!

(MRS. HONEY *looks up.*)

MRS. HONEY. (*Sharply.*) Inferno? Dear, dear. Retsina, you old dog. Now, let's pull ourselves together.

DAVID. I'm so unhappy. I want to die! I want to join a kibbutz!

MRS. HONEY. Well, at least you have a sense of priority.

DAVID. I'm twenty-three . . .

MRS. HONEY. *That* old!

DAVID. So much of me has been washed away . . .

MRS. HONEY. You tend to over-dramatize, did you know that?

DAVID. I'm falling . . . falling . . .

MRS. HONEY. Oh, I'm no good at this. Mothering.

DAVID. Into the abyss . . .

MRS. HONEY. Never suited me. Ask my children. They loathe me for good reason.

DAVID. The abyss . . .

MRS. HONEY. No, child. It's not an inferno. It's not even a brushfire. It's not an abyss. Do you know what an abyss is?

DAVID. What?

MRS. HONEY. Watching the dentist disappear before your eyes. Cancer. That's an abyss. Watching his flesh melt away from his face. Watching a truck drive through his body every night. That's an abyss. Now dry your eyes and go to bed. We mustn't wake the evil Kistos up. The Kisti. Where is his brother? (*She stands up and looks at the sea.*) Not being loved is nothing. Easy. Fact of life. The dentist didn't love me, certainly not after the first year, but then, I never stopped jabbering, so who can blame him? And I didn't love the dentist; he was a fairly tedious man, although that is no reason to die such a cruel death. No, I married him to get away from my parents' home, and I did, God knows, I did. He took me to Utah, to the desert, the clean, quiet, empty desert, which, believe it or not, I much preferred to Mississippi. And I liked his last name. To be called Honey in perpetuity. Who could resist? And when he finally met his humorless maker I found I had nothing to do. But stare at the desert. The dentist was a companion, you see. He rarely spoke, and when he did it was usually about bleeding gums, but still, he was there, sitting next to me, boring me, but not with malice, and we took comfort in being bored together. But left alone, I was useless. All I was trained to do in Mississippi was to read magazines and chatter. My children fled from my endless chatter. My daughter married a man every bit as dull as the dentist; isn't that always the way? And my son, who has some spunk and brains, moved as far away as he could. They were both petrified I'd visit them, so they suggested I take a trip. I packed a suitcase. It's been four years and I'll never return. They send me money every few months. To American Express. And now I chatter in different locations for a few weeks at a time. And move on. And that, too, is an abyss.

DAVID. I'm embarrassed, I didn't mean to . . .

MRS. HONEY. My son sent a letter with his last check. He's left his job. He's heading for San Francisco with his wife. He says the world is changing. There's a new kind of life. He says. He has *hope.* Well. Glory Hallelujah, bless his soul. *And*—his hair is very long. He sent a photograph. I think he looks quite stunning. He's not much older than you. (*She brushes* DAVID*'s hair.*) Please let it grow. (*Pause.*) Well, well, well. Time to return Nikos Kistos to my dreams. Time to close my eyes and see him pulling at my table, like a demented puppy. Down, Nikos, down! (*She brushes her hand across his face.*) Breathe a little. Let some fresh air in. Throw away your camera. Forget your hurt. Forget your family. Buy some shorts. Have adventures. But first—go to sleep. Sleep is good for growing hair.

> (*She kisses him. He stares at her.*)

DAVID. Mrs. Honey?

MRS. HONEY. What?

DAVID. Your nightgown—is on inside out.

MRS. HONEY. Well, so it is. Fancy that.

> (*She leaves.*
>
> DAVID *sits alone at the table. He runs his hand through his hair and starts to pull on it, as if to make it grow.*
> *Silence.*
>
> COSTOS *enters, from the beach. He is wearing a bathing suit. A beach blanket hangs over his shoulder. He sees* DAVID*. He smiles. He starts to hum "Strangers in the Night."* DAVID *looks up at* COSTOS*, startled. He sees* COSTOS *smile and smiles back tentatively, then turns away.* COSTOS *walks into the kitchen.*
>
> DAVID *gathers his notebook, the two glasses, and the empty wine bottle and starts to leave. He is a bit unsteady on his feet. He looks for some place to throw the bottle.*

(COSTOS *re-enters, carrying a large glass of water.* DAVID *stops, transfixed by* COSTOS's *body.*)

COSTOS. Water.

DAVID. What?

COSTOS. You wanted water?

DAVID. No.

COSTOS. Glass of water.

DAVID. No.

COSTOS. I make mistake?

DAVID. Yes.

COSTOS. Think you want water.

DAVID. No.

(*Pause.* DAVID *starts to leave again.*)

COSTOS. I bring it to your room.

DAVID. Bring what?

COSTOS. Water.

DAVID. No.

COSTOS. Room number six?

DAVID. Yes.

COSTOS. I bring it.

DAVID. I don't want water.

COSTOS. I was going to bring at any rate.

DAVID. You were?

COSTOS. After I swim. Tonight. To room six. To you.

DAVID. You were?

COSTOS. Yes.

DAVID. Why?

COSTOS. But now you here. Better. So drink it here.

(*He holds out the glass.*)

DAVID. But I don't want . . . (COSTOS *stares at him.*) Well . . . I suppose . . . (*He takes the glass.*) Thank you.

COSTOS. You see. I know what you want.

DAVID. It's only water.

COSTOS. Drink it.

(*Pause.*)

DAVID. Alright.

(*He drinks the water.*)

274

COSTOS. Is good?

DAVID. Yes.

COSTOS. Greek water is good?

DAVID. Excellent.

COSTOS. You know Barbara Ann?

DAVID. Who?

COSTOS. Barbara Ann.

DAVID. No.

COSTOS. Song. By Beach Boys.

DAVID. Oh. Oh! I see. Beach Boys. No, I don't listen to . . .

COSTOS. I'm still wet. From sea. Dry under stars. Here. Take chairs. (*He goes to the side of the veranda where the beach chairs are piled and drags two to the center of the veranda.*) You help me. (DAVID *helps him with the chairs.*) Good. We lie down. (COSTOS *throws his blanket on one of the chairs and lies on it, stretching out, provocatively.* DAVID *stares at him.*) Go on. You too. (DAVID *doesn't move.* COSTOS—*impatient—taps the chair next to him.*) Here. Here. Under stars.

　　(*Pause.*)

DAVID. Why not? (*He lies down on the other chair.*) My God! (*Staring at the sky.*) Look at them.

COSTOS. Tomorrow big day.

DAVID. Is it?

COSTOS. King is here.

DAVID. I know.

COSTOS. We have good king.

DAVID. Yes.

COSTOS. No king in America.

DAVID. No. So many stars. I feel almost . . .

COSTOS. Greece happy with king . . .

DAVID. Almost . . .

COSTOS. King is like father.

DAVID. Almost someplace else.

COSTOS. You know Sergeant Barry Sadler?

DAVID. Who?

COSTOS. "Ballad of Green Berets." War song. Big hit. Vietnam. You like it?

DAVID. I don't know it.

COSTOS. No wars in Greece any more. You know this—? (*Sings.*) "Under the boardwalk, we'll be fallin' in love. Under the boardwalk, boardwalk."

DAVID. No.

COSTOS. Drifters.

DAVID. Oh. I see.

COSTOS. Move chairs closer. (*He reaches out and pulls* DAVID's *chair directly next to his, then puts his arm on* DAVID's *shoulder.*) I know what you want. I have many brains. I go to university next year. You go to university?

DAVID. I did.

COSTOS. You leave.

DAVID. Graduate.

COSTOS. You smart person too. You study with the camera?

DAVID. A little. Yes.

COSTOS. I can tell. Smart person. Take pictures for money?

DAVID. Not yet. Someday.

COSTOS. (*Sings.*) "Cool cat, lookin' for a kitty. Gonna look in every corner of the city." Know that?

DAVID. No.

COSTOS. Lovin' Spoonful.

DAVID. I never listen to contemporary . . .

COSTOS. (*Sings.*) "And baby, if the music is right, I'll meet you tomorrow, sort of late at night." (*Pause.*) How I learn my English. Sonny. Cher. Mamas. Papas. Simon. Garfunkel. Good teacher. My English good?

DAVID. Very.

(COSTOS *moves his arm past* DAVID's *shoulder and lays it on* DAVID's *chest.*)

COSTOS. You have girlfriend?

DAVID. No.

COSTOS. I have many.

DAVID. Oh.

COSTOS. Boyfriends too.

(*Pause.*)

DAVID. Oh.

(COSTOS *starts to caress* DAVID*'s chest.*)

COSTOS. You have boyfriends?

DAVID. No.

COSTOS. Not even one?

    (*Pause.*)

DAVID. No.

COSTOS. You not serious.

DAVID. I am. Serious. No. (*Sits up.*) I think I am going to sleep now. (*Rises.*) I'm just a little drunk.

    (COSTOS *grabs* DAVID*'s legs.*)

COSTOS. You stay.

DAVID. I can't.

COSTOS. What make you drunk?

DAVID. Retsina.

COSTOS. It is good, retsina?

DAVID. Yes. But bitter.

COSTOS. Bitter—good?

DAVID. Yes. Bitter very good. But too much. I feel strange.

COSTOS. You feel happy?

DAVID. Happy? No! Not happy. (*Pause.*) Strange.

COSTOS. Strange—good?

DAVID. I don't know. I can't answer. (COSTOS *pulls* DAVID *down to his chair.*) What are you doing?

COSTOS. Look at stars. Beautiful. Greek night. Sound of waves. Magic. I know what you want. I have many brains. I will go to university. I will be smart person too. (*Sings.*) "We'll sing in the sunshine. We'll laugh everyday." Know that?

DAVID. No.

COSTOS. Big hit. No sunshine now. Stars.

    (*He brushes his hand across* DAVID*'s mouth.*)

DAVID. Stars.

COSTOS. It is very hot, no?

DAVID. Yes.

    (COSTOS *takes* DAVID*'s hand and places it on his chest, then sings.*)

COSTOS "Then I'll be on my way." (*Pause.*) I am very hot. You also?

DAVID. Yes.

COSTOS. Why you never unbutton? (*He moves* DAVID's *hand across his chest.*) Greece very hot. You like Greece?

(*He puts* DAVID's *hand on his nipple.*)

DAVID. Very much.

COSTOS. You think Greece beautiful?

DAVID. Very.

COSTOS. Unbutton.

(*He starts to unbutton* DAVID's *shirt.*)

DAVID. No.

(*He sits up.*)

COSTOS. What is wrong?

DAVID. Nothing.

COSTOS. I want to look at you.

DAVID. You do? Really?

COSTOS. Yes. Sure. (*Sings.*) "And it's magic, if the music is groovy."

DAVID. Everybody wants me to unbutton. But I don't . . . Oh. What the hell. (*He pulls his shirt open.*) Unbuttoned! Oh, God, I think I tore it. I tore my shirt. This is a catastrophe.

COSTOS. Leave open.

DAVID. I only have a few shirts with me. And this one drip-dries and . . .

COSTOS. Like shirt torn. Sexy.

DAVID. Sexy?

COSTOS. Yes.

DAVID. Really?

COSTOS. Really.

DAVID. Me? No . . .

COSTOS. Your skin so white. No beach?

DAVID. No beach, no. Can't swim. I visit ruins. No beach. My family . . . they think modern bathing suits are . . . Oh, that's silly . . . I don't listen to them anyway . . . I . . . can't swim though . . .

COSTOS. (*Sings.*) "Hey, Mr. Tambourine Man, sing a song for me." I know what you want. I have many brains.

(*He pulls* DAVID's *shirt completely open.*)

DAVID. It's cold. There's a draft.

COSTOS. It's hot. (*Sings.*) "Hot town, summer in the city." (*Pause.*) Put hand here . . . (*He places* DAVID's *hand on his crotch. Sings.*)

"I'm not sleepy and there's no place I'm going to." (*He pulls* DAVID *down.*) Lips here. (*He kisses* DAVID. DAVID *pulls himself up.* COSTOS *pulls him down again, and as he does so takes the beach blanket out from under his body and drapes it over them, covering both of their bodies.*) Here. I make you relax. You like blanket? Pretty Greek blanket. There. Now you do not have to look. Just feel. Better. I have many brains. I know what you want. (*There is now much mutual activity underneath the blanket.*) You like?

DAVID. Yes. I like.

COSTOS. Very much?

DAVID. Very much.

COSTOS. (*Sings.*) "In the jingle-jangle morning, I'll come following you." (*He speaks in a murmur as he explores* DAVID'*s body.*) Do you feel the jingle-jangle? You come following through under the boardwalks? What a day for a daydream. All my thoughts are far away. Do you believe in magic? Homeward bound, I'm homeward bound . . .

DAVID. Oh . . .

COSTOS. These boots are made for walking . . .

DAVID. Ohh . . .

COSTOS. Walk all over you.

DAVID. Yes.

COSTOS. I make you happy?

DAVID. Yes.

COSTOS. Very happy?

DAVID. Yes.

COSTOS. Sputnik. You go up like Sputnik. All the leaves are brown and the sky is grey . . .

DAVID. Yes.

COSTOS. I've been for a walk on a winter's day.

DAVID. Yes.

COSTOS. Sputnik. Into space.

DAVID. Ohh . . .

COSTOS. I'm not sleepy and there is no place I'm going to . . .

DAVID. Ohh . . .

COSTOS. If I didn't tell her, I could leave today . . .

DAVID. Ohhh.

costos. California dreamin' on a winter's day . . .

david. Ohhh!

> (DAVID *has an orgasm.*
>> *Pause.*
>>> costos *sits up, startled.*)

costos. So soon? Sputnik land so soon?

david. I think so.

costos. Too soon.

david. I'm sorry.

costos. I do not give you pleasure?

david. Yes. I'm sorry.

costos. You do not like me?

david. But I do.

costos. Not very much.

david. I do. Honestly. Very much. You give pleasure.

costos. You make joke.

david. No.

costos. This truth?

david. Yes. Truth.

costos. Promise.

david. Yes.

costos. Great pleasure?

david. Yes. (*Pause.*) Great.

costos. I make you happy?

david. Yes. (*Pause.*) Thank you.

costos. Kiss me thank you. (DAVID *kisses him.*) Now I believe.

david. Good.

costos. Now give present.

> (DAVID *sits up.*)

david. Oh. Really?

costos. Yes.

david. I must be dreaming.

costos. No dream. Give present.

david. You don't have to.

> (*Pause.*)

costos. Have to what?

david. Give me a present. (*Smiles.*) You already did.

COSTOS. You make joke?

DAVID. No.

COSTOS. *You* give present.

DAVID. What?

COSTOS. You give present. To me.
  (*Pause.*)

DAVID. Oh.

COSTOS. I close eyes. (COSTOS *closes his eyes and holds out his hand.* DAVID *stares at him in silence.* COSTOS *opens his eyes.*) Little present.

DAVID. Why?

COSTOS. For pleasure.

DAVID. But I thought . . .

COSTOS. Because I give pleasure.

DAVID. I thought . . .

COSTOS. To say you like me.

DAVID. I thought . . . You found me . . .

COSTOS. To show I make you happy.

DAVID. I thought you thought I was . . . I thought you wanted to . . . I thought. (*Pause.*) I am stupid.

COSTOS. (*Sings.*) "Cool town, evenin' in the city, dressin' so fine and lookin' so pretty."

DAVID. I was almost . . . someplace else. I am very stupid.

COSTOS. Watch.

DAVID. What?

COSTOS. Your watch.

DAVID. Yes?

COSTOS. Give me your watch.

DAVID. No.

COSTOS. Little present.

DAVID. Not my watch.

COSTOS. I like your watch.

DAVID. It's *mine.*

COSTOS. I wear watch and think of you . . . underneath stars.

DAVID. No.

COSTOS. You buy another.

DAVID. Absolutely not.

COSTOS. Radio.
DAVID. I don't have one.
COSTOS. You must.
DAVID. I don't.
COSTOS. Americans have radios.
DAVID. I don't.
COSTOS. Listen to music.
DAVID. I don't.
COSTOS. Beatles.
DAVID. No radio.
COSTOS. Ring.
DAVID. No.

    (COSTOS *points to the ring on* DAVID*'s finger.*)

COSTOS. This ring. Very nice.
DAVID. No.
COSTOS. Fit my finger.

    (*He pulls at the ring.*)

DAVID. No.
COSTOS. Same size.
DAVID. No.
COSTOS. Pretty ring . . .
DAVID. No. My grandmother gave it to me.
COSTOS. Grandmother?
DAVID. Yes. Old lady.
COSTOS. Oh. (*Pause.*) Very good. Very good. Grandmother. You keep.
DAVID. Thank you.
COSTOS. Camera.
DAVID. Certainly not.
COSTOS. Not big one. You have a small one too.
DAVID. No. No cameras.
COSTOS. I go to room. Number six. I take camera. Small one.
DAVID. No.
COSTOS. Not big one.
DAVID. Neither one.
COSTOS. You don't like me.
DAVID. I do.

COSTOS. I do not give pleasure.

DAVID. You did.

COSTOS. You make fun of me.

DAVID. I don't.

COSTOS. You insult me.

DAVID. I didn't.

COSTOS. Then give me camera.

DAVID. I won't.

COSTOS. I lie on floor.

DAVID. No camera.

> (COSTOS *lies down on the ground.*)

COSTOS. I lie on floor. I scream. I say you hurt me.

DAVID. Hurt you?

COSTOS. (*Holds his groin.*) Here. In the sex. You do bad things to me. I cannot move. I cry. You hurt me. I call the police.

DAVID. Police?

COSTOS. They come to room. Number six. They put you in prison. I am young. Seventeen. Against the law. I scream.

DAVID. No.

COSTOS. You hurt me. I cannot move. I am screaming. (*Shouts.*) Police!

DAVID. Stop it.

COSTOS. You give me camera?

DAVID. No.

COSTOS. Police!

DAVID. You'll wake everybody up.

COSTOS. Police!

> (DAVID *puts his hand over* COSTOS's *mouth.* COSTOS *bites it.*)

DAVID. Ouch!

COSTOS. You touch me. You hurt me. You hurt my sex. Tomorrow king come. King find me. Under table. Almost dead. King take me in arms. King cry out—"My people, my people!" I screaming now. Police!

DAVID. You will wake the entire hotel.

COSTOS. I scream louder. Police!

DAVID. Alright! The watch! Take it!

(DAVID *takes the watch off his wrist and holds it out.*
   Pause.
      COSTOS *sits up.*)

COSTOS. For me?

DAVID. Yes.

COSTOS. A present?

DAVID. Yes.

COSTOS. Your watch?

DAVID. Yes.

COSTOS. You sure?

DAVID. Yes.

COSTOS. You like me?

DAVID. Yes.

COSTOS. I make you happy?

DAVID. Yes.

   (*Pause.*)

COSTOS. Very happy?

DAVID. Very happy.

COSTOS. Then I take it. (*He grabs the watch.*) What a surprise. A present! (*He puts the watch on.*) I am beautiful, no?

DAVID. No.

COSTOS. Thank you. I am beautiful. I have watch. I make you happy. You make me happy. I give you great pleasure. Now I go to sleep. You are nice. Pretty present. Pretty stars. Pretty night. (*Sings.*) "We'll sing in the sunshine, we'll laugh everyday." (*He picks up his blanket. Sings.*) "We'll sing in the sunshine." (*He drapes the blanket over his shoulders. Sings.*) "And I'll be on my way."

   (COSTOS *leaves.*
      DAVID *sits at a table. He leans back on his chair, closes his eyes, and begins to sing in Hebrew.*)

DAVID. "Ma nishtanah, hililah hazeh, mikahl halalos . . ."

   (*The lights fade.*
      DAVID's *voice is heard.*)

DAVID. (*Voice only.*) When I was a child, I sang it at Passover. "Ma nishtanah . . ." Why is this night different from any other? Why did that song come racing into my head? (*Pause.*) One thing washes over another. How long will it take for my hair to grow?

Why do I sleep in my underwear? Cross this out. Don't write in this journal when you're drunk. Why is this night different? Because they talk to me now. Touch me. But it's still the same! (*Pause.*) If only my hair were long . . . if only something would change . . .

> (*His voice fades away.*
> *The lights rise.*
> *The veranda. The next morning.*
> MRS. HONEY *is sitting at her table.*)

MRS. HONEY. Waiting! I'm waiting. Hello! I'm waiting. (*She rings her bell.*) I demand my breakfast. (*She rings the bell again.* DAVID *enters. He goes to his table.*) This is war, child. Good morning.

DAVID. Good morning.

MRS. HONEY. They have instituted a blockade of my table. They have imposed sanctions. They are attempting to terrorize my stomach. This inn offers room and famine. Did you sleep well?

DAVID. No.

MRS. HONEY. Nor I. I anticipated trouble. (*She rings the bell. Shouts.*) I shall protest to the ambassador! (*Pause.*) They shall not succeed. Mr. Gandhi, decent as politicians go, often went without food, and *he* became a country. I believe your own religion has a day of ritual starvation.

DAVID. Yom Kippur.

MRS. HONEY. Indeed. Then I hereby declare Yom Kippur at this table.

DAVID. On Yom Kippur you atone for your sins.

MRS. HONEY. Fair enough—that will help me pass the time. My primary sin was to book the wrong inn. But book I did, and stay I shall. Nikos Kistos has joined battle with the wrong pain in the neck. (*Pause.*) Did you hear noise last night? Screaming?

DAVID. No.

MRS. HONEY. In my mind, then. There was screaming in my mind. (*She looks at* DAVID.) Do I spy a top button undone? And what is this late hour?

DAVID. I overslept.

MRS. HONEY. Did you?

DAVID. Yes.

MRS. HONEY. Glory be! Has retsina had a salutary effect? A little vice is not to be sneezed at.

DAVID. What?

MRS. HONEY. Too much wine is an excellent thing sometimes. After all, you need something to atone for on—what is it called?

DAVID. Yom Kippur.

MRS. HONEY. "Dear God, I undid my button, forgive me." You're well on your way, boy, well on your way.

DAVID. I'm hungry. I want my breakfast.

MRS. HONEY. It is a pity you were not up slightly earlier, however. You might have witnessed a stupendous argument. The honeymoon couple. It seems she has misplaced her wedding ring and he is none too pleased about it. I had an enormous temptation to offer some solicitous advice and thus make things worse, but it's difficult to cause trouble on an empty stomach. And they did manage to wolf down their tea and toast, no matter how fierce their disagreement. I am not beyond stealing scraps. (*She rings the bell.*) If only this were louder. If it were not so heavy, I would travel with a gong. (COSTOS *enters, humming "What a Day for a Daydream." He winks at* DAVID. DAVID *turns away.* MRS. HONEY *takes it in.* COSTOS *clears the dishes from a nearby table. He totally ignores* MRS. HONEY.) I'm not going to say a word. I know he's going to ignore me. I have been sitting here for exactly one hour, screaming for service and ringing my bell, and he has paid me no mind. (DAVID *shifts uneasily in his chair.*) Have you noticed that he always hums? The dentist hummed, of course, but dentists are supposed to, so they can drive their patients mad. On anyone else it is most unattractive.

(NIKOS *enters, with his deck of cards.*)

NIKOS. Good morning, dear lady.

(*Pause.*)

MRS. HONEY. Well, well, well.

(NIKOS *sits at a table and starts to play solitaire.*)

NIKOS. Beautiful day.

MRS. HONEY. I suppose.

NIKOS. Not a cloud in the sky.

MRS. HONEY. No.

NIKOS. Good for the suntan.

MRS. HONEY. Excellent.

NIKOS. Have you enjoyed breakfast?

MRS. HONEY. Oh, dear—how foolish of me. I forgot all about breakfast. I've been enjoying the view. Do you see that rock jutting out into the sea? There's an old woman dressed in black sitting on it. She has one eye. Most interesting. I could watch her all day.

NIKOS. Would you like breakfast?

MRS. HONEY. Oh. I don't now.

NIKOS. We would be happy to serve you.

MRS. HONEY. Well, if it makes *you* happy, Nikos.

NIKOS. (*To* COSTOS.) Ferte ris to ithico p roime.

COSTOS. Malista, kirie.

> (*He goes into the kitchen.*)

MRS. HONEY. Well, well, well.

NIKOS. She has the evil eye.

MRS. HONEY. Who?

NIKOS. The woman on the rock.

MRS. HONEY. And it's her only one, what a pity. (*Pause.*) Is it aimed at you or me?

NIKOS. You look very pretty this morning, Mrs. Honey.

> (*Pause.*)

MRS. HONEY. I loathe small talk. I practice it all the time, but I loathe it in others. I smell deceit. I can taste it. You won't get the table, Nikos.

NIKOS. I'm winning.

MRS. HONEY. What?

NIKOS. At cards.

> (COSTOS *returns with a large tray containing two breakfasts. He lays a breakfast for* DAVID—*orange juice, toast, and tea.* MRS. HONEY *watches him with hungry eyes.* COSTOS *is humming "Mr. Tambourine Man," making* DAVID *even more uncomfortable.* COSTOS *then brings his tray to* MRS. HONEY's *table and gives her juice, tea, and toast—and an extra plate, covered with a lid, which he lays down with a great flourish.*)

MRS. HONEY. Ah. This is sumptuous.

NIKOS. Of course.

MRS. HONEY. You seem to have given me something special.

NIKOS. Have we?

MRS. HONEY. Something not required. Something not on the menu. Something beyond orange juice, tea, and toast.

NIKOS. A surprise, then.

MRS. HONEY. Indeed. (*She stares at* NIKOS, *sizing up the situation.*) Take it away.

NIKOS. Lift the lid.

MRS. HONEY. I don't want it. Take it away.

NIKOS. Lift the lid.

MRS. HONEY. I'm not hungry. Take it away.

NIKOS. Lift the lid.

MRS. HONEY. I think not. The specialty of the house is trouble. I smell deceit. Take it away. (NIKOS *rises and goes to her table. He lifts the lid off of the plate. A jewel box lies underneath.*) How on earth?

NIKOS. What is it?

MRS. HONEY. My jewel box.

NIKOS. Your jewel box, dear lady?

    (MRS. HONEY *stares at him.*)

MRS. HONEY. Yes.

NIKOS. Astonishing.

MRS. HONEY. Where did you get my jewel box? Have you been rummaging through my room? I shall issue a complaint. I shall go to the police. This was packed away in a suitcase.

NIKOS. It is most attractive.

MRS. HONEY. Yes.

NIKOS. An antique.

MRS. HONEY. The dentist gave it to me. A long time ago. *What is it doing here?*

NIKOS. It is yours, though?

MRS. HONEY. You know it is.

NIKOS. Why don't you open it?

    (*Pause.*)

MRS. HONEY. Ah. (*Pause.*) I think not.

NIKOS. Don't you want to make sure . . . ?

MRS. HONEY. Make sure?

NIKOS. That nothing is missing.

MRS. HONEY. No.

NIKOS. I think you must open it.

MRS. HONEY. I think I must not. (NIKOS *flings the jewel box open.* MRS. HONEY *does not look at it.*) Nothing is missing.

NIKOS. You haven't looked.

MRS. HONEY. No. I haven't.

> (*She closes the box.* NIKOS *opens the box again.*)

NIKOS. Beautiful things.

MRS. HONEY. Yes.

NIKOS. Won't you look?

MRS. HONEY. No.

> (NIKOS *removes a necklace and holds it up.*)

NIKOS. This is lovely.

MRS. HONEY. My mother's.

> (NIKOS *removes a bracelet and holds it up.*)

NIKOS. Exquisite.

MRS. HONEY. My mother's as well.

> (NIKOS *holds up a ring.*)

NIKOS. And this?

MRS. HONEY. I don't know.

NIKOS. You don't know.

MRS. HONEY. I've never seen it before.

NIKOS. You've never seen it before?

MRS. HONEY. It's not mine.

NIKOS. It must be.

MRS. HONEY. It isn't. It's too vulgar. It's not mine.

NIKOS. Then whose is it?

MRS. HONEY. I have no idea.

NIKOS. And what is it doing in your jewel box?

MRS. HONEY. I have no idea.

NIKOS. Ah, but it could be . . . it looks remarkably like . . .

MRS. HONEY. Oh. I see. I see. Oh, yes. I see.

NIKOS. The ring that until this morning adorned the finger of that sweet young girl on her honeymoon. She mislaid it.

MRS. HONEY. Indeed.

NIKOS. Is it hers?

MRS. HONEY. I would not know.

NIKOS. I think it is.

MRS. HONEY. It would not surprise me.

(NIKOS *holds up a watch.*)

NIKOS. And what is this?

MRS. HONEY. A watch.

NIKOS. Yours?

MRS. HONEY. No.

NIKOS. Whose?

MRS. HONEY. I have no idea. I think this game is over.

NIKOS. Whose watch?

MRS. HONEY. I do not know. Nikos, leave it be.

(NIKOS *turns to* DAVID.)

NIKOS. Is this your watch?

DAVID. Mine?

NIKOS. It looks like the watch I have noticed on your wrist.

DAVID. No.

NIKOS. Let me see your wrist. (*Silence.* DAVID *doesn't move.*) Please.
(DAVID *holds out his wrist.*) No watch.

MRS. HONEY. It is yours, child? Tell the truth.

DAVID. Yes. I think it is.

MRS. HONEY. How did it get here?

DAVID. I don't know.

(MRS. HONEY *goes to* DAVID.)

MRS. HONEY. Listen to me, child, this is very important, this is crucial. Relatively few moments are crucial in life. This one is. Do
you have any idea what happened to your watch? Do you have
any idea how your watch has come to be in my jewel box? (DAVID
is silent.) Do you, child?

(*Silence.*)

DAVID. No.

MRS. HONEY. Then I'm lost. (*She returns to her table.*) Lost. (*To*
NIKOS.) And I suppose your cousin is the police chief?

NIKOS. No.

MRS. HONEY. Oh?

NIKOS. My uncle.

MRS. HONEY. (*Smiles.*) Of course.

NIKOS. I'd hate to disturb him.

    (*Pause.*)

MRS. HONEY. You needn't. An Oxford education has served you well. You are clever, you and your brother. What have you done with him? Have you murdered him? There is, of course, no one to help me. I am totally unattached. The king must have his dinner. I believe there is a bus at noon. A local bus filled with livestock. Before I reclaim my jewel box please tell me if it contains any other surprises. Has the French scientist misplaced an ankle bracelet? And the Germans? Have they suffered a loss?

NIKOS. No. Just a ring and a watch.

MRS. HONEY. Well, then . . . (*She closes the jewel box.*) Take the breakfast away, Nikos. I've lost my appetite. (*Rises.*) It *is* stupid. For a table! Good Lord.

    (MRS. HONEY *leaves her table. She walks past* DAVID.)

DAVID. I'm sorry.

MRS. HONEY. It's not your fault. Don't worry. Others will talk to you. You'll see. (*She starts to leave, then turns back.*) I would like the photograph. Send it to me?

DAVID. Yes.

MRS. HONEY. Thank you.

DAVID. Where?

MRS. HONEY. Care of American Express.

DAVID. Which city?

MRS. HONEY. Choose one.

    (MRS. HONEY *leaves.*

        COSTOS *clears her table, humming. He looks over at* DAVID. DAVID *looks away.* NIKOS *is at his table again, playing solitaire.* DAVID *looks out to sea.*

        The lights hold on them as we hear DAVID*'s voice.*)

DAVID. (*Voice only.*) There is a cool breeze tonight. From the Levant. And clouds. You cannot see the stars. You cannot see Albania. And it is raining. The afternoon was glorious, however. Very hot. I wasn't here when she took the bus. I was on the beach. The rain started around five. It's very light rain, more of a drizzle. The king cancelled his dinner. He didn't want to get wet.

(COSTOS *continues to clean the table.*
NIKOS *continues to play solitaire.*
DAVID *continues to stare at the sea.*
Curtain.)

Contributors

BRUCE BENDERSON is the author of seven books, including *Sex and Iso-lation: And Other Essays, The Romanian: Story of an Obsession, User,* and *Pretending to Say No.* He has contributed articles to *New York Times Magazine, Village Voice, nest, Paris Vogue, Blackbook, Libération,* and other media. An accomplished translator and bilingual author, he was awarded the prestigious Prix de Flore for literature in 2004, and he has also taught creative writing, urban culture, and French literature at colleges throughout the United States. He divides his time between New York and Paris.

BRIAN BOULDREY is the author of the nonfiction books *Honorable Ban-dit: A Walk across Corsica, Monster: Adventures in American Machismo,* and *The Autobiography Box;* the novels *The Genius of Desire, Love, the Magician,* and *The Boom Economy;* and the editor of several antholo-gies. Bouldrey is the recipient of fellowships from Yaddo and the East-ern Frontier Society, the Joseph Henry Jackson Award from the San Francisco Foundation, a Lambda Literary Award, and the Western Re-gional Magazine Award. He teaches fiction and creative nonfiction at Northwestern University and the MFA Program at Lesley University.

CLIFFORD CHASE is the author of a novel, *Winkie,* and *The Hurry-Up Song: A Memoir of Losing My Brother.* His stories and memoirs have appeared in *McSweeney's, Threepenny Review, The Yale Review,* and other journals and anthologies. He lives in Brooklyn, where he is at work on a second memoir.

DUNCAN FALLOWELL is a British writer of fiction and nonfiction. He is the author of the novels *Satyrday, The Underbelly,* and *A History of Face-lifting,* the travel books *To Noto, One Hot Summer in St Petersburg,* and *Going as Far as I Can,* and the biography of a transsexual *April Ashley's Odyssey.* Fallowell is also a cultural commentator and journalist who has specialized in interview-portraits of unusual or celebrated personal-ities. A collection of these has been published as *20th Century Charac-ters* and a second volume, *Platinum Peepshow,* will be published in 2009.

MACK FRIEDMAN is the author of *Strapped for Cash: A History of American Hustler Culture* and *Setting the Lawn on Fire,* which won the Edmund White Award for best debut fiction in 2006. His essays have been featured at the Center for Exploratory and Perceptual Art and the Leslie-Lohman Gallery, and his performance art has been showcased at the Andy Warhol Museum. His stories have appeared in the anthologies *Between Men, Wonderlands,* and *Barnstorm.* He has contributed to the magazines *Out Traveler* and *$pread,* among others. He lives in Pennsylvania.

PHILIP GAMBONE is an award-winning essayist, journalist, and fiction writer. His previous work includes *Beijing: A Novel, Something Inside: Conversations with Gay Fiction Writers,* both published by the University of Wisconsin Press, and a book of stories, *The Language We Use Up Here.* He lives in Boston and teaches writing at Harvard University and English at Boston University Academy.

TY GELTMAKER is a historian who has taught history and literature at California Institute of the Arts, the University of Southern California, and community colleges in Los Angeles and New York. Before working in academia, he was an editor at United Press International in New York and a journalist in Rome. He is the author of *Tired of Living: Suicide in Italy from National Unification to World War I, 1860–1915* and "The Queer Nation Acts Up: Health Care, Politics, and Sexual Diversity in the County of Angels," which appeared in the anthology *Queers in Space.* He has recently published review articles on Fascist rhetoric of youth, and Italian criminology in history and fiction, in the *Journal of Modern Italian Studies.* He lives in Los Angeles. "Lamb of God" is a work of fiction.

AARON HAMBURGER was awarded the Rome Prize by the American Academy of Arts and Letters and the American Academy in Rome for his short story collection *The View from Stalin's Head,* which was also nominated for a Violet Quill Award. His novel *Faith for Beginners* was nominated for a Lambda Literary Award. His writing has appeared in *The Village Voice, Poets and Writers, Details, Nerve, Out, The Forward,* and *Time Out New York.* Hamburger is the recipient of a fellowship from the Edward F. Albee Foundation, has won first place in the David J. Dornstein Contest for Young Jewish Writers, and teaches creative writing at Columbia University.

TREBOR HEALEY is the author of a Ferro-Grumley and Violet Quill award-winning novel, *Through It Came Bright Colors,* as well as a poetry collection, *Sweet Son of Pan,* and a book of short stories, *A Perfect Scar and Other Stories.* Healey's poem "Denny" was made into a hit single by the homocore punk band Pansy Division. He lives in Los Angeles, where he is working on his second novel, *A Horse Named Sorrow.*

ANDREW HOLLERAN is the author, most recently, of the award-winning *Grief: A Novel;* a collection of stories, *In September, the Light Changes;* and three highly acclaimed novels: *The Beauty of Men, Nights in Aruba,* and the now classic *Dancer from the Dance,* which is widely regarded as one of the most important gay novels of the twentieth century. Edmund White describes *Dancer from the Dance* as having "accomplished for the 1970s what *The Great Gatsby* achieved for the 1920s . . . the glamorization of a decade and a culture."

RAPHAEL KADUSHIN is an award-winning food and travel writer whose work appears regularly in *Bon Appetit, National Geographic Traveler, Condé Nast Traveler,* the Condé Nast/CondéNet Web sites Epicurious and Concierge, and *OutTraveler.* His fiction and journalism have been widely anthologized, in collections including *Men on Men 5, Best Food Writing 2001* and *2008, Mr. Wrong,* and National Geographic's best-selling *Through the Lens,* and he is the editor of the anthologies *Wonderlands: Good Gay Travel Writing* and *Barnstorm: Contemporary Wisconsin Fiction.* He is the senior acquisitions editor at the University of Wisconsin Press.

MICHAEL KLEIN is an award-winning poet and author. His poetry collections *1990* and *Poets for Life* are winners of the Lambda Literary Award. His memoir, *Track Conditions,* won a Lambda Literary Award for autobiography. He lives in New York City and teaches memoir writing in the summer program at the Fine Arts Work Center in Provincetown.

DOUGLAS A. MARTIN's books include *In the Time of Assignments,* a poetry collection; *Branwell,* a novel of the Brontë brother; and *Your Body Figured,* an experimental narrative. *They Change the Subject,* a collection of stories, was named one of the top ten books of the year in the *San Francisco Bay Times. Outline of My Lover,* Martin's first novel, was named an international book of the year in the *Times Literary Supplement* and adapted by the Forsythe Company for their multimedia ballet and production *Kammer/Kammer.*

DALE PECK is the author of the novels *Now It's Time to Say Goodbye, Martin and John,* and *The Law of Enclosures* (for which he co-wrote the screenplay). His short fiction has appeared in *Artforum, Bookforum, BOMB, London Review of Books, The New Republic, New York Times,* and *The Village Voice.* He received a Guggenheim Fellowship in 1995.

MARTIN SHERMAN has twice been published in collections of "gay plays" and many of his works focus on homosexuality. *Bent* was first performed in a workshop at the O'Neill Theatre Centre in Waterford, Connecticut, in 1978, before premiering in London (with Ian McKellen in the lead) and on Broadway (with Richard Gere) in 1979. This play was the first to deal with the treatment of homosexuals by the Nazis during World War II. Set primarily in a concentration camp, it garnered controversy over two scenes in which the gay inmates achieve climax by words. The Philadelphia-born writer has had a number of stage successes in London (where he permanently settled in 1980). *A Madhouse in Goa* (1989) focuses on the deceptive relationship between a young man and the woman he encounters on a Greek island. Vanessa Redgrave played Isadora Duncan in Sherman's *When She Danced* (1990–91) while Rupert Everett won praise for his turn as the object of the affection of a British Army officer in North Africa in *Some Sunny Day* (1996). Olympia Dukakis appeared in his play *Rose* (1999) in London and New York, and he wrote the book for the Broadway musical *The Boy from Oz* (2003). His latest play, *Aristo,* premiered in 2008. His many screenplays include *Mrs. Henderson Presents* and *Alive and Kicking.*

EDMUND WHITE is an all-around man of letters, known for his novels, plays, literary essays, biographies, memoirs, and travel writing. His trilogy of autobiographical novels—*A Boy's Own Story, The Beautiful Room Is Empty,* and *The Farewell Symphony*—mapped out the itinerary of an entire generation of gay men. He has written three biographies of French gay writers—Jean Genet, Marcel Proust, and Arthur Rimbaud. His essays have been collected in two books, *The Burning Library* and *Arts and Letters.* His 1980 travelogue, *States of Desire: Travels in Gay America,* remains a classic if insouciant (and now poignant) look at gay life at a particular cultural moment just before the onslaught of AIDS. His short stories, collected in *Skinned Alive,* represented one of the first serious literary responses to the disease. He has edited numerous anthologies of gay fiction, including *The Faber Book of Gay Short Fiction* and *Fresh Men: New Voices in Gay Fiction.* He reviews regularly for *The New York Review of Books.* He is an officer in the French Order of Arts and Letters and has won the National Book Critics Circle Award. He teaches at Princeton. His most recent novel is *Hotel de Dream.*